How to Rebuild
NISSAN/DATSUN
OHC Engine

by Tom Monroe, P.E., S.A.E., A.S.E. Master Mechanic

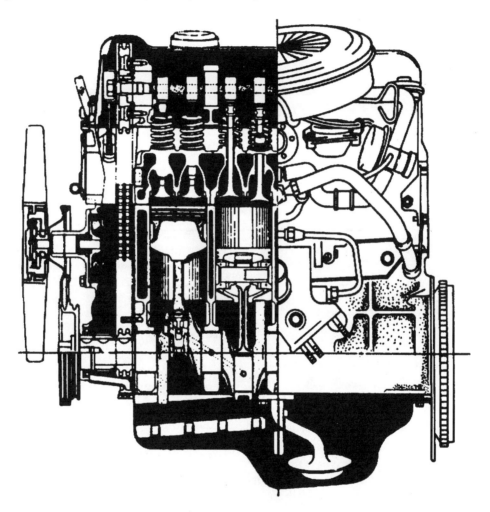

Covers L-Series Engines:
4-cylinder 1968-1978
6-cylinder 1970-1984

Another Fact-Packed Automotive Book from

California Bill's
Automotive Handbooks

The cooperation of Nissan Motor Corporation in U.S.A. is gratefully acknowledged. However, this publication is a wholly independent production of California Bill's Automotive Handbooks.

Contents

Notice: The information in this book is true and complete to the best of our knowledge. It is offered with no guarantees on the part of the author or California Bill's Automotive Handbooks. The author and publisher disclaim all liability in connection with the use of this book.

Thanks

To build engines and gather research data for writing a comprehensive book such as this requires help from many quarters. Those worthy of mention who supplied parts or information include Bob Bub of Cloyes Gear and Products, John Thompson of Federal Mogul, Bob Morris of Fel-Pro, Cal DeBruin of Sealed Power Corporation, and Louis Cohn of TRW.

Thanks also to Allen Osborn, a former Nissan instructor who double-checked the 1998 revision and added some extra-helpful tips and advice.

Special thanks to Denny Wyckoff of Motor Machine, Tucson, Arizona, who allowed me the use of his engine machine shop. This allowed me to photograph many of the inspection and machining operations illustrated throughout this book.

Thanks also to Mickey Meyer for assisting with cyliner-head removal and replacement.

Finally, thanks to Frank Honsowetz of Nissan Motorsports. Frank read behind me, making sure what I said was right. He also helped by supplying tips from his vast experience and knowledge on the Nissan/Datsun L-series engine.

Publishers: Howard Fisher
Helen Fisher

Revised Edition Editor: Bill Fisher

Editorial Assistant: Alison Fisher

Revised Edition Technical Editor: Allen Osborne

Original Editor: Ron Sessions, A.S.A.E.

Cover Design: Gary Smith
Performance Design

Cover Photo: Bill Keller

Photos: Tom Monroe, except as noted

© 1998, 2001 Tom Monroe

Published by:
California Bill's Automotive Handbooks, LLC
PO Box 91858
Tucson, AZ 85752-1858

Previously published by Fisher Books.

Printed in U.S.A.

Printing 10 9 8 7 6 5 4 3

ISBN 1-931128-03-0

Introduction

The L-series Nissan/Datsun engine began its life powering the 1966 Type 130S. Big production numbers started in 1967 with the introduction of the Bluebird, or 510, or in Europe, the Datsun 1600. The first ones in the U.S. were 1968 models. The L-series engine has been used in many family sedans, sports cars and pickup trucks, in four- and six-cylinder configurations.

Similar to the BMW 2002 engine, the L-series Datsun in-line engine has a chain-driven overhead camshaft, intake and exhaust ports on the left side of the head and five main bearings for fours and seven mains for six-cylinder engines. The block extends below the center of the main bearings for added rigidity. Five or seven main bearings are used at the front and rear and between each crank throw; five for fours and seven in the sixes. The induction system varies from the single, two-throat Hitachi and SU-type twin carburetors to Bosch L-Jetronic fuel injection. The L-series induction system was topped off with turbocharging on the '81 280ZX.

Not only has the L-series engine proved its durability over thousands of miles in family sedans, sports cars and pickup trucks, it's a formidable competitor in many types of racing. Notable are offroad-racing pickup trucks and road-racing sedans and sports cars. In turbocharged, fuel-injected form, the L28 has produced in excess of 800 HP!

There are nine basic L-series engines: L13, L14, L16, L18, L20A, L20B, L24, L26 and L28. The nearby chart shows the displacement, number of cylinders, and bore and stroke of each engine:

HOW TO USE THIS BOOK

How To Rebuild Your Nissan/Datsun OHC Engine is organized to demonstrate how an engine rebuild should be done. I start with showing you how to determine whether a rebuild is necessary and why. If cylinder-head work is all that's needed, I describe how to remove and replace it without removing the engine. If you need to rebuild, the chapters that follow cover engine removal and teardown.

A diversion from the actual rebuilding process is the chapter on parts identifica-

240Z such as this is worth keeping in top-running condition. So are many other Nissan/Datsun cars or trucks. Photo courtesy Nissan.

BASIC ENGINE SPECIFICATIONS

Engine	(CID/cc)	Cylinders	Bore (in./mm)	Stroke (in./mm)
L13*	79.1/1296	4	3.268/83	2.358/59.9
L14*	87.2/1428	4	3.268/83	2.598/66.0
L16	97.3/1595	4	3.268/83	2.902/73.7
L18	108.0/1770	4	3.346/85	3.071/78.0
L20A*	121.9/1998	6	3.071/78	2.744/69.7
L20B	119.1/1952	4	3.346/85	3.390/86.0
L24	146.0/2393	6	3.268/83	2.902/73.7
L26	156.5/2565	6	3.268/83	3.110/79.0
L28	168.0/2753	6	3.386/86	3.110/79.0

*Not sold in the U.S.

tion and interchange. If a major engine component must be replaced, this information can prove valuable.

The book guides you through the basic inspection, reconditioning and assembly stages required for a rebuild. Once the engine is assembled, I show how to install it and give some tips on engine tuning so you'll get maximum performance from your new rebuild.

CHAPTER ONE

Time To Rebuild?

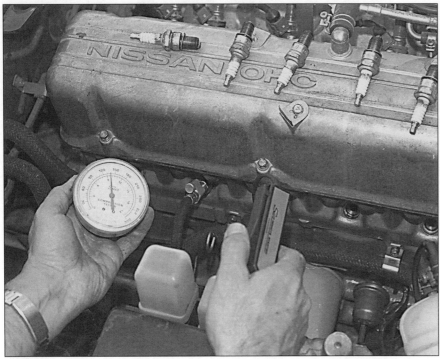

Compression tester gives quick indication of cylinder sealing. With all plugs removed, crank engine the same number of revolutions when checking each one. Four compression strokes is about right. Gage shows 145-psi compression for number-1 cylinder, a good reading.

Read this chapter before you make the final decision to do rebuild your L-series Nissan/Datsun engine. Rebuilding an engine just because it has accumulated a lot of miles isn't necessarily required. More important than miles is how the engine was maintained and operated. For instance, a Z-car engine that received regular servicing and was driven primarily on highways will go many more miles than a pickup-truck engine that was serviced erratically and was used in a dusty environment.

Performance should be the primary consideration when determining whether or not to rebuild. The engine must be consuming excessive amounts of oil, getting poor mileage or noticeably down on power. If oil consumption is the problem, the cause may be a clogged positive crankcase ventilation (PCV) system. Such a condition may pressurize the crankcase, forcing oil up

past the pistons and past the seals. Replacing the PCV valve may be all that's necessary to correct this. If power or mileage is the problem, a thorough tuneup—possibly a carburetor rebuild (if one is used) and ignition servicing may be all that's needed.

Let's examine how to determine if your engine needs to be rebuilt.

LUBRICATION SYSTEM

Oil consumption and pressure are two of the best ways to judge engine condition. High oil consumption or low oil pressure indicate increased clearances—wear—at the pistons, valves or bearings.

Oil Consumption—An engine must use some oil for proper lubrication. Otherwise, the pistons, piston rings and valves would not receive lubrication. The question is, "How much oil should an engine use?" This, of course, depends on how the engine is used and its

compression. An engine that works extremely hard or operates at high rpm will use more oil. The same goes for a higher-compression engine. But generally, if an engine uses a quart of oil every 600 miles or less, it is using too much.

Before you label your engine an *oil burner,* check whether the oil is leaking from a gasket or seal. For example, a damaged cam-cover gasket or rear main crankshaft seal may be causing the oil loss. Oil spots on the driveway can mean a lot of oil is being lost on the road. Check this by looking under the car immediately after parking it. If you detect dripping oil and the underside of the car is wet with oil, the problem is poor sealing somewhere in the engine. Find and fix it. However, if it doesn't leak oil, there are other possibilities.

Piston Rings—All L-series pistons use three piston rings. The top two rings share the job of sealing the combustion chamber; the bottom ring handles oil control. The oil ring scrapes off most of the oil sprayed or splashed onto the cylinder wall, but some is left to lubricate and seal the piston and rings.

Although the rings may not be worn, oil can get into the combustion chamber when excess oil is splashed on the cylinder walls. This is caused by excessive bearing-to-journal clearances at the main or connecting-rod journals. The additional oil may be too much for the oil rings to control. Excess clearances will be detected as low oil pressure when you perform an oil-pressure check.

Just as oil can get past the rings and into the combustion chamber, combustion gases can blow back past the compression rings into the crankcase. This is referred to as *blowby.* Crankcase gases or vapors have to be vented or excess pressure will build up in the crankcase, overtaxing the PCV system.

Excess blowby causes smoke at the exhaust or breather cap, providing the breather is not connected to the induction

How much oil an engine uses is a good indication of its condition. An engine using more than one quart every 600 miles has a problem. Excess oil may be going down valve guides or past the piston rings. If there are visible oil leaks, this could be another reason for high oil consumption.

system. If the breather is connected to the induction system, excess blowby will deposit oil on the air filter and oily carbon deposits in the combustion chamber. The valves, spark plugs, piston tops, piston-ring lands and the insides of the intake and exhaust manifolds will be also coated.

Valve Guides & Seals—Guides and stems have built-in clearance to allow a slight amount of oil to pass for lubrication. As clearance grows with wear, so does oil passage, particularly at the intake valves. This is due to vacuum created during the intake stroke—unless the engine is a Turbo 280ZX under boost. In the case of the turbocharged engine, the induction system is pressurized. Oil loss down the valve guides is also aggravated by blowby. Excess blowby indicates the engine may need to be rebuilt; worn guides mean the cylinder head needs to be rebuilt.

A similar result occurs if the valve-stem seals are worn, cracked or missing. This allows excessive oil flow down the guides, regardless of stem or guide condition.

Replacing bad valve-stem seals can bring oil consumption within an acceptable level if the engine is in otherwise good condition. This can be done without removing the engine or cylinder

head, but the cam followers and valve springs must be removed.

Cracked Oil Passage—An often-seen problem with the L-series engine is a cracked cylinder-head oil passage. This passage feeds oil from the center of the cylinder block longitudinally through the head and up to each cam tower to lubricate the cam, cam followers and valves.

When a crack occurs between the oil passage and water jacket, oil mixes with the coolant. Oil flows into the cooling system while the engine is running; coolant gets into the crankcase when the engine is shut off.

To check for a cracked oil passage, inspect the radiator coolant. Oil will appear on the surface as a multicolored oil slick. Because a blown head gasket will also force coolant into the lubrication system, check crankcase oil immediately after running the engine. A milky substance in the oil is coolant. Or, after the engine has been shut off for some time—at least overnight—drain some oil from the crankcase. If there's coolant in the oil, it will come out first—it's heavier than oil. Unfortunately, a cracked cylinder head means the cylinder head must be replaced.

If you only see coolant in the oil, but no oil in the coolant, it may be something as simple as the front cover has corroded through behind the water pump. This can happen if the engine has run for quite some time without any antifreeze in the cooling system to prevent corrosion.

PERFORMANCE LOSS

If fuel economy isn't what it should be or power seems low, there are a few checks you can make to pinpoint the problem. Numerous problems can cause poor performance and not require a rebuild to correct them.

First, make sure the engine is in tune. Too much or too little fuel, or incorrect ignition operation can hurt performance. Also, excessive drag from the brakes or drive line reduces power where you need it—at the rear wheels. You should also perform a *compression* or *leak-down* test, page 11.

A good way to check power is to take your vehicle to a shop with a *chassis dynamometer*. A chassis dyno can be used to check power at the *wheels—road horsepower*. While the engine is operating under road load, the operator can check various engine components, such as the fuel and ignition systems. A chassis dyno allows direct comparisons of power before and after changes are made.

Have the engine tuned and checked on a dyno only if you suspect the engine is in good condition, or you want to spend the money to see how much power is gained after you do a rebuild. If the engine hasn't had a tuneup recently, its performance should improve.

Before getting into engine-problem diagnosis, let's take a look at other causes of performance loss.

Non-Engine-Related Problems—Don't blame the engine for poor performance unless you're sure the rest of the drive line is in good condition. Make sure the clutch is not slipping, if a manual transmission is used. And, an automatic transmission should shift correctly and not slip between shifts. Don't forget the brakes. Find a place where you can coast in neutral from highway speed to make sure the brakes don't drag.

Poor Fuel Supply—A restriction in the fuel line or filter, or a faulty fuel pump can account for poor performance. This can cause the air/fuel mixture to lean out as engine speed increases. Also make sure the throttle plate(s) are opening and closing all the way. Check the induction system for air leaks. This will also cause air/fuel-mixture lean out and hurt engine performance.

Faulty Ignition—Check the ignition system. Make sure the engine is getting good spark at the correct time. Incorrect spark plugs, faulty wires or coil, a cracked or worn distributor cap and rotor or incorrect timing can cause a huge performance loss.

Have the engine checked on an engine analyzer or oscilloscope, commonly called a *scope*. If the scope finds nothing amiss with a breaker-point ignition system, yet you still feel something is wrong, check the distributor's vacuum- and mechanical-advance mechanisms. Electronic-ignition advance curve can be checked on the engine analyzer. Or, remove the distributor and take it to an ignition-specialty shop.

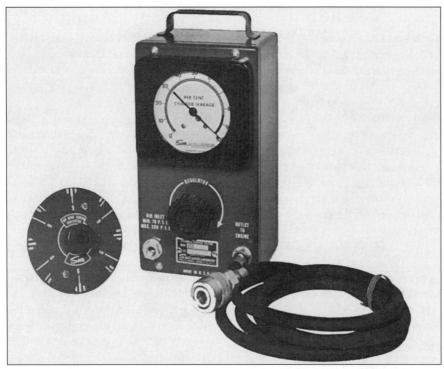

Leak-down test is done without cranking engine, thus cranking speed, valve timing or cam condition doesn't affect results. Leak-down tester requires a compressed air source. Photo courtesy Sun Corporation.

If you've come this far and still haven't found the problem, check for the following: blown head gasket, restricted exhaust, worn timing chain, worn camshaft lobes, burned exhaust valves and carbon deposits.

Sometimes head gaskets can seep coolant overnight, causing excessive amounts of steam or white smoke from the exhaust, which will go away when the engine is hot. With most L-series engines you can stick a subminiature lamp through the sparkplug holes and actually see the tops of the pistons. Coolant or water leaks will usually clean most of the carbon off of the tops of the pistons.

Blown Head Gasket—Often there will be a power loss and increased engine noise when a head gasket blows. If the leak occurs to the outside of the engine, you'll hear it. The noise will sound like a rapid off-and-on release of high-pressure air. The rate increases with engine speed.

Some head-gasket leaks enter the cooling system, showing up as a multicolored oil slick on the surface of the coolant. These leaks are relatively easy to diagnose. Large white deposits will also appear on the spark plugs. There may also be white "smoke"—steam—in the exhaust from coolant being drawn into the combustion chambers and exhausted. Overheating will eventually

occur as combustion gases overpressurize the cooling system and force out coolant.

A combustion leak into an adjacent cylinder is harder to detect. Symptoms include misfiring at idle, causing the engine to run rough, and significant power loss. The cylinders at fault can be detected by doing a compression or leak-down test. A compression test should be done when the engine is warm because some head gaskets leak only when the engine is warm or hot.

Cracked Cylinder Head—If oil showed up in your engine's coolant and coolant in the oil, refer to page 89 to check for cracks between the cylinder head's oil passage and water jacket. Because engine oil pressure is higher than cooling-system pressure, oil will leak into the coolant when the engine is operating. The reverse will happen when the engine is shut off. Oil pressure drops to zero and coolant pressure increases—no more than the pressure cap will allow—causing coolant to leak into the oil passage.

If you only see coolant in the oil, but no oil in the coolant, it may be something as simple as the front cover has corroded through behind the water pump. This can happen if the engine has run for quite some time without any antifreeze in the cooling system to prevent corrosion.

Plugged Exhaust—A restricted exhaust

system has perplexed many a mechanic. It doesn't happen often, but when it does it is usually found only after *everything else* has been checked.

A plugged exhaust usually allows an engine to start and idle. But the engine will lose power and not be able to reach high rpm, depending on how badly the exhaust is plugged. This will show up as low intake manifold vacuum as engine rpm increases.

Likely causes of a plugged exhaust are a crushed exhaust pipe or muffler, loose baffle in the muffler or clogged catalytic converter, if the car or truck is so equipped. One cause that can be very frustrating to find is a collapsed inner wall of a double-wall exhaust pipe. Also, it's not uncommon for a converter to plug, particularly if it was overheated from a rich air/fuel mixture. Listen for whistling at the exhaust.

To check for a plugged exhaust, start with the simplest test: Hold your hand over the tail pipe while the engine is running. Have someone rev the engine. You should feel a definite exhaust pulse. You may be able to recognize the choking sound of a plugged exhaust system.

If you suspect a restriction, look underneath for a crimped or collapsed pipe or muffler. If the pipe doesn't appear to be collapsed, don't assume it's OK. The inner exhaust-pipe wall or catalytic converter may be collapsed or plugged, or a muffler baffle may have broken loose. Any of these can block exhaust flow. Also, the pipe behind the restriction will be colder. Be careful not to get burned if you touch the pipe along its length. Spray water on it just to be safe.

As a last-resort check, disconnect the exhaust system at the exhaust manifold. Run the engine to see if the condition improves. It will be noisy, so make sure you do this where and when it won't arouse the neighbors. Do it only long enough to make the check.

Worn Timing Chain—If the timing chain is badly worn, valve timing will be retarded. This can affect performance severely, even to the point of the engine not running. It can also cause severe mechanical damage. Many an L-series engine front cover has been destroyed as a result of a worn timing chain.

To check timing-chain wear, turn the crankshaft clockwise to top center (TC), and look at the cam-sprocket timing mark.

To check cam and timing chain, pull off cam cover. Visual inspection is all that's needed to determine cam condition. Also, check valve lash while cover is off. Push on backside (right side) of chain to check for excess slack.

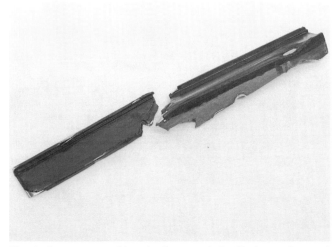

Here's damage caused by a badly worn chain. Chain caught top of tight-side guide and tore it loose from block.

The crankshaft timing mark must be on **0**, or **TC**. The front two rocker arms will feel loose when the number-l cylinder is at TC of its *firing stroke.* The loose-rocker check won't work on L-28 turbos because these have hydraulic valve lifters built into the rocker pivots. Also, the distributor rotor will point at the number-1 distributor-cap post. If the rockers aren't loose, turn the crank 360° and recheck. Turn the crank clockwise slowly until it's on the TC mark and stop. Don't go past the mark, then back up to it. Instead, go back past the mark and start over in the clockwise direction.

Turn to page 131 and read about where the timing marks—a notch in the cam-sprocket hub and an oblong groove in the camshaft thrust plate—should be in relation to one another. Both are behind the cam sprocket.

Worn Cam Lobes—Although uncommon with the L-series engines, severe cam-lobe wear can affect performance. If one cam lobe or follower wears more than the others, the engine will run rough, especially under load. If all lobes or followers are worn excessively, engine power will be severely reduced.

If an intake valve doesn't open enough, there won't be sufficient air/fuel mixture to supply that cylinder, regardless of throttle-plate opening. If an exhaust valve doesn't open enough, the incoming air/fuel mixture will be diluted with exhaust gases. Either way, the engine loses power.

If all cam lobes are worn, suspect that the oil-jet-restriction in the oil gallery—at the block deck is clogged. This will block oil flow from the block to the cylinder head. To check for a clogged jet, run the engine with the cam cover loose. Gradually lift up on the cover to check for oil flow from the cam or oil-spray bar. If there isn't any or it's very little, the oil jet is probably clogged. You'll have to pull the head to clear the jet.

Burned Valves—A burned exhaust valve can't seal the combustion chamber. The result is lower compression and power. A burned valve can be caused by retarded timing, lean air/fuel mixture or by the valve not seating fully, usually due to inadequate valve lash, or clearance. Sometimes, burned valves are caused by a combination of these.

Inadequate valve lash on L-series engines is common because the exhaust valves lose lash, unlike the intakes, which gain lash with time.

A burned exhaust valve will show poor cylinder sealing during a compression or leak-down test, page 11. A quick check is to hang a dollar bill over the tail pipe with the engine running. The bill will be sucked against the pipe if a valve is burned. There will also be a put-put noise.

Carbon Deposits—The brownish or gray-black particulates pouring from an exhaust at wide-open throttle are carbon deposits being burned and knocked off the combustion-chamber walls, piston domes, valves and exhaust port and pipe walls.

These deposits form in the combustion

Oil deposits on back side of intake valve indicate excessive oil loss through valve guide. Such deposits also reduce flow efficiency of that port.

chambers of an engine in poor tune or condition, or in a healthy engine that is idled for extended period or driven at slow speeds. Carbon deposits have a number of causes: rich fuel mixture, high oil consumption, cold operating temperature or extended low-speed driving or idling.

Carbon deposits can cause a number of problems: First, carbon accumulates on the pistons, valves and combustion chamber walls. This raises the compression ratio.

If compression gets too high, the engine *detonates,* or *pings.* During normal combustion, combustion-chamber pressure builds to the point that the air/fuel charge in the combustion chamber explodes—*detonates*—instead of burning.

Engine needs more than a rebuild; it needs to be replaced. Hole in block was caused by nut coming off connecting-rod-cap bolt, resulting in loose rod cap followed by destroyed block, rod and crankshaft.

Here's what crank looked like from holed block. Grooved rod-bearing journal at left resulted from lost oil pressure when rod left journal at right. Evidently, driver kept going even though rod punched hole in block!

If the engine has a problem with detonation, don't assume it's due to carbon build-up. Detonation can also be caused by using fuel with an octane rating too low for the engine's compression ratio—a common occurrence with today's low-octane gas. If you use the highest-octane gas you can find and the engine still detonates, it's unfortunate. Aside from avgas and expensive racing gas, genuine high-octane pump gasoline is difficult to find, courtesy of the bureaucrats and the oil companies.

Other causes of detonation may be overheating, excessive ignition advance or an oil-rich intake charge due to worn valve guides, bad valve-stem seals or worn rings. A leaking automatic-transmission-modulator diaphragm that allows automatic-transmission fluid (ATF) to be drawn into the engine will also cause detonation. Engine oil or ATF dilutes the intake charge, causing a drop in octane rating.

Before enough carbon accumulates to cause detonation, it can cause *preignition*. Carbon deposits in the combustion chamber glow hot enough to ignite the intake charge *before* the spark plug does—like the glow plug of a diesel or model-airplane engine.

Detonation and preignition are both hard on an engine. They put excessive loads on the pistons, rods, crank, cylinder heads and, finally, your wallet.

Carbon also causes problems at the valves. As carbon accumulates around a valve seat, it can prevent the valve from closing. Then the hot exhaust gases act like an acetylene torch and burn or cut the edge of the valve as they escape into the exhaust port. Once burned, the valve cannot seal combustion-chamber pressures and the cylinder loses compression. Meanwhile, the valve continues to burn.

There's more: Carbon deposits on valves, around valve seats, and on port walls reduce air/fuel-mixture flow into and exhaust flow out of the combustion chambers. This robs an engine of power and cuts fuel economy, particularly at high rpm. Carbon also acts as a sponge, soaking up gasoline and causing drivability problems.

A number of "tuneup-in-a-can" elixirs for removing carbon buildup are available. The problem is that these elixirs often work too well. Carbon comes off in big chunks, which is akin to throwing grit into the combustion chambers. The carbon chunks increase ring wear and may become lodged between a valve and its seat. You know what the possible result of this is—a burned valve.

Additives are OK to use if carbon buildup is light. But judging the amount of buildup is difficult with an assembled engine. Rather than using an additive, cure the problem causing the buildup. Do this and the carbon deposits will eventually burn away.

Valve Adjustment—Check valve clearance. A few extra thousandths of an inch between the cam and the rockers can increase valve noise considerably. This extra valve clearance causes lost power, too, because of less *duration*—the valves open later and close earlier. Too little valve lash can be worse. The valves can be held off their seats, causing cylinder leakage and even valve burning.

DIAGNOSIS

Keep in mind that the potential problems I've just discussed are the most common. The problem with your engine, if it has one, may be unusual or unique. Let's take a close look at how to check engine condition.

> **DANGER**
> Use CAUTION when working on a running engine. Make sure that you, your clothing and equipment stay clear of the fan, pulleys and belts. Keep neckties and jewelry in your closet or dresser. Stay out of the plane of the fan. Wear safety glasses. Things can be thrown from an engine and at you. Be safety conscious. Accidents do happen!

NOISES

Any moving part can make a noise, but determining the origin of that noise can be difficult. The first thing to do is narrow the possibilities.

Start your search by determining if the noise is at *engine speed* or *half engine speed*. This will give you some clue as to where the problem lies. Noises at half engine speed are usually in the valve train. Two exceptions are piston slap and fuel-pump noise—if your engine has a mechanical pump. These also occur at half engine speed. Noises occurring at engine speed are usually crankshaft-related in the *bottom end* of the engine.

Use a timing light to determine the frequency of the noise as it relates to engine speed. Hook up your timing light and run the engine. Observe the timing-light flashes and listen. If the noise occurs once

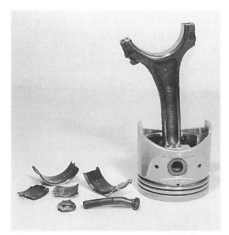

Rod started events that destroyed block.

Noises can be pinpointed with automotive stethoscope. Instead of placing stethoscope against cam cover or front cover, put it against an attaching bolt. Cover gaskets and air space muffle some noises. Long screwdriver with one end against your skull immediately behind an ear and other end against engine can also be used.

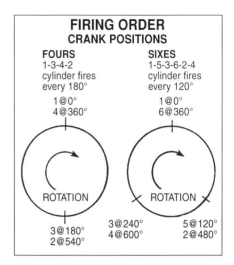

every time the light flashes, the noise is at half engine speed. If it occurs twice for every flash, the noise is at engine speed.

Once you determine the frequency of the noise, you may need a listening device to pinpoint its location. A mechanic's *stethoscope* works best. It is flexible and picks up sound well. You can make do with a screwdriver, piece of wood or a short length of hose.

A 3—4-ft section of hose works similarly to the stethoscope. Use a plastic hose if possible—it transmits sound better than rubber. A screwdriver or wood dowel transmits sound well, but is not flexible.

Unfortunately, sounds are also carried by the cylinder block, which makes pinpointing the noise more difficult. If you use a screwdriver, press the blade end against the engine. Press the other end against your ear or touch it to your skull behind an ear.

Whatever you use as a listening probe, move it to different spots on the engine until you find where the noise is loudest. Place the probe next to a spark plug. This is an excellent way to locate noise from one cylinder—especially from the piston or connecting rod.

An erratic banging or slapping noise at the front of the engine may be a very loose, worn timing chain. Listen with the probe placed against the front cover.

If the noise seems to be coming from the upper part of the engine—the valve train—move the probe until the sound is the loudest. Then alternate between the

intake and exhaust ports of the noisy cylinder to pinpoint the source. Don't forget the mechanical fuel pump. It also operates at half engine speed. Read on for more details about this problem.

Valve-Train Noise—A loud clicking sound from the valve train is normally caused by excessive valve lash. If the noise appears to be in this area, remove the cam cover.

Don't run the engine with the cover off, particularly if the cam lobes are drilled for lobe and follower lubrication. Do it and you'll oil yourself, any onlookers, the engine compartment, and garage floor or driveway.

Dig out your feeler gages and check valve lash for each cylinder at top center (TC). Valve clearance for intake and exhaust valves is 0.008 in. (0.20mm) and 0.010 in. (0.24mm), respectively, for a "stone-cold" engine. If the engine is hot—at operating temperature—set lash to 0.0l0 in. (0.24mm) intake and 0.012 in. (0.30mm) exhaust. If the engine is warm, let it cool before checking lash.

Turn to pages 111 and 155 for the specific valve-lashing procedure.

Piston Slap—This is a hollow or dull noise. If you were to tap a piston thrust surface—either skirt just below the piston pin—with a plastic mallet, it would make

a similar sound. The same noise that comes from the engine is muffled by the cast-iron cylinder block and coolant.

Piston slap is loudest when an engine is cold. Piston-to-bore clearance is maximum on a cold engine. If the noise gradually goes away as the engine warms up, the condition isn't serious.

To determine if a noise is piston slap, loosen the bolt(s) at the base of the distributor so you can turn the distributor. With the engine running, *retard* the ignition slowly by rotating the distributor housing counterclockwise. Retarded timing reduces the combustion load on the pistons. Therefore, the noise should diminish or cease if it's piston slap. Reset timing and tighten the bolt(s) after performing this check.

A hole in a piston makes a noise similar to piston slap. It can be detected by removing the dipstick and listening to the dipstick tube. You should hear the noise followed by a pressure pulse.

Main Bearing—A main bearing with excess clearance will knock at half engine speed. The noise will sound distant—muffled—in the engine. You can sometimes feel such a noise through the accelerator pedal. The noise usually occurs when the engine is first started, hot or cold, before oil pressure builds. It can also be detected under hard acceleration. Disabling a cylinder on either side of the problem bearing should quiet the noise.

Don't be fooled by detonation which usually occurs under hard acceleration. It is higher pitched than the knock caused by excessive main-bearing clearance, with a tinny, rattling sound.

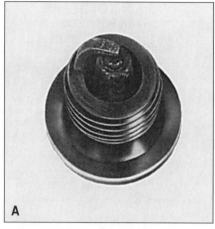

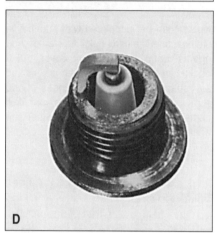

Spark plugs can yield important troubleshooting clues. Plug A suffers from heavily rounded electrodes and pitted insulator—it's worn out. Replace such plugs and engine performance will improve. Plug B is oil-fouled. Shiny black coating indicated excess oil consumption, possibly from worn rings and valve guides. Plug C is carbon-fouled—don't confuse it with oil-fouling. A carbon-fouled plug's dry, flat-black coating comes from excessively rich air/fuel mixture, stop-and-go driving or a too-cold plug heat range. Note: Plug D is normal. Electrode rounding is moderate and insulator is even tan or gray, indicating all is well in combustion chamber. Photos courtesy of Champion Spark Plug Company.

Connecting Rod—A connecting rod will knock or pound if oil pressure is low or connecting-rod bearing-to-journal clearance is excessive. The noise will be loudest just after releasing the accelerator after maintaining a constant speed.

Piston Pin—Piston-pin noise has a pronounced double click. This sound is normally heard while the engine is idling or at low speed. Piston slap or noise at the pin or rod bearing can be checked by grounding the plug at that cylinder while the engine idles. The clicking noise will diminish or stop when the problem cylinder is disabled.

Piston Rings—Defective piston rings make a chattering sound that is most noticeable during acceleration. The chattering is usually caused by broken rings, but it may occur due to the rings losing their *tension,*

or springiness. Either condition should show up as low compression during a compression or leak-down test.

Fuel Pump—Before you tear down your engine because of a valve-train noise or whatever, check the fuel pump. Mechanical fuel-pump noise will normally be a fairly loud, double click at half engine speed.

To confirm a faulty fuel pump, disconnect the fuel line at the pump and remove the pump. Temporarily tape over the fuel-pump hole in the head so oil doesn't get tossed out the open hole. Run the engine—there will be enough fuel in the carburetor for a few minutes of idling. If the click is gone, the pump is most likely the problem, but the noise could be caused by a loose fuel-pump eccentric. It's on the nose of the cam.

PERFORMANCE PROBLEMS

Read the Plugs—Spark plugs allow you to "see" into each cylinder of an engine. Remove the plugs, but keep them in order.

Two major things to look for are a plug with a wet, shiny-black insulator or one with blister marks on the insulator or shell. Wet, black deposits indicate excessive oil being drawn into the combustion chamber. Blistering on the insulator indicates excessive heat. See photos.

If the plug insulators have a dry gray or black coating on them, check for an over-rich mixture or weak ignition. Extensive low-speed driving or excessive idling can also cause this condition. Other problems—if the engine is carburetor-equipped—there may be a float level problem, sunken float or a stuck choke. Malfunctioning fuel-injector nozzles can also be the cause.

Vacuum Test—An internal-combustion engine is basically an air pump. How well it pumps is a good indicator of its overall condition. When idling, an engine produces a vacuum in the intake manifold, turbocharged or not. If each cylinder doesn't contribute its share, a vacuum gage will show it.

The first test should be done with the engine running. Hook the vacuum gage to a fitting on the intake manifold, not a carburetor. Start the engine. At idle, the reading should be about 16—18 inches of mercury (in. Hg). Altitude, ignition timing and cam design all affect manifold vacuum. Vacuum will be less at high altitude and on engines with high-overlap cams—mostly in high-performance engines.

A reading of 15 in. Hg or less indicates either incorrect ignition timing or a worn engine. Set the timing and recheck manifold vacuum. If the gage needle *floats*—moves slowly back and forth—the mixture is probably over-rich. Turn the idle-mixture screws—if a carburetor is used—or increase engine speed to 2000—2500 rpm to see if this corrects the problem. If the reading is low—12 in. Hg or less—the engine may have a blown head gasket or an air leak.

Next, accelerate the engine rapidly and release the throttle. When the engine is accelerating, the vacuum reading should drop, but remain steady. If the reading fluctuates at higher rpm, the valve springs may be weak.

When you release the throttle, the reading should jump about 5 in. Hg above that at idle, then settle back to the original

When an engine's sealing is subpar, it can't "pull" adequate vacuum. Causes of poor vacuum include poorly adjusted valves, burned valves, worn cam lobes, a blown head gasket, and worn cylinders, pistons and rings. A fluctuating needle indicates trouble in at least one cylinder.

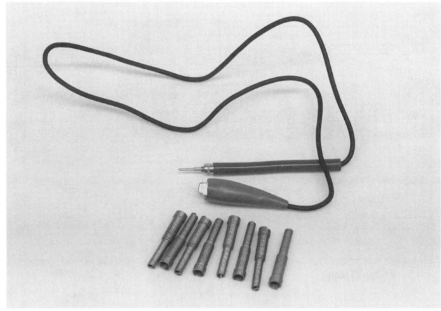

Plug jumpers and ground wire make power-balance testing easy. Setup can help prevent a high-voltage shock and damage to expensive electronic-ignition module, if so equipped.

idle reading. If the reading does not go that high, the pistons and rings are not sealing well.

If you get a normal reading that soon drops back to zero when you first start the engine, suspect a plugged exhaust system.

Once the engine is warm, perform some *cranking vacuum tests.* First, disable the ignition. If the engine has a conventional point-type distributor, disconnect the primary battery lead to the coil. With electronic ignition, disconnect the distributor-to-amplifier lead.

Now, with a helper or a remote starter, crank the engine. The vacuum-gage needle should remain fairly steady while the engine is cranked. If it fluctuates, one of the cylinders is not doing its share. The cause of this could be one of the following: incorrect valve adjustment, worn camshaft lobe, leaky valve, worn cylinder bore or piston rings, broken piston rings, holed piston or a leaky head gasket. The following test will pinpoint which cylinder(s) is at fault.

Power-Balance Test—This is a good test for finding a problem cylinder. Aircraft mechanics use a test similar to this on reciprocating engines.

If each cylinder is contributing an equal amount of power, eliminating any one will result in the same power or rpm reduction. A good engine analyzer with an oscilloscope will have a power-

balance-test feature. With this capability, any combination of cylinders can be disabled to perform the test.

During the power-balance test, disable the cylinders one at a time as the engine runs at a fixed throttle setting. Note rpm drop with the cylinder disabled.

For the test, idle the engine at about 1000 rpm. Disable one cylinder and allow engine speed to stabilize. Note rpm drop for each cylinder. The greater the drop, the more power that cylinder produces. Conversely, the less rpm drop, the less that cylinder produces.

Most engine analyzers have a built-in *power-balance tester* that simplifies this test. Regardless, the home method is not so difficult, but be careful. Touch the business end of a spark-plug lead and you can get a 20,000—60,000-volt shock. And on vehicles with electronic ignition, the resulting high-voltage surge may damage the ignition-control unit if the spark-plug lead isn't grounded when it's disconnected from the spark plug.

One way of doing a power-balance test is to pull each plug wire off its spark plug. Then place a 4-in.-long section of solid wire into the boot so it touches the lead. Bend the wire at the bottom of the boot and install the lead back on the plug. Bend the wire so it is as far away from the surrounding metal as possible. Do this for

all four or six plugs and you're ready to do the test. By using a ground wire or jumper cable, you can ground each plug individually to disable that cylinder.

This same method can also be used at the distributor cap, but care must be taken to avoid arcing between cap towers. Trace each plug wire back from its plug to determine which cylinder you're disabling.

A number of manufacturers make power-balance test kits. As shown, these kits consist of a jumper wire and eight springs only four or six springs will be needed. The springs install between the plugs and wire boots. By touching the exposed spring with the grounded jumper, each plug can be shorted without damaging the ignition or your nerves.

The last method is one I don't recommend. Pull each plug wire off using insulated pliers while the engine runs. Although this method definitely works, be prepared to get shocked. Restrict the use of this method to engines using point-type ignition systems. Do not use this procedure with an electronic-ignition-equipped engine.

Compression Test—This is the easiest way to check the sealing quality of a cylinder. Compression testing should be done with the engine warm to give the most accurate indication of engine condition. Run the engine to bring it up to operating

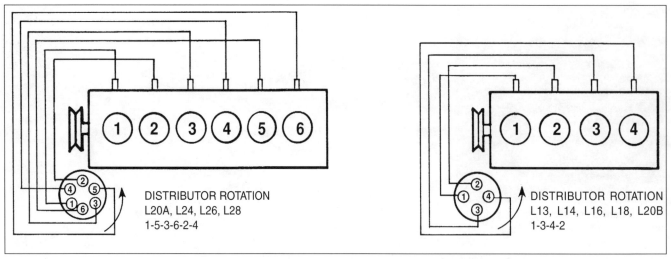

Firing order for six- and four-cylinder L-series engines with distributor rotation and spark-plug leads: Remove distributor cap to determine firing position of each cylinder.

temperature, then remove the spark plugs. Disable the ignition system. Do this by disconnecting the battery lead (+) at the coil. Block the throttle wide open so the cylinder can get a full air charge. Make sure the carburetor choke is wide open. On fuel-injected engines, pull the leads off the injectors so they don't squirt fuel into the cylinders. Or, better yet, crank the engine with a remote starter switch and the ignition off so the injectors don't squirt.

Install the compression tester in number-1 spark-plug hole. The best testers thread into the spark-plug hole and have a long hose so you can position the gage for easier reading. Inexpensive testers have a rigid steel tube extending from the gage with a rubber cone at the end. This cone must be held tightly over the hole for positive sealing.

Once you have the gage installed or in position, crank over the engine at least four times and record the highest reading. Release the gage pressure and go to the next cylinder. Once you've tested all cylinders, compare the readings. The lowest reading should be at least 75% of the highest.

For example, if the highest reading is 140 psi, the lowest should be 0.75 X 140 = 105 psi minimum. Consider 75% the *absolute lowest percentage* for street use. For a performance vehicle, the minimum should be in the high 90% range.

WARNING: When doing a compression test on a carbureted engine, an explosive air/fuel charge shoots out the spark-plug holes while the engine is cranking. A spark or flame could cause a small explo-

sion. Make sure the immediate area is free of any open flames—*don't smoke*. And always disable the ignition because it is a ready source of sparks.

What readings should you see? Certainly, the compression of an engine from the "good-fuel era" should be higher than that of a unleaded engine. For example, an early L16 or L24 in good condition should give about 180 psi versus 140 psi for a Turbo L28.

If all cylinders except one are good, squirt about a *teaspoon* of 20W or 30W oil through the spark-plug hole. Too much oil will raise compression and give you a false reading. Wait a minute, then recheck the compression.

If cylinder pressure comes up near the others, the rings are not sealing. If pressure remains unchanged, suspect a burned or stuck valve or a blown head gasket.

Leak-Down Test—This test is similar to a compression test, with a little more sophistication, more answers and more money. The major difference between the two is that a leak-down test uses externally applied pressure. The advantage of leak-down testing is that it eliminates factors not affecting an engine's sealing ability; primarily, engine-cranking speed and valve timing. Rather than reading in pressure, *percent leakage* at a given pressure indicates the cylinder's sealing ability.

The disadvantage of a leak-down tester is its cost—too expensive for the typical toolbox. And, it requires a compressed-air source. But, except for the *percent-leakage gauge,* the test can be done with a simple air tank and spark-plug-hole adapter. You

just won't be able to read percent leakage. Thus, you won't be able to compare cylinders. However, you'll be able to find severe leaks.

A leak-down test is performed with the piston at *exactly* TC on its *compression stroke*—both valves closed. Air is supplied to the cylinder via a special fitting that adapts the air hose to the spark-plug hole. The cylinder *should* do a good job of holding pressure. If it doesn't, the test can give you an indication of what's wrong.

WARNING: Be sure to stay away from the fan, accessory-drive belts and pulleys while doing a leak-down test. Because the cylinder is pressurized, the engine can turn over with a short burst if the piston is not right on TC of its firing stroke. Remember that two cylinders are at TC in this crank position, but one is firing while the other is between its intake and exhaust stroke—both valves are slightly open. Consequently, the crank must be turned 360° to test the other cylinder.

To minimize the possibility of the crank spinning during leak-down testing, set each piston at TC. Start by marking the distributor housing directly in line with each spark-plug tower. The marks must be accurate. Remove the distributor cap and crank the engine to align the rotor with the next mark, then back the crank up about 10°. Firing orders are: 1-3-4-2 for four-cylinder engines and 1-5-3-6-2-4 for sixes.

This will only get you very close to TC because the ignition fires a few degrees before TC (BTC). To find cylinder-l TC, simply align the crankshaft-pulley timing mark with the pointer. For four-cylinder engines, cylinder 4 also fires in this position, but 360° later; for six-cylinder engines, cylinder 6 fires 60° later.

To find TC of the other cylinders, use the rotor to get close. You'll need a helper to turn the crankshaft. Then, with a 2-in. piece of wire stuck down in the spark-plug hole so it butts square against the piston, have your helper rotate the crank *backward*, or counterclockwise. The wire will back out of the hole, then go back in. The instant the wire changes direction is when the piston is at TC. Rotate the crank back and forth until you find this *neutral* or TC position.

For four-cylinder engines, once you find cylinder-3 TC, mark the pulley in line with the timing pointer—it will be exactly 180° of crank rotation from cylinder-1 TC mark. You'll then be able to find cylinder-2 TC without using the wire—it occurs 360° afterward. Just align the mark with the pointer after you've turned the crank one complete rotation.

For six-cylinder engines, there are three instead of two TC positions at the pulley—120° apart. Cylinder 5 fires 120° after cylinder 1. Mark this position after finding it using the wire; you'll use it for finding cylinder-2 TC, which occurs 360° later. Turn the crank another 120° for cylinder 3. Again, mark it—you'll use it for finding cylinder-4 TC.

You may be thoroughly confused by now. If so, see the crank-pulley drawings, page 9, for four- and six-cylinder TC positions and firing orders.

While testing, have the oil-filler and radiator caps off and the carburetors—if so equipped—blocked wide open. With fuel injection, you can disconnect the duct at the airflow meter on the engine side.

Connect the air hose and pressurize the cylinder. This is when the leak-down gage comes in handy. The gage indicates what percentage of air supplied to the cylinder leaks out past the piston, a valve, head gasket or a crack. It is not unusual to hear a small amount of leakage at the oil-filler hole in the cam if the engine is worn. Normal leak-down is 5-10%; 20% or more is considered excessive.

If you don't have the gage, listen for air leaking at the exhaust pipe, radiator, oil-filler hole, dipstick tube and carburetor—or manifold, if you removed the airflow

meter on a fuel-injected engine.

If you hear air escaping through the carburetor or manifold, the intake valve is leaking. If you can hear it at the exhaust, it's the exhaust valve. If either valve is leaking, be sure the piston is still at TC *on the compression stroke.*

A head-gasket leak will show up as air leaking out an adjacent cylinder or through the radiator-filler neck. A cracked cylinder wall or head will also show up as air leaking from the radiator-filler neck. If you hear leakage at the oil-filler hole or dipstick tube, the pistons and rings are not sealing satisfactorily.

Head Gasket—If pressure is down on two adjacent cylinders, chances are the head gasket has blown between them. A compression test of the two cylinders will show high leakage or low pressure. During a leak-down test, a blown head gasket will reveal itself as air escaping from one spark-plug hole while the other cylinder is pressurized, and vice versa.

A head gasket can also blow between the cylinder and the cooling system. This allows combustion-chamber pressure to escape into the cooling system and coolant into the combustion chamber. If the problem is severe, you can find the leak by pressurizing the cooling system. You'll be able to hear air or coolant escaping into that cylinder through the spark-plug hole.

A blown head gasket is also indicated by the spark plugs. If one or two plugs show white fluffy deposits and the others look OK, suspect a blown head gasket.

Valves—As I noted earlier, a leak-down test will indicate a bad valve by allowing air to escape from the carburetor or manifold, or exhaust. If you don't have a leak-down tester, you'll have to depend on a compression check and further testing. If oil in the cylinder didn't correct a low-compression reading, chances are one of the valves isn't sealing.

The first thing to do is to make sure the valve is closing all the way. Remove the cam cover. Rotate the crankshaft until the piston in the bad cylinder is at TC on the compression stroke—the distributor rotor should point at that cylinder's distributor-cap tower and the rocker arms should be loose

If there is too much clearance—a rocker arm is extremely loose—look at the cam

Listen to engine while watching timing-light flashes. If light flashes every time noise occurs, noise is at camshaft speed that is half crankshaft speed. Noises occurring twice for every flash of light are at crankshaft speed.

lobe. It and the rocker may be worn. This will require cam and rocker-arm replacement. If you're lucky, it may only require setting valve clearance to the proper specs.

CAMSHAFT-LOBE WEAR

Camshaft-lobe *and* rocker-arm wear occur rapidly. Once the hardened contact surface of either a lobe or rocker is worn through, the softer material is easily galled and quickly removed. The resulting metal particles also remove the hardened rubbing surface of the mating part. Therefore, regardless of which of the two components begins to wear in this chain of events, both the lobe and follower are quickly destroyed. Consequently, valve lift and engine performance gradually deteriorate with increasing cam-lobe and rocker-arm wear as gas flow in or out of that cylinder diminishes.

Unlike a conventional rocker-arm engine that has its cam buried deep in the engine block, the L-series camshaft is easily inspected. It's right under the cam cover. So, if you suspect that poor engine performance may be caused by a worn cam and rocker, remove the cam cover and take a look.

Inspect Lobe & Rocker Arm—A worn cam lobe is easily recognized by visually comparing it to other lobes. The worn lobe's *nose (toe)* will be galled and rounded off. Usually, only one cam lobe is at fault. Good lobes are shiny all the way around. A bad one will be rounded off and galled. See the following illustration for cam-lobe terminology. Stick a

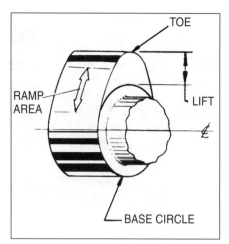

When cam-lobe base circle is on rocker arm, valve is fully closed. When tip of lobe toe is against rocker arm, valve is fully open.

finger in the oil laying in the head. If you feel metal filings when rubbing your fingers together, they probably came from a *wiped* lobe and rocker arm.

Rotate the camshaft so you can get a good look at each lobe. Crank the engine a few degrees, take a look; then crank it a few more degrees. While you're looking, also check the rocker arms. Although a wiped cam lobe is much easier to spot, a worn rocker-arm pad will be obvious. **Check Valve Lift & Lash**—Although visually inspecting the cam and rockers should be sufficient, a valve-lift check will

confirm whether a lobe and its rocker are OK. Before doing this, make sure valve lash is correct. If it's not, valve lift won't be right, either. Lash is 0.008 in. (0.20mm) intake and 0.010 in. (0.24mm) exhaust, cold; 0.010 in. (0.24mm) intake and 0.012 in. (0.30mm) exhaust, hot.

Go through the firing order when adjusting valve lash. Start with cylinder-1 valves by setting the crank on TC with cylinder-1 in its *firing position*. Mark the distributor housing in line with the cylinder-1 plug-wire post. While you're at it, also mark the positions of the others. Remove the distributor cap, then align the rotor to this mark. Cylinder-1 exhaust and intake rocker arms should be loose. Also, the two cam-lobe toes should be pointing away from the rocker arms. If the rotor is pointing away from the number-1 mark and the cam-lobe toes are down, the crank is 360° out of position.

After checking and adjusting the first two valves, if required, rotate the crank 180° (four-cylinder engines) or 120° (six-cylinder engines) to the next cylinder in the firing order. As indicated on page 12, this will be cylinder 3 for fours, or cylinder 5 for sixes. The distributor will turn counterclockwise 90° or 60°, respectively. Continue this process until you've checked and adjusted all valves.

To measure valve lift, start with the

rocker arm on the base of its cam lobe—piston at TC on its compression stroke. This is the reference height for the closed valve. The best place to measure is from the spring seat to the spring retainer. Check all intake valves, then all exhausts. Record the results and compare. One that's obviously low—with a difference of 0.015 in. (0.381mm) or more—is excessively worn.

Note: A 0.010 in. (0.25mm) lift variation is acceptable on stock engines because of rocker-arm size—ratio—and geometry differences.

Several types of instruments can be used for checking valve lift. Best is a vernier caliper or dial indicator. Because the head is aluminum, a magnetic-base dial indicator won't work. You can remedy this by bolting the indicator or a steel plate to the head at a cam-cover bolt hole on the spark-plug side of the head.

With the follower on the camshaft base circle, measure from the spring seat to the top of the spring retainer with a vernier, ruler or divider. Record your reading. Or, with a dial indicator, set the indicator plunger square against the top of the retainer and zero the dial. Rotate the crank until the valve is fully opened. Remeasure and record this figure. The difference between the two figures is valve lift. Lift is read directly with a dial indicator. Continue this process until you've checked all of the valves. Note each valve's position and whether it's an intake or exhaust valve.

Compare the readings after you've finished. Any reading that is low probably is due to a worn lobe and rocker arm. This can be visually verified. Then check your findings against the chart at left. **Replace Cam & Rocker**—If you find a bad cam lobe and rocker, but compression is good and oil consumption is not excessive, you can replace the cam and the bad rocker and be relatively confident that the engine will be OK.

To remove the camshaft, you must first disconnect the timing chain from the cam. This is covered in the next chapter. You can then replace the camshaft and rocker arm. This procedure is covered on page 107, Chapter 7. Once the rocker arm and cam is replaced, turn back to page 23 for details on reconnecting the timing chain.

CAMSHAFT LOBE LIFT						
		\multicolumn{5}{c}{mm (in)}				
Engine	Year	\multicolumn{2}{c}{Intake}		\multicolumn{2}{c}{Exhaust}	
		@ Lobe	@ Valve	@Lobe	@ Valve
L13, L14	All	6.65 (0.2618)	10.0 (0.3937)	6.65 (0.2618)	10.0 (0.3937)
L16	68-72	6.65 (0.2618)	10.0 (0.3937)	6.65 (0.2618)	10.5 (0.3937)
L16	73	7.00 (0.2756)	10.5 (0.4134)	7.00 (0.2756)	10.5 (0.4134)
L18	73-74	7.00 (0.2756)	10.5 (0.4134)	7.00 (0.2756)	10.5 (0.4134)
L20B	75-80	7.00 (0.2756)	10.5 (0.4134)	7.00 (0.2756)	10.5 (0.4134)
L20A1 L20A2	66-73	7.05 (0.2776) 7.35 (0.2894)	10.4 (0.4094) 10.8 (0.4252)	7.05 (0.2776) 7.35 (0.2894)	10.4 (0.4094) 10.8 (0.4252)
L24	77-84 (810) 70-73 (240Z)	6.65 (0.2618) 7.00 (0.2756)	10.0 (0.3937) 10.5 (0.4134)	7.00 (0.2756) 7.00 (0.2756)	10.5 (0.4134) 10.5 (0.4134)
L26	74-75	7.00 (0.2756)	11.0 (0.4333)	7.00 (0.2756)	11.0 (0.4333)
L28	75-83	7.00 (0.2756)	11.0 (0.4333)	7.00 (0.2756)	11.0 (0.4333)

1 Single carburetor
2 Twin carburetor

CHAPTER TWO

In-Car Repairs: Cylinder Head & Timing Chain

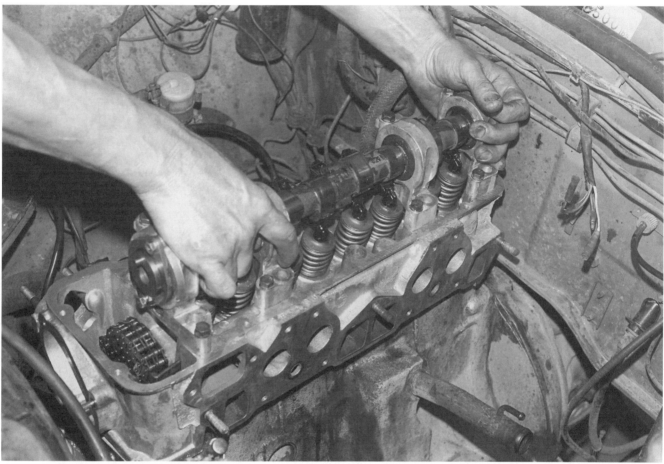

L-series engine is durable, but cylinder head and timing chain will require more attention than block. When installing head, make sure it engages locating dowels on block.

Although the L-series Nissan/Datsun engine is rugged, the cylinder head is sensitive to overheating. This is primarily because it is an aluminum cylinder head bolted to a cast-iron block. The durability of the cylinder head can also be shortened by poor or improper maintenance. This is particularly true in North America where car owners are accustomed to understressed, large-displacement, cast-iron sixes and V8s that are more tolerant of neglect and abuse. Poor maintenance habits have unfortunately been carried over to smaller, more highly stressed fours and sixes such as the L-series Nissan/Datsun.

Because of this, I include a chapter devoted to in-car cylinder-head removal and replacement along with how to check and correct for timing-chain wear. Rather than providing the details of component inspection in this chapter, I cover only the in-car aspects of the repair. You can fill in the blanks by referring to the engine teardown and assembly chapters starting on pages 37 and 112, respectively.

The cylinder head shown being removed is on an L16 engine installed in a 1973 PL620 pickup truck. This represents the simplest installation of the L-series

engines. For details on cylinder-head removal and installation on the more complicated fuel-injected Z-car engine, refer to the engine removal and installation chapters on pages 27 and 141, respectively.

If your car has a front-hinged hood, the first thing to do is get the hood out of the way. Refer to page 28 for how to do this.

CYLINDER-HEAD REMOVAL

Find TC—Rotate the crank so number-1 piston is at TC of its *firing stroke*. Doing this necessary job now is easier than doing it later.

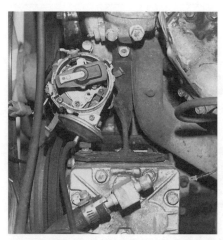

Set number-1 cylinder at top center (TC) before removing cylinder head. After matchmarking position of number-1 distributor cap on distributor housing, remove cap. Rotate crank so pulley timing mark aligns with TC mark and distributor rotor is near mark you just made on housing.

If equipped with mechanical fuel pump, remove pump after you disconnect fuel lines and attaching bolts.

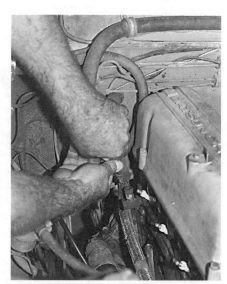

Disconnect heater hose at cylinder head.

Remove cam cover. A sharp whack with heel of your palm should break it loose.

Make sure that the piston is in this position and not at TC between the exhaust and intake strokes. One way to do this is to remove the cam cover and see if the number-1 intake and exhaust valves are fully closed when the crank-pulley TC mark aligns with the pointer. At this position, the rocker arms will be on the base circle of the cam lobe and will feel loose.

Another way to check for TC is to remove the number-1 spark plug, then crank the engine with your thumb sealing the plug hole. The instant you feel cylinder pressure building, rotate the crank so the TC mark aligns with the pointer.

Still another way to verify TC is to mark the position of the number-1 spark-plug post on the distributor housing, then remove the distributor cap. If the distributor rotor points at the mark with the crank on TC, you've got it. If not, rotate the crank 360° to bring it into position.

Fuel Pump—Skip this step if your car is equipped only with an electric fuel pump. However, if it has a mechanical pump mounted on the right front of the cylinder head—you'll have to remove it before you can remove the cam sprocket. Disconnect the fuel line to the carburetor/s. The supply line can be left attached to the pump. Remove the two pump attaching bolts, the pump and its spacer. Lay the pump back out of the way. Remove the engine-lifting lug, if your engine is so equipped. It'll be directly behind the fuel pump or where the pump would be. An engine ground strap may be under one of the lug mounting bolts.

Cam Cover—Remove all cam-cover bolts, then bump the cover loose with the butt of your hand. It should come off easily. *Don't pry the cam cover off.* The risk of damage is high and cast-aluminum covers are fragile—and expensive!

TC Check—Although you already set number-1 piston at TC, recheck it. There are three timing notches on the cam-sprocket hub, one for each of the three dowel holes in the sprocket. The timing notches, or marks, are directly in line with the dowel holes. The dowel holes are behind the fuel-pump eccentric.

There's another timing mark—an oblong groove—in the front of the cam thrust plate, just to the left, of the plate's top mounting bolt as viewed from the front. You should be able to see both timing marks through one of the sprocket lightening holes. If the marks don't line up, they should be close. If they aren't, rotate the crank clockwise 360° to line up the crank TC mark, and recheck.

TIMING-CHAIN INSPECTION

Because L-series Nissan/Datsun engines often suffer from timing-chain *elongation*—commonly referred to as *stretch*—now is the time to check it.

As the links of a timing chain wear, overall chain length increases—or *elongates*. This results in the cam getting "behind" the crankshaft, opening and closing the valves *later* in relation to the crankshaft and piston positions. The power band is then moved higher in the rpm range, increasing power at higher rpm. This may be OK if your car is being used for high-speed operation, but overall power output also suffers as chain wear progresses.

If cam timing can't be restored by repositioning the cam sprocket, the chain must be replaced. The picture on page 7 shows what can happen with a badly

Before removing head, check timing-chain condition. With crank set on TC, cam-sprocket-hub notch should line up with groove in cam thrust plate.

Hardwood block wedged between tight and slack sides of timing chain will keep chain from falling down into engine. Taper on end as shown. Be sure to include a retrieving wire or cord to assist in removing it. The wire or cord can hang out of the front of the engine as a good reminder to be sure to remove it.

worn chain. To determine if the chain needs to be replaced, or if it can be corrected by simply repositioning the cam sprocket, see the nearby sidebar, *Cam-Sprocket Timing Marks.*

Cam-Timing Check—With the number-1 piston at TC, find the cam-sprocket timing marks through the sprocket "window" at the top. The marks will be just to the left of the top thrust-plate mounting bolt as you look at it. If the sprocket timing notch lines up with the right end of the plate's timing groove, cam timing is right on. If it's to the left, the cam is retarded. Use your discretion if the mark is in between. Just keep in mind that the chain will continue to wear.

If cam timing needs to be advanced, reinstall the sprocket in the next highest-numbered camshaft-dowel hole, then recheck timing. Now you've come to the first critical teardown step, whether you are removing the cylinder head or just replacing the timing chain.

Wood Block—One of the cheapest, but most important tools for working on L-series engines is a wood block about 1/2 in. thick X l in. wide X 7 in. long. Carve one from 1/2 in. thick wood using the photo as reference. This little chunk of wood will be the difference between a two-hour or a two-day job. When in place, it will keep the chain-tensioning piston from popping out or the chain from dropping.

Cam-Sprocket Bolt—Loosen the cam-sprocket bolt using a 19mm socket and breaker bar. To keep a four-cylinder engine from turning over while loosening

the bolt, put an adjustable wrench on the square bosses cast onto the camshaft at its center. Large Vise-Grip pliers can be clamped onto a 6-cylinder cam. Position the wrench or Vise-Grips so it will rotate down against the right-side cam-cover gasket surface. Put a wood block between the tool and the head. This will prevent the tool from damaging the cam-cover gasket surface. You can now apply enough force to break loose the bolt.

If you have a vehicle with a 4-speed transmission, use first gear to keep the engine from turning. On automatic-transmission vehicles use a 26mm wrench on the crank bolt. Finally, you could remove the cam bolt with an impact wrench.

Turn the crank in its normal direction of rotation back to TC after breaking loose the sprocket bolt. This keeps the normally *tight side* of the timing chain tight.

Mark Chain Link—Looking at the front of the sprocket, find the numbered *dimple* at the outer periphery of the sprocket to the right of the sprocket's center. It corresponds to the numbered dowel hole above the sprocket's center and is engaged by the cam dowel: **1** for **1**; **2** for **2**; and **3** for **3**. Mark the chain link that lines up with the dimple. White or yellow grease pencil or paint is easy to see and will stay on. You'll use this mark as a reference when reinstalling the sprocket.

If the cam sprocket is already installed to the number-3 notch and it's retarded, plan on replacing the chain. Do the same if cam timing can't be restored by reinstalling the sprocket to the number-3 notch.

Install Wood Block—The most critical part of the cylinder-head installation-and-removal process is installing the wood block.

Timing marks 1, 2 and 3 (arrows) are at outer periphery and corresponding dowel holes of sprocket. Drawing of timing marks is on page 131.

CAM-SPROCKET TIMING MARKS
There are three timing positions on the cam sprocket: 1, 2 and 3. Due to different dowel-hole offsets, each represents a 4° difference in camshaft timing in crankshaft degrees. If the sprocket is installed on the camshaft dowel to the number-1 mark, reinstalling it to the number-2 mark advances the cam four crankshaft degrees. Likewise, reinstalling the sprocket timed to the number-3 mark advances it another 4°. So, if the cam was originally timed to the number-1 notch and it became retarded 4° because of chain wear, timing can be restored to specs by reinstalling the sprocket to the number-2 notch. This will compensate for chain wear.

If chain wear cannot be compensated for by installing the sprocket to the number-3 notch—in this case, a total of 8°—the chain must be replaced. Doing this requires removing the crankshaft damper, distributor and front cover. The fan, its shroud, radiator and some engine accessories will have to come off, too.

To keep cam from turning while loosening sprocket bolt, put wrench on center of cam at bosses. Hold wrench so it doesn't come down hard against head and damage cam-cover gasket surface.

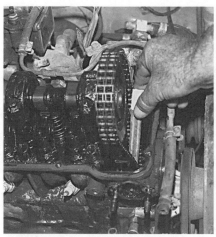

Insert hardwood block between chain and drive firmly in place. Do this before you remove sprocket. Another photo on page 22 shows this from a different angle.

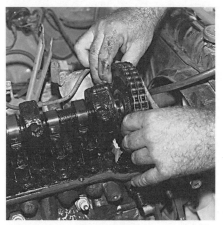

Work sprocket off cam and from under chain. Lay chain on top of wood block.

Remove battery and store out of way. Battery-terminal puller makes job easy and does not stress battery post.

Make sure the manual transmission is in neutral, then slip the block down between the tight and slack sides of the timing chain, below the cam sprocket. Wedge it between the chain so it's *real tight.* A long socket-set extension and a soft mallet are good for doing this. Drive it in good. Here's one situation where almost too much is better than not enough. If the spring-loaded tensioner pops out, be ready for a lot of unnecessary work, such as removing the radiator, accessories, crank damper, distributor and front cover.

After the wedge is *securely* in place, remove the cam-sprocket bolt and fuel-pump eccentric. With the bolt out, work the sprocket off the end of the camshaft. Remove the sprocket and let the timing chain drop on top of the block.

Reposition Cam Sprocket—Now is the time the "tale will be told." Reinstall the cam sprocket to its *next-highest-numbered* timing mark. If your engine is a four-cylinder, have a Crescent wrench ready to rotate the cam slightly. Because it doesn't take much torque to rotate the cam, you can use Vise-Grip pliers on a six-cylinder's cam. *Don't clamp on a lobe!*

Fit the sprocket to the chain, aligning the numbered dimple with the marked chain link. Engage the sprocket's dowel hole with the cam dowel. Hold the sprocket against the end of the cam, then rotate the cam about 2E—clockwise looking at the front of the engine—until the sprocket engages the cam's center boss. Use a soft mallet to tap the sprocket on the cam until it bottoms. Be careful here. It doesn't take much force to break the dowel.

Wood-Block Removal—To remove the wood block, either now or after you've installed the sprocket, bump the engine over slightly *after the sprocket is in place.* This is best done with a socket on the crank-pulley bolt. Remove the wood block while pulling up on it with that wire or cord you put on the block. The block should pull free when the chain moves.

Recheck Cam Timing—If the left side of the sprocket notch lines up with the right end of the thrust-plate timing groove, you're in luck. Take note of the cam-sprocket position and make sure the wood block is firmly in place. You can now remove the sprocket and proceed with removing the head.

However, if the sprocket is fitted to the number-2 position and the cam is still retarded, refit it to the number-3 position and recheck it. If it's already in the number-3 position, your job just got bigger. The timing chain has to be replaced. Refer to Chapters 3, 4, 8 and 9 for doing this job.

Remove Battery—Disconnect the battery cables, remove the battery hold down and battery if you think the job will drag on for more than two weeks. Store it out of the way in a cool, dry area.

Remove Carburetor—If you plan to rebuild your carburetor(s), now is a good time to remove it. On the other hand, if it doesn't need rebuilding, leave the carburetor(s) in place. You'll remove it with the manifold later.

Distributor—Don't remove the distributor unless necessary. If the vacuum-advance diaphragm is in the way, note the position of the distributor, loosen its adjusting bolt, then rotate it out of the way. **STOP:** Read about the intake and exhaust manifolds, below, before disconnecting the exhaust, fuel lines and manifold connections. You'll save some time and trouble later on when it's time to reconnect them.

Disconnect Exhaust—Disconnecting the exhaust pipe at the manifold is the one job you'll have to do from underneath, so don't take chances. A truck has sufficient ground clearance, but a passenger car must be jacked up. Block the rear wheels, jack the car up at the front, then support the front using two jack or safety stands placed under structural members. The number-2 crossmember or the front-suspension strut-rod brackets are good supports, depending on the vehicle. **Once the vehicle is on the stands, jostle it from side to side to make sure everything is substantial before climbing underneath.**

This is where a ratchet and a swivel-head socket with a long extension come in handy. Trick from the pros: Wrap the swivel joint with electrical tape to keep it from flopping around. This eases getting the socket on a hard-to-get-to bolt or nut.

With the nuts off their studs, break the exhaust flange loose. The exhaust pipe should then pull free. If it doesn't, check back along the exhaust pipe for a rigid bracket like that on the 280Z I used for engine installation and removal. It will have to be loosened to pull the pipe back and down to free the flange from the manifold studs.

Remove Air Cleaner—On carburetor-equipped vehicles, remove the air cleaner. Make sure you label any hoses by wrapping them with masking tape, making a "flag" about 1 in. long. Use a ballpoint pen or a Sharpie® pen to write with. Felt-tip ink will wash away, and is easily faded by sunlight.

Drain Coolant—Drain coolant from the radiator and engine. To save good antifreeze, drain it into a clean bucket and transfer it into a closed container. Wipe up any spills and keep your pets away from it because it is terribly poisonous.

Start by draining coolant from the radiator. You may need to jack up the front of your car slightly to be able to get the con-

tainer underneath and still have room to loosen the drain cock. To complete the coolant-draining job, set the heater control to the ON position and remove the plug from the right side of the engine block.

Radiator & Heater Hoses—Disconnect the top radiator hose at the thermostat housing and the heater-outlet hose at the right-rear of the cylinder head. Don't pry off hoses with a screwdriver. Loosen the hose clamp, twist the hose at its connection to break it loose, then pull the hose off.

Miscellaneous Hoses & Wires—Disconnect any hoses or wires that run to the cylinder head, intake manifold or carburetor(s). These include fuel lines, vacuum and heater hoses, fuel-injector and sending-unit leads, etc. Don't think you can get away with remembering where all those hoses and wires connect, particularly if yours is one of the complicated installations. Label them. Take some snapshots, too. You'll be glad you did.

Intake & Exhaust Manifolds—Removing the manifolds before removing the head is not always necessary or possible, but it was in my situation. The L16 in the subject 1971 PL620 pickup has a rigid positive crankcase ventilation (PCV) tube routed under the intake manifold and over the exhaust. The cylinder head cannot be removed with the exhaust manifold in place—both manifolds have to come off first. This is no big deal as they have to come off the head in most instances anyway, so you might as well do it now.

If your engine is equipped with fuel injection, it is next to impossible to remove the manifolds before removing the head. The reason is obvious when you look at your fuel-injected engine—all those connections and lack of access to the manifold-to-head fasteners.

Unbolt the manifolds, move them a few inches to the side, and you can leave most everything connected. I've found that it's a lot easier to remove and install the manifolds under the hood to avoid the nightmarish task of reconnecting all the fuel-injection and emissions leads later. But first, disconnect the throttle linkage, fuel lines and air-intake duct. Removing these connections gives you sufficient intake-manifold movement to get to the exhaust manifold.

The intake manifold must come off

Electrical tape around flex joint keeps socket from flopping around while you're trying to fit it to exhaust-pipe bolts. Joint remains flexible.

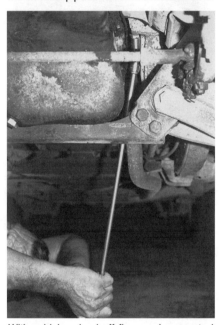

With vehicle raised off floor and supported with jack stands on firm base, loosen exhaust-to-header-pipe nuts. Long extension makes job easier.

before you can get to the exhaust. Both manifolds are mounted with studs, nuts, bolts and washers. The top of the intake is attached by bolts and washers; the bottom by bolts and heavy washers that bridge the intake- and exhaust-manifold flanges. Access to the lower bolts is difficult, but they only need to be loosened to remove the intake manifold once the top bolts are out. Remove the intake manifold first, or block it up off the exhaust manifold on fuel-injected engines.

With the intake manifold out of the way, finish removing the bolts with their heavy washers and the nuts from the exhaust-manifold studs. Then, break the exhaust manifold loose from the head. With it still connected to the exhaust pipe, lay it over to one side. On fuel-injected

With wood block in place and timing chain and sprocket off cam, head can be removed.

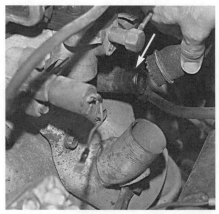

It is unfortunate that manifolds must be removed before head. Note breather tube extending from block above exhaust manifold and below intake (arrow). Depending on engine, job can range from extremely difficult to nearly impossible.

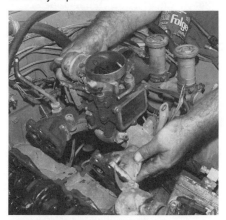

Intake manifold comes off first . . .

. . . followed by exhaust manifold.

engines, rest the intake manifold on the exhaust manifold. Disconnect any braces or brackets attached to the head, such as the one that mounted the hang-on A/C compressor on my L16.

Head Bolts—Remove the two small bolts that thread down through the forward-projecting cylinder-head flange and into the front cover *before removing any head bolts*. Forget these two little bolts before removing the cylinder head and you'll be buying a new cylinder head or front cover. Look carefully. These are often covered with grease and gunk and are very easy to miss. The right-side bolt is hidden under the fuel-pump mounting boss.

Because the head bolts have hex-socket heads, you'll need a 10mm Allen socket wrench, or plain Allen wrench to remove them. A standard 10mm Allen wrench and a short section of 1/2-in. pipe slipped over it is fine for removing the head bolts, but you'll need a socket-type Allen wrench come installation time. You need this to be able to use your torque wrench to tighten the head bolts accurately.

If you don't want to buy an Allen-socket drive, use your ingenuity. Hacksaw about a straight 3-in. section from a standard Allen wrench, chamfer the cut-off end, then use a six-point, 10mm socket with it. That's all a socket-drive Allen wrench is anyway.

IMPORTANT! Before attempting to loosen the head bolts, clean out the recess in each bolt head. They tend to fill up with sludge and other deposits, making full wrench engagement impossible. If you mess up a bolt head, it's an ordeal to remove the bolt! Don't risk this. Use a scribe, small punch or small screwdriver to dig out the deposits in the bolt heads.

Remove Bolts in Sequence—Unlike rigid cast-iron heads, aluminum heads are easily warped or bent. Consequently, the L-series Nissan/Datsun head bolts *must be loosened in sequence—reverse order of the tightening sequence*. Refer to the head bolt-sequence drawings, page 44. Loosen the bolts, alternating in pairs as you work from the ends toward the center, then remove them.

Remove Head—With all head bolts out, break the head loose from the block. First, double-check that nothing will prevent it from coming off. Above all, make sure those two head-to-front-cover bolts have been removed. Heads and front covers don't come cheap!

Don't wedge between the cylinder block and head to break the head loose. Lever it off with a bar inserted in an intake or exhaust port, page 45. If you left the manifolds in place, use a pry bar on top of the exhaust manifold and under the intake to lever the head off. Once broken free, it's nice to have a friend standing at the opposite fender to help lift off the head, particularly if the intake and exhaust manifolds are still in place.

Inspection—What interesting things you'll find inside an engine! Engine in photos had *wet* pistons, a sure sign that oil got into the combustion chambers. I thought the problem was "upstairs" because troubleshooting pointed to bad valve guides or seals—high oil consumption, oil-fouled spark plugs and good cylinder pressures. The bores appeared to

Breather tube that caused extra work is pressed into block. It is difficult to remove without damaging it.

If you don't have a set of metric Allen sockets, make one for removing head bolts. This short 10mm hex was hacksawed from Allen wrench for use with a 10mm socket.

Before attempting to loosen head bolts, make sure socket fully engages with bolt head. With a small screwdriver or scribe, dig out sludge and crud from bolt head. Otherwise, you may strip out bolt head. Then you'll be in real trouble.

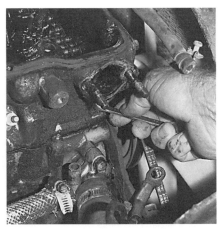

Don't forget to remove two small bolts at front that secure head to front cover. If you try to remove head with them in place, you'll damage head, front cover, or both.

Once head is broken loose, lift it off. If it doesn't break loose, double-check that you removed all bolts. Don't force it.

be in good condition—virtually no wear after 100,000 miles on the odometer. Upon inspection, I found badly worn intake-valve guides. The exhaust-valve guides were worn, too, of course. Consequently, I was prepared to install new valves, guides and seals, and resurface the head. But the bright, clean edges around the pistons indicate oil was coming up past the pistons, indicating a need for new piston rings.

After the head is off, head-gasket problems are relatively easy to spot. Peel the head gasket off the block or head and look it over. Blown areas may appear discolored, or the blown section simply won't

be there. A burned valve should also be evident to the eye. Look for cracks shaped like pie slices or notches around the periphery of the valves. For specifics on cylinder-head inspection and reconditioning, turn to page 85.

DECK SURFACE
Scrape, Scrape, Scrape—The cylinder-block *deck* surface must be clean so the new head gasket will seal. It must also be clean before you can inspect for warpage.

Your gasket-scraping job will go a lot easier if you use a gasket scraper rather than trying to wrestle with a putty knife. The gasket scraper is rigid and you can really "lean into it."

It's best to keep carbon and gasket particles out of the bores. So, stuff some rags in each bore on top of the pistons *before you start scraping*. You won't be able to do this with pistons at TC. However, if you're also replacing the timing chain, rotate the crank so all pistons are down in their bores.

Clean edges around pistons indicate oil leaked up past rings. This engine needs a ring job. Unless you plan on removing front cover to replace timing chain, don't turn crank to expose other cylinders.

Chain is securely wedged in place. It'll stay there until you are ready to install reconditioned head.

While head was off I chased head-bolt threads, cleaned block deck and piston tops. Gasket is in place and ready for cylinder head. IMPORTANT: Don't use a sanding block or body shop "air board" to clean the block or head surfaces. It can round off the outer edges and induce leaks.

Otherwise, keep small particles from getting between the end pistons and bores by shoving a piece of oily string down on top of each top compression ring and around each piston.

After the deck is scraped down to bare metal, lift each rag or string out carefully, bringing most of the debris with it. *Don't use compressed air* to blow out the bores. This will wedge particles between the piston and bore, causing possible bore or ring damage when the engine is restarted. If you do it right, the few particles remaining will either be burned or blown out the exhaust.

It's unlikely that the deck surface will be warped. However, if the engine has suffered chronic head-gasket leakage problems, check the deck for flatness, page 91. Do this with an *accurate* straight-edge, if you can get your hands on one. If not, take the head to an engine machine shop for checking.

BORE INSPECTION

Check Bores—Even though Nissan/Datsun cylinder bores are incredibly tough, it's a good idea to check them now while the head is off. Refer to page 64 for how to check bore wear.

Because your engine block is fully assembled, the end pistons are at TC—number-1 and -4 with a four cylinder and number-1 and -6 with a six. Consequently, you won't be able to check bore wear on these cylinders. The crank can't be turned because of the timing chain. This, of course, doesn't apply if timing-chain replacement is part of your current engine project. But if you are not replacing the chain, don't worry. If the middle bores are OK, it's a safe bet the end bores will be, too. This is assuming these cylinders had good compression, or low compression was due to a blown gasket or burned valve. A special Nissan tool holds up the sprocket with the head off and allows turning the crank.

Use any of the methods described in Chapter 6 for measuring the bores, with one variation. *Taper,* page 64, is measured by comparing the worn and unworn sections of a bore. Maximum wear occurs immediately below the bore *ridge*—the unworn section at the top of the bore. However, you can't go to the bottom of the bore to get an unworn measurement because the piston is in the way. The solution is to scrape carbon from the ridge at the top of the bore, then measure across it to get the bore's unworn diameter.

Before scraping the ridges, stuff some rags in each bore on top of the pistons—just like you did when cleaning the deck surface. Remember, don't use compressed air to blow out the debris.

After the ridges are clean, measure and compare the bores. Have a pencil and writing pad handy to record data. Refer to page 65 to interpret this data.

INSTALL CYLINDER HEAD

Now that you've reconditioned the cylinder head or found and corrected its problem, it's time to get it back where it can do some good—on the block. Although I show the intake and exhaust manifolds being installed afterward, you can bench-assemble the manifolds to the head before it goes on the block. If you were able to remove the head with them intact, you can install them that way. Just be aware that the head will be extremely awkward to handle and heavier, an important consideration during assembly.

Check Crank & Cam Position— Before setting the cylinder head on the block, make doubly sure that the crankshaft and camshaft are correctly timed. Regardless of whether you replaced the timing chain or not, your engine's crank should be on TC—number-1 piston at the top of its bore—provided you followed the correct procedures. The same goes for the camshaft. It should be timed as outlined on page 17. The dowel at the front of the cam should be vertical. Temporarily fit the cam sprocket to the nose of the cam. The notch in the sprocket hub should align with the camshaft thrust-plate groove. Double-check to avoid damaging valves and the pistons they'd be jammed into if not timed correctly.

Head Gasket—Although there are sealers specifically for this purpose, I spray both sides of the gasket with *high-temperature* aluminum paint to ensure good head-gasket sealing. However, if you are using a no-torque gasket such as that pictured or a stock Nissan gasket, don't use sealer.

Fit the gasket to the block over the dowels. Pile the timing chain on top of the wood block so it won't get in the way when installing the cylinder head. You're now ready to set the head on the block.

Position Cylinder Head—The cam is a good handle for lifting the head. Set the head on the block carefully, lining it up so it engages the dowels. Before installing the head bolts, make sure their threads are

After head bolts are cleaned, oiled and threaded into block torque them to spec and in sequence, page 129. Again, don't forget two head-to-front cover bolts.

clean. Use a wire brush to clean them. With the hardened-steel washers installed on each bolt, oil the bolt threads, then thread them into the block. The longer bolts fit into the cam pillars. There are six short and four long bolts for four-cylinder engines, and nine short and five long bolts for sixes. Don't tighten the bolts yet; run them in a couple of turns.

Note: It may be necessary to fit the intake and exhaust manifolds to the head before tightening the head bolts because of interference with the *hang-on* A/C-compressor bracket. Although you may not have the same situation, save some time by making sure. I discovered the problem *after* the cam sprocket was installed and head bolts were torqued. The sprocket had to come back off and the head bolts had to be loosened to install the exhaust manifold.

ASSEMBLY TIP

When installing a component or assembly, it's best to install all fasteners loosely first, then snug them—lightly tighten. Follow this by tightening all nuts or bolts in steps. Do this with a simple mental calculation. For example, a torque specification of 60 ft-lb can be divided into thirds: 20 ft-lb for the first step, 40 ft-lb or the second and 60 ft-lb for the final. This is not always necessary, but little things count when assembling an engine, particularly when there's a gasket between parts being joined.

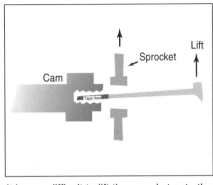

It is very difficult to lift the sprocket onto the cam nose if the chain is new or tight. Allen Osborne suggests using a long pointed bar which reaches back into the cam-bolt hole to lift the sprocket. Wrap the end of the bar with electrical tape to avoid damaging threads in cam.

Torque Head Bolts—It's time to put your socket-drive Allen wrench to work. Tighten the head bolts using the drawings, page 129. The cylinder-head bolts *must be torqued in steps and in sequence*. Start with the center bolts, then work toward the ends. Alternate from end to end until all bolts are fully tightened. I recommend retightening head bolts after running the engine for the first time. Do the retorquing after the engine has cooled. It is very important that you do not retorque the head bolts while the engine is still hot!!

Don't forget the two bolts at the front. *Tighten head-to-front-cover bolts 2.9—5.8 ft-lb (0.4—0.8 kg-m).*

TIMING CHAIN & CAM SPROCKET

Using the notes from your timing-chain and sprocket inspection, line up the appropriate notch at the back of the cam sprocket with the groove in the cam thrust plate. The camshaft dowel should be vertical. While holding the sprocket in line with the cam, lift the timing chain up over the sprocket, fitting the chain to the sprocket teeth. With the sprocket partially fitted to the nose of the cam, look through the top window in the sprocket and check the position of the timing notch.

Whatever position you're installing the cam sprocket in—**1**, **2** or **3**—the notch on the sprocket hub should line up with the right end of the thrust-plate groove as you're viewing it. If it doesn't, refit the chain to the sprocket by jumping a sprocket

Position cam so dowel aligns with thrust-plate groove, then install sprocket.

Rotate cam slightly to align dowel with sprocket. Check cam timing by observing relationship between notch in sprocket and groove in plate.

Tap sprocket into place with soft mallet.

Install fuel-pump eccentric and sprocket bolt. Although some applications don't use a mechanical fuel pump, eccentric may still be used. Torque bolt 86—116 ft-lb (11.6—15.7 kg-m).

Pull out wood block after chain and sprocket are installed. While Channel-lock® pliers were used here, a retrieving wire on the block would be a better way to pull it out.

tooth in the appropriate direction, then recheck. When you've got it, push the sprocket all the way onto the cam.

Unless you're very lucky, the sprocket won't go on the cam all the way. The camshaft dowel has to be in perfect alignment with the hole in the sprocket—it probably won't be. To line them up, use the Vise-Grip pliers or Crescent-wrench trick to turn the camshaft.

Push the sprocket back against the nose of the cam while a friend turns the cam. You can tell him which way to turn it by sighting through the dowel hole in the sprocket. After the sprocket engages the dowel, slide the sprocket all the way onto the camshaft nose.

Carefully use a soft mallet to drive on the sprocket if it's too tight to push on by hand. The weight of the cam and the force of the rocker arms against it should prevent the cam from moving rearward. However, if the cam slides rearward through the cam-bearing towers, back it up with something to keep it from moving. If a hammer will fit between the fire wall and the rear of the cam, hold it against the end cam-bearing journal.

Secure the sprocket with its bolt and lock washer. Don't forget the fuel-pump eccentric. Even though your engine may not be equipped with a mechanical fuel pump, install the sprocket. It acts as a big flat washer.

Torque the cam-sprocket bolt 86—116 ft-lb (12—16 kg-m). To keep the cam and engine from turning while tightening the bolt, put the transmission in gear or hold the cam with a wrench as shown.

Remove Wedge—Don't forget to remove the wood wedge. If you leave it in, the timing chain, chain guides and front cover may be damaged. Worse, the crankcase will be full of splinters that will block the oil pickup. Remove the wedge by grasping the end of it with Channellock pliers, then turn the crankshaft a *few* degrees. This can be done with a wrench on the crank-pulley bolt or by "bumping" the engine over backward with the transmission in gear. Pull the wedge free at the same time you turn the crank.

Fuel Pump—If your engine is equipped with a mechanical fuel pump, install it now. Smear some moly grease—MoS_2, or molybdenum disulfide—on the fuel-pump eccentric first. Make sure the *phenolic insulator* gets installed. It insulates the fuel pump from much of the heat that would otherwise be conducted from the cylinder head, helping prevent *vapor lock*.

If your engine doesn't have a mechanical fuel pump, it'll have a cover that seals the fuel-pump opening. If you removed it, replace it now.

With all fuel-pump gasket surfaces clean and free of old gasket material, place the *first* gasket, pump insulator and *second* gasket against the head over the mounting studs. Fit the pump over the studs and secure it with two washers and nuts. If your engine has only the cover, install it with its gasket. Tighten the fuel-pump nuts 8.7—13 ft-lb (1.2—1.8 kg-m).

Lubricate fuel-pump eccentric.

Install fuel pump with insulator and two new gaskets. Push on pump to compress pump-return spring and start bolts. Torque bolts 8.7—13 ft-lb (1.2—1.8 kg-m).

Double-check that cam lobes are prelubed, then install cam cover. Pretend manifolds haven't been installed yet. I prefer installing cam cover first to keep out dirt or any other foreign material that could harm engine.

Now is time to install manifolds. Start by placing intake/exhaust-manifold gasket on head studs.

Install Intake & Exhaust Manifolds— Be sure to use the correct intake manifold gasket for your engine. Allen Osborne says that he has seen L24/L26 gaskets for a carbureted engine put onto an L28. While the gasket fits, it blocks the injector flow and the engine won't run. He says this was one of the most difficult driveability problems he ever diagnosed: the car would run, but just barely.

Start manifold installation by placing the intake/exhaust-manifold gasket against the head. The exhaust-manifold studs will hold it in place. The exhaust manifold

goes on first. Fit it over the studs and hold it in place using the nuts and washers. Run the nuts down finger-tight.

The manifold bolts that go between the intake- and exhaust-manifold flanges can be installed loosely before the intake manifold goes on. With the thick washers on the bolts—domed or convex side against the bolt head—run them in a couple of turns. The manifold can now be installed by sliding it down between the head and washers. The bolts would be nearly impossible to install with the intake manifold in place. Install the remaining bolts

and washers.

Torque 8mm bolts 8.7—11.6 ft-lb (1.2—1.6 kg-m) and 10mm bolts 25—35 ft-lb (3.4—4.7 kg-m). The 10mm bolts are used on fuel-injected engines only. Torque nuts 8.7—11.6 ft-lb (1.2—1.6 kg-m).

Carburetor(s)— If your engine is carburetor-equipped, install the carburetor(s) now. Install the carburetor(s), new gasket(s) and any spacers that go between the carburetor(s) and manifold. A 12mm open-end wrench with the handle bent about 45° and the sides of the open end

Next, slide exhaust manifold over mounting studs and secure it with washers and nuts.

Thread in bolts with heavy washers that straddle intake and exhaust-manifold flanges. Leave them loose for now.

Slip intake manifold down in behind washers. Finish dressing engine as shown on page 138.

ground for access makes this operation much easier. Overtightened and stripped studs or nuts are common, so be careful. Torque carburetor nuts 3.6—7.2 ft-lb (0.5—1.0 kg-m).

Thermostat Housing—If the thermostat housing was removed from the head, install it now. Use a new gasket with some sealer, then install the housing. Torque thermostat-housing bolts 9—14 ft-lb (1.2—1.0 kg-m).

CAUTION: Make certain to use the correct length bolts. There is a short one and a long one. The short one installs in the front hole. If the front thermostat-housing bolt is too long, it will run into the back of the tight-side timing chain guide. This bends the guide and forces it into the

chain. The guide will be destroyed immediately when the engine is started.

Look down between the chain guide and inside surface of the head to check bolt-to-guide clearance when installing the front bolt.

Cam Cover—Although I show installing the cam cover later, it's a good idea to do it as soon as possible to eliminate the chance of dropping any foreign objects into the engine. If nothing else, it keeps dust and dirt off the camshaft. Or, you can accomplish the same thing by setting the cover loosely on the head—the gaskets and bolts don't have to be installed.

Radiator & Heater Hoses—Unless the heater and radiator hoses are relatively new, it's a good idea to replace them now. Think of this as cheap insurance. Inspect them. If the radiator hose feels soft and pliable, and no cracks appear when you bend it, it'll be OK to reuse. Otherwise, replace it *and* the bottom hose. If the heater hoses are cracked, oil-soaked or in otherwise bad shape, replace them, too. Factory hoses have a string-like wrap around them. If this is at all frayed, it is time to replace the hoses.

Exhaust Pipe—It's time to get your car or truck back up in the air. Again, make sure it's solidly supported on jack stands. You don't want to be injured—or worse—while in the process of saving a few bucks.

Hook up the exhaust pipe to the manifold using a new gasket. Slip the new gasket over the manifold studs, then fit the pipe to the manifold. Torque the exhaust-

pipe-to-manifold nuts 14—18 ft-lb (2.0—2.5 kg-m).

Hoses & Wires—Install all those wires and hoses you labeled—at least I hope you did. A late-model, injected Z-car can be a nightmare as you can see from the engine installation beginning on page 149. Install and connect the fuel line, too.

Fill Radiator—Top off the radiator with fresh antifreeze if what you drained out was unusable. *Don't use plain water*. Corrosion and overheating causes the premature death of more aluminum cylinder heads than anything else. If you live in a warm climate and insist on using water, add a can of *rust inhibitor*/water-pump lubricant. It will protect the cooling system and provide lubrication for the water-pump seal.

Antifreeze has three highly desirable features: protects against corrosion, lubricates the water-pump seal, and has a higher boiling temperature than water. The last feature is a good case for using antifreeze in warm climates. Not using antifreeze can ruin a perfectly good engine.

Oil—Make sure the oil level is to the full mark on the dipstick. In fact, it's a good idea to treat your rebuilt cylinder head to clean oil and a new filter.

New Camshaft?—If a new camshaft was installed, *don't idle the engine less than 2000 rpm for the first half hour of running time*. This ensures that the cam is well oiled during the critical break-in period. Otherwise, the engine can be operated and the car driven normally.

CHAPTER THREE

Engine Removal

"Pulling" an engine is the most grimy, troublesome and potentially dangerous part of rebuilding an engine. These problems can be compounded when it comes time to install the engine. So, a careful and orderly removal job avoids or minimizes problems at both ends of the project.

PREPARATION

Removing an engine is like diagnosing one; you'll need some special equipment other than a standard set of tools. You should have something to drain liquids into, a jack and some jack or safety stands to raise and support your vehicle. You'll need something to lift your engine from the engine compartment and a couple of fender protectors to prevent nicking and scratching the paint. A must is masking tape for identifying those loose ends so you can tell where they go when it's time to reinstall your newly rebuilt engine. Remember some rags and hand cleaner, too.

Lifting Engine—One of the more common ways of lifting an engine is to sling a chain over a garage-roof beam or tree limb and hang a chain hoist from it. The car is jacked up and supported by jack stands or driven up some ramps, followed by getting the engine ready for removing. After the engine is hoisted out of the engine compartment, the car is set back down on the ground and rolled out of the way to wait for its rejuvenated engine. The engine can then be lowered to the ground for teardown.

The order is reversed at installation time.

Unfortunately, the money saved by doing the rebuild job yourself is often negated by the expense involved in rebuilding the garage—or worse yet, paying the hospital bills. If the chain-hoist support is strong enough, the drawback is you'll have to move your car before lowering the engine. And once the engine is lowered, you'll have to move it again. A

Cherry picker is best device for removing and installing engine.

final word of caution about using this method: I've rarely found a conventional passenger-car garage with a beam sturdy enough to support an engine safely, so make sure your health- and life-insurance premiums are paid if you insist on trying it.

Then there is the "shade-tree" approach. Set up an A-frame made from three 12- or 15-ft.-long, 5- or 6-in.-diameter poles—preferably under a shade tree, of course. Chain them together at the top and hang a chain hoist from the chain. A

come-along will also do the job. Drive your car up two ramps positioned so the engine ends up directly under the hoist. Block the rear wheels so the car won't roll back down the ramps about the time you start pulling the engine. Get the engine ready for removal and lift it up clear of the car, then roll the car off the ramps and lower the engine to the ground. Even though I'm jesting about the shade tree, an A-frame like I've just described is a lot stronger than a garage beam.

The most convenient device for removing

Start engine removal by removing battery. Store in an area that's not wet, hot or cold.

Mark around hood hinges before loosening bolts. These will be your reference marks when reinstalling hood.

an engine is a "cherry picker." You can rent one from your nearest tool-rental outlet on a daily basis for a reasonable price. Most are equipped so they can be towed behind a car. You'll need one for an hour or so for removing, and again when installing your engine. This neat device lets you lift your engine out, then move it where you're going to do the teardown. The vehicle stays put.

With my sermon over, let's get on with pulling your engine. Because the L-series Nissan/Datsun engine has been installed in so many types of vehicles and in so many configurations, there isn't enough room in this book to show them all. I picked one of the most complex installations, a fuel-injected 280Z with all of the goodies and external plumbing. Chances are your vehicle is different, but the principles are the same. Let your common sense fill in the voids. I get specific in the engine-rebuild chapters.

Clean Engine—Before immobilizing your vehicle, clean its engine and engine compartment. Remove as much dirt and grease as possible. Concentrate on the fasteners—bolts, nuts and screws. Finding these and getting a wrench or screwdriver on them will be much easier.

The most effective and simplest way of doing this is with a can of spray degreaser and high-pressure water. If your car will run, take it to a car wash. After you've let the cleaner soak in, spray off the engine compartment using hot, high-pressure water. If you do this job at home, take

heed; What's on your engine ends up under the car afterward. A messy driveway isn't much fun either. Although your engine may not look new after you've finished, it will be a whole lot easier to work on just because it is cleaner.

Fender Protection—Cover the fenders with fender protectors, blankets or throw rugs to protect the finish. This also makes the fenders more comfortable to lay on and your tools won't slide off as easily.

Battery—*With ignition off,* disconnect the battery *ground* cable. If your vehicle is equipped with a manual transmission, finish removing the battery and store it in a warm, well-ventilated area—somewhere that battery-acid fumes won't cause damage. On automatic-transmission vehicles, disconnect the ground cable, but leave the battery in place. It will come in handy later to bump the starter for converter-bolt removal. Disconnect the coil-to-distributor lead—the one coming out the center of the distributor cap.

Remove Hood—Before removing the hood, drive a nail in a garage stud or whatever so you'll have something to tie the hood to for storage. This will keep it from falling over between now and installation time. Have some wire or rope handy, too. This is absolutely necessary if you want to avoid hood damage. If you can provide protection for the hood with taped-on pieces of cardboard or a moving blanket, so much the better. You cannot imagine all of the dumb and crazy things that can happen to a hood while it is off of the car.

Placing the hood upside down on a blanket on top of the car works very well.

It's possible to remove a front-pivoted hood equipped with sprung hinges by yourself, but it is a whole lot easier with help. If you lose the balancing act, expect hood and fender damage. As for rear-pivoted hoods, it's very difficult to remove the hood alone without damaging it, the fenders and the cowl.

Regardless of the type of hinging the hood has, tape a rag or piece of cardboard around each *rear corner* of the hood to protect them. This is the end you'll stand the hood on for storing. Mark hood alignment by outlining each hinge at the hood with a permanent felt-tip marker or a grease pencil. Loosen the hinge-to-hood bolts.

Another trick is to drill a 1/8-in. hole through the hinge and hood bracket or inner panel—*don't drill through the hood!* To reinstall the hood, bolt it loosely to the hinges, insert an ice pick or an awl through the hole to align the hood to the hinge, then tighten the bolts. Then do the other hinge. The result—perfect alignment.

Front-hinged: Although I don't recommend it, here's the "solo" method of removing a hood. You may want to use it for the same reason I did—finding yourself without help when it's time to remove the hood.

Remove either bolt from one hinge, then insert a punch in the hole—it's tapered and will wedge tight. Remove the other bolt. Go to the other hinge, but don't remove either bolt without holding the hood—it will come crashing down. With another punch handy, remove one bolt while holding the hood. Insert the punch as you did with the other side. This will support the hood so it won't fall. Hold the hood firmly and remove the remaining bolt. Don't let it slide off the punch. This is the tricky part. While still supporting the hood, get in front of the hood and slip a punch out from one side, then slide the hood off the other punch.

If you have help, remove the bolts from one hinge while your partner holds the hood upright at the other side. Return the favor while he removes the bolts from his side.

Rear-hinged: There are two types:

Label and disconnect hoses from carbon canister.

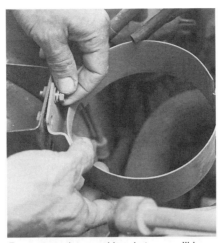

Remove canister and bracket so you'll have better access to engine.

On 260Z, 280Z and 280ZX, remove air-cleaner housing and snorkel to provide access to radiator bolts that thread rearward into weld nuts on radiator.

Remove attaching bolts and loosen hose clamp, then remove Z-car air-cleaner base.

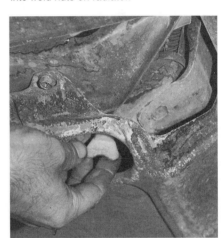

With pan underneath, drain coolant from radiator. To complete draining job, remove plug from right side of engine. Save antifreeze if it's in good shape.

prop-supported and torsion-bar-supported. On torsion-bar hoods, the bars must be removed before the hood. With someone supporting the end of the hood, pry the end of each bar off its operating link using a screwdriver, then remove it. Releasing these torsion bars can be tricky and dangerous. Be careful! After the bars are removed, the remainder of the hood-removal process is virtually the same for both prop and torsion-bar types.

With you on one side and someone on the other, loosen all the hinge bolts, but don't remove them. Get firm grips on the hood, then finish removing the bolts and lift off the hood. Store it in an out-of-the-way place. Tie it to a stud or nail in the wall—and cover it with cardboard or a moving blanket for more protection.

Carbon Canister—Remove the fuel-vapor carbon canister and bracket. It blocked removal of the radiator and fan in this case. Before disconnecting the canister hoses, label them. Use pliers to squeeze the factory clamps together, then slide them back on their hose. To break the hoses loose and not the plastic canister nipples, rotate each hose at its connection with pliers and pull on the hose. Be careful not to break the plastic. Gradually work off the hose.

Lift out the canister after unclipping the bracket. Finish the job by unbolting and removing the bracket.

PLAN AHEAD

It's tempting to disconnect everything in sight without stopping to think that it'll have to be reconnected exactly the same. Don't rely on your memory. Even if there are only five hoses, there are 120 ways they could be installed, and 119 are wrong! Mark all items you will disconnect—wires and hoses. Wrap masking tape around the end of wires or hoses, making a little "flag" for writing where the ends go. Put similar flags on the connection itself so you can get it all back together. Put your camera to use. Snap a few pictures of the engine from various angles; then you'll have a backup just in case a friend plays a trick and switches your flags around. Finally, collect some cans or small boxes for storing and separating bolts, nuts and washers. If your engine is loaded with accessories, you'll find it especially helpful to label the containers as to where each group of fasteners goes.

Remove top radiator hose. After loosening clamp, work hose loose from radiator inlet. Don't use excessive force that might damage radiator neck. Instead, slit hose and replace it.

If so equipped, remove splash shield to allow access to front of engine from underneath. Thread bolts back in so you don't lose them.

Unbolt fan shroud from radiator and remove top half of shroud to gain access to fan.

With an open-end wrench, remove four fan-and-pulley-to-pump-flange bolts. Loosen belts so you can rotate pulley. To keep pump from turning while loosening bolts, push against back side of belt.

Air Cleaner & Coolant-Recovery Bottle—If the coolant-recovery bottle or any other components restrict access to the radiator-mounting bolts, remove it. I also removed the Z-car's air cleaner.

Remove the air-cleaner top and snorkel together. One bolt attaches the snorkel end to the radiator support. Remove the air-cleaner-base bolts in view at the top and two nuts and washers on studs that are well hidden underneath. You'll have to use the "Braille" method here. Disconnect the air-cleaner-to-flowmeter hose, then lift out the air-cleaner housing. Next comes the coolant-recovery bottle. It slips up off its bayonet-style bracket. The bracket is held on with one radiator bolt.

Radiator & Fan—It's a good idea to get

the radiator out now. This will give you more access to the front of your engine for removing accessories. It also must be removed before the engine to prevent core damage. One nudge from the engine can ruin the radiator.

Jack up the front of the car so you'll have some working space and room for the bucket. Slide a couple of jack stands underneath for safety. Drain the coolant into a bucket. Loosening the radiator cap will let it drain faster. Complete the draining job by removing the plug from the left side of the block. If the antifreeze is in good shape, save it—they don't give it away these days. Make sure you clean up any spills and store the antifreeze in closed containers. You don't want your pets to

lap it up because it is terribly poisonous.

If your car is equipped with a splash shield that attaches to the underside of the radiator support and the number-2 cross-member like the 280Z pictured, remove it now while the car is still in the air. This will let that bolt or screw that you'll inevitably drop fall to the ground. You'll also be able to get to the A/C-compressor mounting bolts from underneath.

Loosen both top radiator-hose clamps and the bottom hose clamp at the engine. Don't pry the hoses off their connections. Twist them to break them loose, then pull them off. Remove the top hose and pull the bottom one off at the engine. You can leave it connected to the radiator.

If your vehicle has an automatic transmission, disconnect the transmission-cooler lines. Disconnect the hoses connecting the cooler lines to the radiator. If these hoses are in bad shape, replace them.

How you remove the radiator depends on whether it's equipped with a fan shroud. If there is no fan shroud, simply unbolt the radiator from the radiator support and lift it straight up and out. You can then remove the fan. However, if the radiator has a fan shroud bolted to it, fan and radiator removal is more involved.

There are two types of Nissan/Datsun fan shrouds, split horizontally—like that pictured—or split vertically. The shrouds are split so they can be removed prior to removing the fan. The vertically split fan shroud interlocks. It is unlocked by unbolting one half, then pushing it toward the other half. The horizontally split shroud is bolted together with sheet-metal screws and *Tinnerman*-style sheet-metal nuts.

Unbolt radiator and carefully lift it out. Store radiator out of harm's way so core fins don't get damaged.

There are also two basic types of fan attachments: bolts that thread into the pulley between the fan and the radiator; and bolts or nuts behind the fan.

Now for the second type of fan attachment: To avoid any more "knuckle-busting" work than is necessary, partially unbolt one half of the fan shroud and move it out of the way. This provides access to the fan. The radiator and fan shroud can then be removed. An open-end wrench works best. For more access to the nuts, slacken the alternator/water-pump drive belt at the alternator so the water-pump pulley can be turned. Tighten the alternator adjusting bolt. To keep the pulley from turning when loosening fan nuts or bolts, simply push on the belt in the center of its run. When removing fan nuts or bolts and washers, keep a hand underneath to catch them. They are easy to lose.

With the fan off, you can now remove the radiator. It's bolted to the radiator support through the front. The bolts also mount the condenser with some factory A/C systems.

Viscous-Fan Storage—Store a viscous-drive fan *face down*, water-pump-mounting surface up. This prevents silicone fluid from leaking from the viscous-drive coupler. Replace washers and nuts or bolts on the water-pump flange.

On injected Z-car, remove airflow meter after unbolting it from mounting bracket. Disconnect wiring harness and hose.

Airflow Meter—Loosen the airflow-meter hose clamp at the manifold. Slip the hose off by pushing in the center of the hose. Remove three meter-to-bracket screws—one has a ground wire underneath. Lift the meter from its bracket and disconnect the control-unit wiring-harness connector by pulling back the spring clip at both ends of the connector. This is harder than it looks! With age, these wires and connectors become brittle and break very

Label all hoses and wires, then disconnect them. Carefully loosen tie-wraps and bands with small screwdriver so they can be reused. Refer to drawing, page 150, when labeling connections.

easily. Don't just rip it off or you'll damage the plug. A small 90º dentist's pick can be used to release the wire holder.

Little hands help here, Handle the airflow meter like a carton of eggs—it's easily damaged.

Disconnect Wires & Vacuum Hoses—I said it before and I'll say it again: Label all wire and vacuum-hose ends *before disconnecting them*. Do this especially if you're working on a late-model "emissions

Loosen clamps to free engine wiring harness. Connectors for electronic fuel injection and sensors are fragile. Handle with care.

Replace wire retainer on fuel-injection connector after disconnecting.

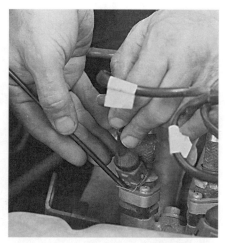

Wire retainer is slipped off connector at fuel injector with scribe. Take care not to lose retainer.

Stick wire retaining clips to a strip of tape to keep them from getting lost.

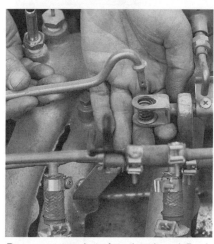

Remove cotter pin to free throttle rod. Don't lose spring and washer. After disconnecting throttle rod, replace spring, washer and pin on rod and swing to side, out of way. Wire up to hold in place.

Disconnect wires from ignition junction block. Note different size terminals, studs, nuts and washers.

engine" or one equipped with electronic fuel injection (EFI). Use the following suggestions to save yourself a lot of time and grief. Save the plastic tie-wraps by prying back their locking tabs. Use a scribe or similar tool to pry back or remove connector retaining clips. A dentist's tool works well here, too.

If you remove any connector retaining clips—required with EFI-injector leads— keep them from getting lost by sticking them to a strip of masking tape. I'll guarantee that it's a bunch easier to find the strip of tape than the tiny clips at the bottom of a cardboard box. Final tip: When pulling a connector off, pull on the connector, not the wire. If the connector does not come off easily, stop and check to see what the problem is. Plastic connectors are

easily broken and difficult to replace.

Fuel-Injection Notes—Even though EFI leads are numbered, don't leave anything to chance. Label them! After removing all the EFI-connector clips and sticking them to a piece of tape, put them in a secure place for safe keeping—on top of the car's instrument panel is a good place. EFI connector U-clips slide off their connectors easily. They don't hook in place like the G-clips used on many of the other connectors. Push one end off, then hook it off the rest of the way. Again, pull on the connector body to remove it, not the wire.

Throttle Rod—Rather than being a "pull-type" linkage, all 240Z, 260Z and 280Z throttle rods rotate. To remove this type of throttle rod, first remove the cotter pin.

With your hand underneath to catch the spring and washer, lift the rod up out of the throttle shaft. Slide the rod out of the rod-and-boot assembly at the fire wall. Pull on it and it should come right out. Replace the spring and washer on the rod. Install its cotter pin to keep everything in place.

Distributor Leads—Disconnect the ground wire from the ballast resistor at the distributor base, unless yours' is an EFI/electronic-ignition Z. Disconnect the distributor leads from the junction block on the left-front inner-fender panel. Three different connectors, threaded studs, lock washers and nuts are used on this model, but all nuts have a 12mm hex—nearly foolproof! Store the special nuts and lock washers on their studs.

Loosen clamps and disconnect radiator hoses. Break hoses loose by twisting them.

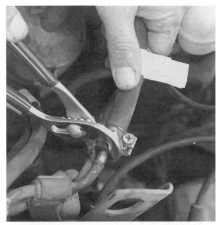

Use pliers to twist loose fuel hose. Plug hose with bolt pushed in end.

Disconnect oil-pressure-sender lead.

Heater Hoses—It's easiest to disconnect the heater hoses at the fire wall. Treat these with even more care than you took with the radiator-hose connections. Heater-core hose nipples are easily bent. Loosen the clamps, twist the hoses to break them loose, then pull the hoses off.

Fuel Lines—Disconnect the fuel-filter and fuel-pressure-regulator hoses at the tubes on the engine. Loosen the clamps, then break the hoses loose by twisting them with pliers.

Warning: Fuel will drain from the lines, so have a 5/16-in. or 8mm bolt ready to push into the end of the line to avoid a fire hazard. The bolt should not be fully threaded. Otherwise, fuel may leak around the threads.

CAUTION: If there's a gas water heater or furnace nearby, turn off the appliance and extinguish the pilot lights whenever there's any chance of leaking or spilling gasoline.

Right-Side Wiring—Disconnect the oil-pressure-sender connector, starter-solenoid connector, and unclip the wiring harness secured to the right side of the engine under the heater-hose clips. The heater hose is routed along the right side of the engine block and bolted to the block with clips.

Starter Motor—Unless you plan to unbolt the automatic-transmission torque converter by using the starter motor to rotate the crankshaft, label and disconnect the leads to the starter-motor solenoid. Loosen the starter-motor mounting bolts. Remove the bottom one first with a ratchet and socket with a long extension. Hold the starter while removing the top bolt. The top bolt also mounts the engine-ground lead. Slide the starter forward out of the bell housing.

Disconnect starter leads, then remove mounting bolts. Using a deep socket and long extension, remove bottom bolt first. Note ground-wire terminal under top bolt.

Power-Steering Pump—At the front of the engine, remove all engine accessories. Start with the power-steering pump, if your car is a ZX. The adjustable idler pulley is attached to the front of the cylinder head. Loosen the belt by first loosening the nut at the center of the pulley, then backing off the adjusting bolt. If the pulley doesn't move, lightly tap the adjusting-bolt head. Slip the belt off the pump pulley.

Remove the three pump-mounting bolts, but don't disconnect the hoses. With the mounting bolts out, lay the pump over to the right. Wire it up against the inner-fender panel to keep it out of the way.

Alternator—Loosen the two pivot bolts at the bottom of the alternator. There is one at the front and one at the back. Label and disconnect the top and bottom leads at the back of the alternator. Loosen the top adjusting bolt. Remove the drive belt. Finish removing the bottom pivot bolts and adjusting bolt and remove the

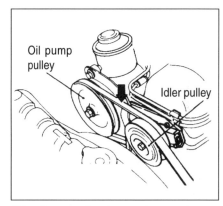

After disconnecting hoses at pump, loosen power-steering-pump adjuster, then belt. Then, remove pump. Drawing courtesy Nissan.

alternator.

Air Pump—The 280Z is not equipped with an air-injection pump, smog pump or whatever, so one is not shown. If your engine has an air-injection pump it will be mounted on the left side of the engine above the A/C compressor, if so equipped. If your engine has factory air conditioning, you'll have to remove the air pump before the A/C compressor. Otherwise, you can remove it after the engine is out.

Disconnect and remove the air-injection hoses. Loosen the pump's adjusting and mounting bolts, remove its drive belt, then finish removing the pump. Remove the adjusting bracket, too.

A/C Compressor—Loosen the center nut for the A/C-compressor-belt adjustable idler—it's in the center of the pulley. Back off the adjusting screw until it projects up from its bracket about an inch, then lightly tap the adjusting bolt or pulley to loosen the belt. Remove the belt from the idler and A/C compressor.

Disconnect alternator drive belt and wires, then remove alternator.

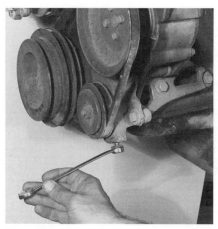

On models so equipped, back out air-pump idler/adjuster bolt . . .

. . . and loosen clamping bolt at center pulley to loosen belt tension.

Unbolt air pump from block.

If equipped with A/C, relieve A/C-compressor belt tension by loosening clamping bolt at center of pulley, then backing out adjusting bolt at top of idler pulley. Loosen pulley by tapping on adjusting bolt.

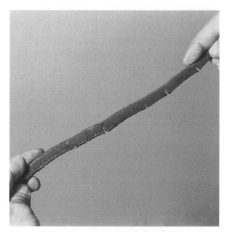

Inspect belts as you remove them. If in doubt about condition of belt, replace it. There's no doubt about this one.

Remove the top compressor mounting bolts. One threads into the upper mounting ear from the front and the other threads into the rear ear from the rear. Access to the factory-installed A/C-compressor lower mounting bolts is from underneath, so the next move is to get your car in the air.

Jack It Up—A passenger car doesn't have enough crawl space underneath without jacking it up. There's no mystery what happens if it falls when you're underneath. The obituary column in the newspaper will probably record the result. So make sure your car stays up in the air until you want it back down.

Aside from a vehicle hoist at a service station, the best device for raising a vehicle is a hydraulic floor jack. Jack under the number-2 crossmember of a passenger car, or the number-1 crossmember of a truck. After blocking the rear wheels, raise it a little higher than you'll need, then place a

couple of jack stands underneath. Don't ever rely on a jack to keep your car in the air and you alive. And never put the wheels of your car on concrete blocks. That's totally unsafe and amateur mechanics are killed every year when concrete blocks collapse and their cars fall on them.

Only the front needs to be raised, but I set the rear tires on 4 X 4-in. wood blocks because I had to get to the exhaust mount at the transmission—it gets a bit tight back there. You'll have to assess your particular situation about whether or not to raise the back. As for the front, support it with jack stands under two solid points along the front box member or frame rail. Don't place each jack stand under the front suspension. It's too easy for the vehicle to shift sideways and fall off the stand. A good point for a Z-car is under the front-suspension lower control-arm pivot point,

as illustrated. Whichever lift points you use, leave a clear area to work in while you're underneath.

If you're working on dirt or asphalt, place the jack stands on wood blocks or a small piece of plywood. This spreads the load of the jack-stand legs, reducing the possibility of their sinking into the ground or asphalt drive.

After setting your car down on the jack stands, joggle it from side to side. Now is the time to find out whether or not it's supported firmly on the stands, not after you're below.

Remove A/C Compressor—Remove the two bottom compressor-mounting bolts. They thread up into the compressor housing. After the compressor is free from its bracket, move it out of the way for removing the engine. Do this so you won't have to open the suction or pressure lines

Jack up vehicle and support firmly under frame member or box member with jack stands, one on each side. Jack stands must be on firm base, not directly on dirt or asphalt. Check stability of vehicle on stands before going underneath.

Remove bell housing-to-engine-plate or converter cover. On automatic-transmission models, unbolt converter from flexplate. Then remove bell housing-to-engine bolts. Remove them completely after hooking up lifting device.

and lose refrigerant. This saves time and money at installation time. It also eliminates the risk of contaminating the A/C system.

All of these systems use R-12 refrigerant that has become very expensive and hard to find. DON'T WASTE IT! Have it removed at an A/C recycling shop and reinstall it when you are done. SAVE MONEY!

Be very careful when moving the compressor with the lines attached. When refrigerant lines get old, they become brittle. Consequently, if they are bent too much, they will crack at their crimped ends, resulting in a leak. All your efforts to save the refrigerant will have been for naught if this happens. Prop the A/C com-

Unbolt A/C-compressor bracket from underneath. Don't disconnect freon lines. Using wire, tie A/C compressor to one side.

pressor up against the inner fender. I wired it to the airflow-meter bracket.

Exhaust Pipe—Disconnect the exhaust header pipe at the manifold. This job is made easier with penetrating oil, such as WD40 or CRC. Apply it to the manifold studs or bolts and let it soak for a few minutes. You may be able to get to some or all of the nuts or bolts from the top. If doing the job from below, use a ratchet and a six-point, flex-type socket with a long extension. With the nuts or bolts off, pull the pipe loose.

If the header pipe bolts to the manifold with studs you'll have to move the exhaust system down and to the rear to clear the mounting studs. Consequently, you may have to do what I did—disconnect the exhaust pipe from its mounting bracket at the transmission to disengage the pipe from the manifold studs. The pipe will then be free to slide back.

Bellhousing—While the car is up, remove the two engine plate-to-bellhousing bolts and nuts. Remove the bellhousing bolt under the starter, too. It threads forward from the bellhousing into the back of the engine.

Automatic Transmission—With an automatic transmission, you'll have to remove the flexplate-to-converter bolts. Start by removing the bellhousing cover plate—it's directly in front of the flywheel. *Before* removing any of the torque-converter bolts, use light-colored paint, chalk or grease pencil to put index marks on the flexplate and converter. The flexplate and torque-converter holes must line up perfectly before the bolts can be installed, so here's one more variable you'll eliminate

After disconnecting exhaust header pipe at manifold, remove engine-mount bolts at insulator, not at engine.

at installation time.

To expose each bolt, turn the crank with a socket and breaker bar on the crank-pulley bolt. This job is considerably easier with the spark plugs out. Or, reconnect the battery and bump the engine over with the starter motor to expose each flexplate-to-converter bolt. If you use this method, make sure your helper at the ignition switch understands that he is to operate the starter only when you say so. Otherwise, you could be injured.

It is really better to use a remote switch and thereby eliminate any possibility of hurting yourself. After the first bolt is out, turn the crank to expose the next bolt—and so on. If you used the starter to bump the engine over, disconnect the battery and remove the starter now.

Set your car back on the ground to complete engine removal.

Engine Mounts—Unbolt the mounting bracket from the *insulator*—one-piece rubber-and-steel assembly—not from the engine. Two bolts thread into each insulator. Remove the oil filter to gain access to the right engine mount.

For 280ZX automatic-transmission turbos, the two engine-oil-cooler lines must be disconnected. These lines are routed forward from the oil-filter adapter to a junction block. Another set of lines run to the cooler, located behind the lower, right grille. Disconnect the lines at the filter adapter, then stow the hose ends up high on the inner fender panel to keep oil from siphoning from the cooler. Cover the open ends with a plastic bag, rag or the like to keep them free of dirt or dust. Masking tape will hold the bag or rag in place.

Use lifting lugs to hook up chain, cable or lifting strap. Support transmission with jack so it doesn't fall when engine is pulled free.

Hang transmission from fire wall with wire. This will allow you to remove jack from under transmission so car or truck can be moved.

Support Transmission—It's time to put your floor jack back into service—a simple scissors jack works well, too. Place the jack under the bellhousing of a manual transmission and under the oil pan of an automatic—use a block of wood between the pan and the jack. The transmission must be supported before the engine is removed. Otherwise, it will fall and do some needless damage.

With the jack in place, remove the rest of the bellhousing bolts. Don't lose track of any clips or their locations.

Remove Engine—After disconnecting all electrical leads, hoses, linkages, accessories and other items that could interfere with engine removal, you can lift out the engine. In addition to a hoist, you'll also need a chain or nylon lifting strap or cable. Rental outfits usually supply this with their cherry pickers.

Using the engine-lifting lugs—one at the right front and one at the left rear—attach the chain or strap short enough so the engine can be lifted over the front of your vehicle, but long enough so it can be set all the way down once it's out. A quick measurement should tell you how long the strap or chain should be. Keep in mind that the front end of the vehicle will rise about 2 in. when the weight of the engine is removed.

Lift the engine off its mounts. Make sure the exhaust-manifold studs clear the exhaust pipe. Make sure the engine will

clear the number-2 crossmember, then bring the jack up under the transmission. Separate the engine and transmission. This will require some joggling and pulling. You may also have to pry between the rear face of the engine block and the transmission bellhousing—do this carefully! If the engine doesn't separate relatively easily, don't force it. Check to make sure everything is disconnected.

Slide the engine forward. On manual-transmission vehicles, do so until it clears the transmission input shaft. Then lift it high enough so it'll clear the radiator support. If you're using a cherry picker, roll it and the engine clear. Otherwise, wire up the transmission to something sturdy at the fire wall. I used the hood-latch bracket. You can now remove the jack and roll your car or truck out from under the engine.

Secure All Loose Parts—If you don't want to leave the jack under the transmission or need to roll your car to another location, support the transmission so you can remove the jack. Wire coat hangers are great for doing this job. This is easy on a Z-car. Run the wires through a couple of bellhousing bolt holes and up and over the hood-latch bracket at the fire wall. Wire up the exhaust while you're at it. This will keep it from dragging on the ground. Let the jack down slowly and check the wires. Remove the jack.

If you haven't already done so, now is

the time to drain the oil. It'll avoid a terrible mess later on. While you're at it, finish draining coolant by removing the *block drain plug* at the rear corner of the block on the left side. This is a threaded pipe plug that screws out.

Think about where you're going to store the external engine parts before you start stripping them off. Store them in a secure dry, clean area where they won't get mixed in with your lawnmower, motorcycle, snowmobile or any other miscellaneous parts you may have lying about. The trunk of your car or bed of your truck is a good place. Go one better by getting most of the grease, oil and dirt off the parts first and put them in containers.

Electric Fuel Pump—If your engine is equipped with an electric fuel pump—fuel-injected Z-car or 810—it's best to remove and store the pump in a plastic bag. Twin SU-equipped 260Z's use *both* a mechanical and an electric fuel pump. This will greatly reduce the risk of it being damaged from corrosion or old gas while the car sits during the engine rebuild. You'll find the electric fuel pump near the fuel tank. Disconnect the two fuel lines from the pump, plug them with a bolt pushed into each hose, then remove the pump. Mark the wires as they can sometimes be put on backward and the pump will then run backward and you will not have any fuel flow or pressure.

CHAPTER FOUR

Teardown

Just as with cylinder-head removal and installation, and engine removal and installation, I use a typical L-series engine for the four rebuild chapters. But when there is an important difference between this engine—an L20B from a 200SX—and other L-series engines, I note the difference.

REMOVE EXTERNAL HARDWARE

While your engine is still "on the hook" after being lifted from the engine compartment, remove as much external hardware as possible before setting it down. It is more convenient to do it now rather than after the engine is on the floor or workbench. Another tip: Use small boxes or cans to store fasteners and small parts. Store them in groups according to their function. For example, keep the exhaust- and intake-manifold bolts in the same container rather than mixed in one container with all other fasteners.

Be sure to label the cans or boxes. Or, if you are unsure as to where all the bolts and nuts go, put them in paper cups (alternator bolts in one, pan bolts in another) and write what they are on the cup. This will save you hours putting it all back together. Another trick is to use sealable plastic bags. You can write on these with a Sharpie® pen.

Drain the crankcase oil and coolant if you haven't already done so. This will prevent that big mess I alluded to previously. The job is going to be messy enough anyway.

Clutch & Flywheel or Flexplate—If you are going to use an engine stand, remove the clutch and flywheel or converter *driveplate* (flexplate) now. In the case of the clutch, punch-mark the pressure-plate cover *and* flywheel for reference so you can reinstall the pressure plate in the same position.

Don't remove any pressure-plate bolts completely. First loosen them in rotation, a couple of turns at a time, until the pressure plate is unloaded. Then remove them. This helps prevent pressure-plate-cover warpage. Gradually work the pressure plate off its locating dowels, keeping ready

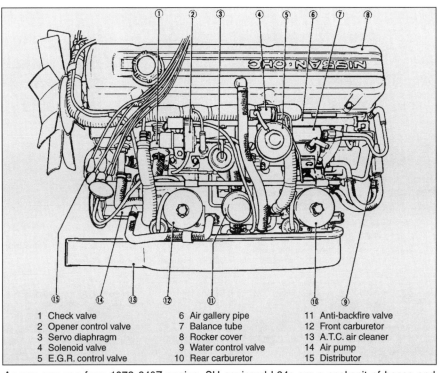

1 Check valve
2 Opener control valve
3 Servo diaphragm
4 Solenoid valve
5 E.G.R. control valve
6 Air gallery pipe
7 Balance tube
8 Rocker cover
9 Water control valve
10 Rear carburetor
11 Anti-backfire valve
12 Front carburetor
13 A.T.C. air cleaner
14 Air pump
15 Distributor

As you can see from 1973 240Z engine, SU-equipped L24s are a snakepit of hoses and wires. Label all disconnects. Drawing courtesy Nissan.

to handle about 35 lb of pressure plate *and* disc when it pulls free.

Except for compensating for the weight difference, flywheel and flexplate removal is the same. You'll have to keep the crankshaft from turning when trying to break the flywheel or flexplate bolts loose—unless you have an impact wrench. Reinstalling the spark plugs will help, but only slightly. Or, you can hold the crank from turning with a 26mm wrench on the crankshaft-pulley bolt. As shown, I took the easy way out by using a Mr. Gasket® flywheel-locking tool. A flywheel turner or two bolts threaded in the pressure-plate bolt holes bridge with a prybar or large screwdriver also works.

After all bolts are out—leave one partially threaded in if you're working with a flywheel—remove the flywheel or flexplate by working it off its crankshaft pilot. It's very wise to leave the one bolt in the flywheel because it keeps it from accidentally falling off the crank onto the floor or your foot. A ring gear with the weight of a flywheel behind it makes a nasty wound.

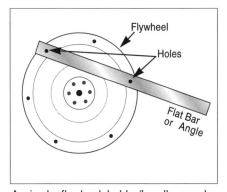

A simple flywheel holder/handle can be made from a 3-foot-long piece of 1/4 X 2 in. bar stock. Just drill two holes to match two of the clutch-cover bolts. Install it with two bolts.

You may have to use a small bar or large screwdriver to work the flywheel or flexplate off the crank. The fit is tight and just a little corrosion locks the flywheel or flexplate to the crankshaft.

An engine plate is the next item to remove. It fits tightly to the bellhousing dowels, so it may require a little coaxing with a screwdriver.

Engine Stand—If you're going to use an engine stand, you'll have to remove the

Breaking loose pressure-plate bolts with "poor-man's" impact, a combination wrench and soft mallet. Back out each bolt no more than two turns at a time. Work pressure plate off dowels, then grasp pressure plate and disc and remove together.

Break loose flywheel bolts. Note flywheel-holding clamp at upper right.

With one bolt left in crankshaft to keep flywheel from falling, lever off flywheel.

Remove engine plate. It fits tightly on dowel.

If you'll be using an engine stand, remove bellhousing locating dowels. Vise-Grip pliers work well for this.

hollow dowel that's concentric with the left, bottom bellhousing-bolt hole. It interferes with mounting the engine to the engine stand. The dowel is split, so it is easily removed by compressing it with Vise-Grip® pliers. Work the dowel out of its bore.

Before getting to the engine proper, remove any remaining external hardware. First, strip off any accessories and their brackets.

Air Pump—If your engine didn't have factory A/C, but did have an air pump,

remove it now. Loosen the nut in the center of the idler pulley, back out the adjusting bolt, then lightly tap on the bolt head to move the pulley and loosen the belt.

To get the belt off the crank pulley, you'll have to partially remove the timing pointer—it covers the back crank-pulley groove. The top pointer screw is threaded into the front cover. Remove it with a Phillips screwdriver. Next, loosen the bottom bolt that goes through the pointer, front cover and into the block. Swing the pointer over and out of the way. Now

remove the belt.

After removing the pump-support bracket from the top of the pump, remove the pump, its idler pulley and bracket as an assembly. Just make sure the bottom air-pump mounting bolts are tight before you remove the support bracket. This keeps the pump from swinging down over the bracket-to-block bolts or onto your hands. Remove the bracket bolts and the pump-and-bracket assembly.

A/C-Compressor Bracket—The factory A/C-compressor bracket is in the same neighborhood as the air pump. Remove its four mounting bolts, then the bracket.

Alternator Bracket—Over on the right side of the engine, remove the alternator-mounting bracket. Considering all the brackets you're removing, it's a good idea to keep the mounting bolts with their bracket. This eliminates any confusion at installation time.

Induction System—There are many variations on the L-series induction system. These can range from a single two-barrel, to twin SU-type carburetors, to fuel injection—that may or may not have turbocharging. The engine shown is equipped with the single, *staged* two-barrel Hitachi—one primary barrel and one secondary. I'll concentrate on this installation, but will cover any important points about the others.

Carburetor—Although it's not necessary, remove the carburetor(s) so the manifold bolts will be easier to get at. Start by disconnecting hoses or wires that will interfere with carburetor removal: fuel lines, choke wire, vacuum hoses, air-pump hose, PCV hose and so on. Remove the carburetor nuts, then lift the carburetor(s) off and store it. If you're not going to rebuild the carburetor(s), make sure it is kept clean and dry.

Turbocharger—Now is a good time to remove the turbocharger if yours is a 280ZX Turbo. Start by disconnecting three lines at the turbocharger assembly: oil-feed line, EGR tube and the oil-return pipe. Disconnect the turbo oil-feed line using a flare-nut wrench. It joins the turbocharger between the turbine and compressor housings. Disconnect the EGR tube at the manifold—it's easier that way.

As for the oil-return pipe, start by loosening the hose clamps at the oil pan. Next, remove the two bolts that thread up into the turbocharger. Be ready for some oil spillage. Twist and pull the pipe loose from the oil pan.

The only thing left before removing the turbocharger is the O_2 sensor—disconnect it. Now, remove the four nuts from the exhaust-manifold studs and remove the turbocharger.

Fuel Pipes—On *carbureted engines only*, remove the two fuel *pipes* (steel lines) that run along the top of the intake manifold and around the front of the cylinder head to the right side. Depending on your engine, its fuel-pipe brackets will be secured by intake-manifold, thermostat-housing and fuel-pump bolts. Remove these bolts, then the pipe assembly.

As for fuel injection, leave the fuel-rail assembly with the manifold. There are too many small, delicate and expensive components involved in removing the pipe assembly from the manifold—and for no

Remove carburetor and store in plastic bag.

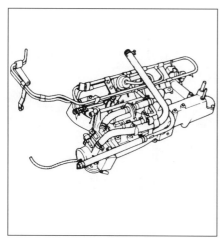

When removing manifold from fuel-injected L28, leave hardware intact on manifold. Drawing courtesy Nissan.

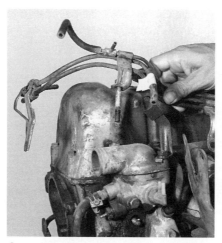

On carbureted models, remove fuel pipes from engine. While you're at it, remove mechanical fuel pump, if so equipped.

Removing intake and exhaust manifolds now is much easier than when engine is installed in vehicle. Remove all nuts and bolts . . . .

. . . . then pull manifolds off mounting studs. If manifolds are bolted together remove them as a single unit. There's no need to separate them unless one is damaged.

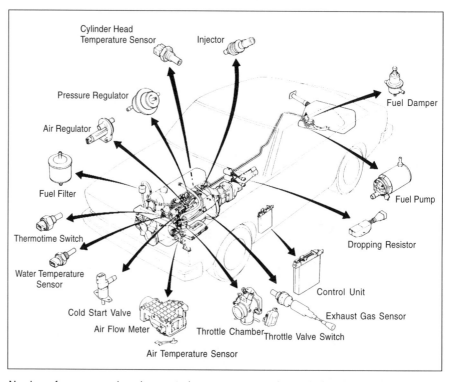

Number of sensors and engine-control components on electronic fuel-injected engines can be mind-boggling. Be gentle with these components; they are easily damaged and expensive to replace. Drawing courtesy Nissan.

good reason. Otherwise, you'll risk damaging or losing them. So, on fuel-injected engines, leave as much intact as possible. Just don't forget to remove the bolts holding the two pipe brackets to the front and right-front side of the head before removing the manifold.

Other Manifold Connections—Label and disconnect all other hoses from the intake manifold. Among the possibilities are hoses or tubes for the EGR, PCV and cooling systems.

Intake & Exhaust Manifolds—There are several L-series intake/exhaust-manifold configurations: Water-heated intake with separate exhaust; exhaust-heated

intake manifold cast integral with the exhaust manifold; intakes with two SU carburetors; intakes with one 2-barrel Hitachi carburetor; fuel injection with and without turbocharging. Regardless of the complexity, intake and exhaust manifolds are secured to cylinder heads with bolts and studs and nuts with heavy washers.

Unless the intake manifold is exhaust-heated like that used on our L20—as

opposed to water-heated—it can be removed before the exhaust manifold. With the intake manifold out of the way, you'll find it considerably easier to get to the combined intake/exhaust-manifold bolts under the two manifolds.

To remove an intake manifold that is separate from its exhaust manifold, loosen the bottom bolts, and remove the top bolts and their washers. Break the manifold loose from the head and lift it off. Finish removing the exhaust manifold after removing all bolts, nuts and washers.

On some 280Zs and ZXs a small tin cover covers up the center exhaust-manifold bolt. Don't forget to remove it. It is secured by a single screw.

To remove the combined intake/exhaust manifolds, all the bolts, nuts and washers have to come off first. You'll have to use the "Braille method" to remove the bottom bolts—they are hard to see and reach. Remove the bottom bolts first.

PCV Tube—Most L-series Nissan/Datsun engines are equipped with a PCV tube that exits the left side of the block. It's best not to remove this force-fit steel tube because it frequently ends up loose when reinstalled, with the result being constant oil seepage down the side of the block. Just don't use the tube for a lifting handle or let the block fall over on its side. This will wreck the tube for good. You'll clean out the tube and PCV passages from inside the block after the engine is disassembled.

If, however, you insist on removing the PCV tube, work it out of the block gradually. In the case of a tube with a bend, rotate the tube back and forth while prying up on it with a screwdriver. As for the straight type, you'll have to pull and wiggle the tube out. Again, don't do this unless it's absolutely necessary, particularly if you're working with a straight tube.

Core Plugs—Now is a good time to remove the core plugs—*freeze plugs* they are sometimes called. You'll find three—two if you already removed one—in the right or oil-filter side of a four-cylinder block and four in a six-cylinder block. Both blocks have two core plugs in the left side, plus one in each end.

Although core plugs may appear difficult to remove, the job is relatively easy. Using a punch and hammer, drive against the edge of the plug, driving it into the block. This rotates the plug in its bore, making it easy to grab with pliers. Now, lever the plug from the block using Channel-lock® or Vise-Grip pliers as pictured.

This procedure won't work with core plugs in the front and rear faces of the block. These are so close to the end cylinders that they can't be driven into the block. Consequently, you'll have to pull them out. Using a 1/8-in. drill or a prick punch, drill or drive a hole in the plug at

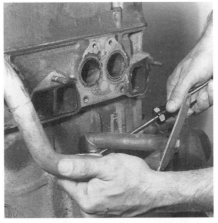

I removed rigid crankcase vent tube to prevent damaging it during rebuild. If you want to remove yours, carefully pry up and rotate tube to work it out of hole in block.

To remove core plugs from side of block, drive edge of each plug into block . . .

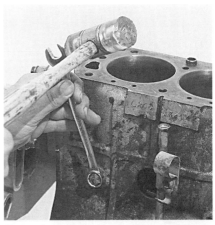

If you haven't already removed block's coolant drain plug, do it now. I'm using my "manual impact wrench" to break loose plug.

. . . then lever out plug with Channel-lock pliers.

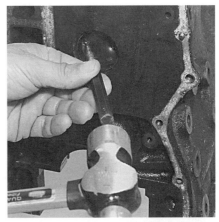

Core plugs at ends of block cannot be driven in because of close proximity to cylinders. To remove them, punch hole in each plug at an angle.

an angle at one side or the other of the plug as shown. Go too deep and you'll drill a hole into the cylinder. Just be careful.

Thread a #6 or other medium-size sheet-metal screw into the hole until it has a good grip. Clamp onto the screw head with Vise-Grip pliers. Now, using a sturdy screwdriver, lever against the pliers to pull out the core plug.

Thermostat Housing—The thermostat housing is one of several items that don't need to be removed during engine teardown. However, it's easier to remove it now than after the head is removed.

After its two bolts are out, remove the upper half of the thermostat housing. Break it loose by tapping under its snout with a soft mallet or bumping it with a wood handle.

Lift the thermostat from the bottom half of its housing. It may resist because of old gasket material overlapping its flange. So peel the gasket away, then lift the thermostat out. Save the thermostat because it's probably reusable. You can bet it's OK if your engine didn't have overheating or warm-up problems.

Run sheet-metal screw into plug. This gives something to grab hold of.

Clamp onto screw head with Vise-Grip pliers. With screwdriver behind pliers' jaws, lever out plug.

After removing bolts, break loose top half of thermostat housing by tapping lightly under hose neck.

WHAT LENGTH BOLT GOES WHERE?
It seems that nearly all L-series Nissan/Datsun-engine fasteners are different lengths—and for no apparent reason. But there are reasons. A short bolt in a "long hole" may not engage enough threads to hold full tightening torque. Conversely, a long bolt may bottom out in a "short" hole before clamping, or worse yet, interfere with another engine component. This may result in catastrophic engine failure.

Therefore, make certain each bolt goes back in the right hole at reassembly. With this is mind, return each bolt to its hole in the component it retains and wrap some tape around its threaded end to keep it there. Do this immediately after removing each component. At the very least, segregate all engine fasteners by function in labeled boxes or cans. For instance, put manifold bolts, nuts and washers in one container, water-pump fasteners in another, and so on. This will minimize confusion later on and help prevent fastener misuse during engine assembly.

Disconnect bypass hose and finish removing thermostat housing. Make sure bolts stay with housing. If too long a bolt is used in front hole, it can do serious harm to your engine, page 137.

Remove water-pump inlet.

There are probably more good thermostats tossed away than bad ones. If you have any doubts, check the thermostat in a pan of water on the kitchen stove. If the thermostat opens just before the water boils, it's OK. This varies depending on altitude, so it's best to use a thermometer. It should start to open at 170-190F and be fully open at 195-212F. For hot climates, the thermostat should open sooner and vice versa for a cold climate.

Disconnect the thermostat-bypass hose and any other remaining electrical leads or hoses that run to the housing and label them. The number of connections varies, depending on the engine and model year.

For instance, the L20B shown is relatively simple with only a bypass hose, water-temperature-sender lead and a couple of vacuum hoses. On the other hand, a 280ZX Turbo can be mind-boggling.

Remove the bottom thermostat-housing half. There is a long bolt and a short one. Break the housing free from the cylinder head, then reassemble the top and bottom thermostat-housing halves. Return the thermostat housing-to-head bolts to their holes in the housing and wrap tape around their threads. This keeps the bolts in place.

Water-Pump Inlet—While you're at it, remove the water-pump inlet. It's mounted to the right side of the front cover. Remove it the same way you did the thermostat housing: Remove the two mounting bolts and tap the inlet lightly. Wha'da'ya know. These bolts are the same length!

Cam Cover—It's time to get a look inside your engine. Remove all of the cam-cover bolts. A speed handle and 10mm socket will hurry this job along. The bolts aren't tight, but they are threaded-in a long way.

Don't drive a screwdriver or anything of the kind between the cam cover and the head to break it loose. Hit it *lightly* at the front corner with a soft mallet or with the butt of your hand to pop it loose.

After removing bolts, bump loose cam cover with butt of your hand.

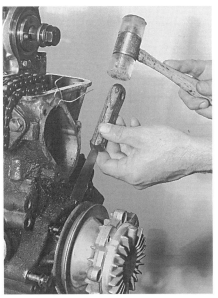

Once all bolts are backed out, break loose water pump by driving putty knife between pump and front cover. Note that drive pulley prevents complete removal of two mounting bolts.

As you remove last oil-pump bolt, remove pump with it. Store four bolts with pump.

Damaging a cam cover will definitely ruin your day—they are *expensive*.

Water Pump—Unlike the cam cover, the water pump *should* be pried loose. After all the water-pump bolts are out, wedge the thin blade of a putty knife between it and the front cover. This is better than shocking the viscous-drive unit or water-pump-shaft bearings.

Note the assortment of different-length water-pump bolts and the two that have to stay with the pump. The backside of the water-pump pulley prevents their removal from the water-pump housing.

Keep the bolts with the water pump and store the pump with the viscous drive *face down* and the pump impeller up. This keeps the silicone drive fluid from leaking from the drive unit.

Oil Pump—If the alternator bracket is still bolted to the block, remove it. Although not necessary, it will make it easier to see the oil pump and its drive gear as you remove them.

When removing the last of the four oil-pump bolts, break the pump loose from the front cover and pull it out of engagement with its drive shaft.

Oil-Pump/Distributor Drive—Remove the oil-pump/distributor-drive spindle now. If you forget it and attempt to remove the front cover, the result could be front-cover or gear damage.

To remove the pump/distributor drive, push on its distributor-drive end while pulling on the lower end. It will rotate counterclockwise—looking at its upper endless it disengages from its drive gear at the crankshaft.

Don't forget to remove oil-pump-drive spindle. If you try to remove front cover with spindle in place, you'll damage spindle, cover or both.

Here's where impact wrench would come in handy. Instead, use a bar through two flywheel bolts at rear of crank or between crankshaft counterweight and block—after oil pan is off—to keep crank from turning while you break loose crankshaft-pulley/damper bolt.

Crank Pulley—You will need a breaker bar and a 1-1/16 in. (26mm) socket to break the crankshaft-pulley bolt loose. Unless you have an impact wrench, you'll also have to keep the crankshaft from turning so you can break the bolt loose. Do this by simply threading a couple of

flywheel bolts into the crankshaft-flywheel flange. Bridge the bolts with a pry bar or a large screwdriver and rotate the crank counterclockwise until the bar or screwdriver is loaded against the workbench or an engine-stand mounting post.

You can also wait until the oil pan is

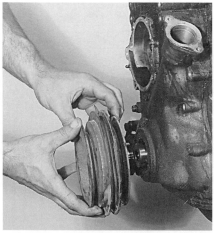

Pulley should slide off crankshaft nose with little resistance.

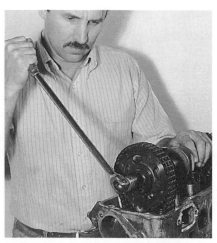

Up top, break loose cam-sprocket bolt.

Remove sprocket bolt, washer and, if used, Fuel-pump eccentric.

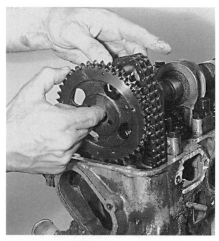

Pull sprocket off cam nose and lift chain off sprocket.

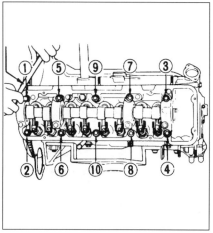

Don't indiscriminately loosen cylinder-head bolts. They must be loosened in reverse order of tightening sequence as shown for four- and six-cylinder heads. Drawings courtesy Nissan.

While you're at front of engine, remove those easily missed head-to-front-cover bolts.

off before removing the crank pulley. Then all you'll need to keep the crank from turning is a block of wood between the block and a crankshaft counterweight. Still another method is to insert a 1/2-in. drive socket set extension into a crankshaft-counterweight lightening hole. Rotate the crankshaft counterclockwise to bring the extension around against the block pan surface.

After the pulley bolt and its large flat washer are removed, the pulley should slide off the crankshaft nose easily. Whatever you do, don't pry against the expensive cast-aluminum front cover. If the pulley is stubborn, tap against its backside with a soft mallet or a wood block and a hammer to loosen it.

Cam Sprocket & Chain—Turn your attention back upstairs and remove the camshaft sprocket. Remove the bolt that threads into the center of the camshaft nose, its lock washer and the fuel-pump eccentric. Even though your engine may not use a mechanical fuel pump, there may be a fuel-pump eccentric or heavy flat washer bolted on with the cam sprocket.

After noting the position of the sprocket on the cam, work the sprocket off the nose of the cam, then disengage it from the timing chain and set it aside. Unlike an in-car cylinder-head removal and replacement job, you can let the chain drop and not worry about it. The head and front cover are coming off shortly, anyway.

Cylinder Head—Before you even think about removing the cylinder head, remove the two cylinder head-to-front cover bolts.

Forget these two bolts before breaking the cylinder head loose and you'll succeed in damaging the cylinder head or front cover. More than likely, they are hidden under a gob of grease at the cylinder-head flange. Scrape any grease away and remove the bolts.

Because socket-head head bolts are used, you'll need a 10mm Allen-type, or hex wrench to remove them. A conventional Allen-type wrench with a pipe slipped over it for leverage works well for removing the head bolts. However, consider getting a hex-head driver that can be used with your torque wrench. A 1/2-in. drive, impact-type is best. It's easier to use, and you'll eventually need it for installing the cylinder head. One more possibility: Because I like to save a penny when possible, I made my own hex-head driver by sawing a 3 in. straight section from a 10mm Allen wrench and used it with a 10mm socket. It's best to use a 6-point impact socket because an ordinary 12-point socket will break every time. **Note: The cylinder-head bolts must be removed in sequence.** This sequence is the reverse of the tightening sequence. Loosen them starting at the end bolts and alternating to the center bolts. This avoids the very real possibility of warping that expensive aluminum cylinder head. Use the accompanying chart as reference for loosening the head bolts.

After you've removed *all* head bolts and the two front cover-to-head bolts, remove the cylinder head. Break the head loose from the block with a bar inserted into one of the intake ports. Pry up on the bar. The head should break loose with relatively little force. If it doesn't, shock the end of the bar with the butt of one hand while holding the bar up tight against the intake port with the other hand. After the head breaks free, lift it off and set it aside with its bolts.

Oil Pan—If you haven't already drained the oil pan, now is your last chance to do so without creating a big mess. With this done, turn the engine on its side or upside down.

Not all L-series engines have the two cast-iron engine-to-transmission supports like those pictured. If your engine has these, remove them before removing the oil pan. Each is retained with two bolts. Likewise, there may be a fuel line(s) bolted to the underside of the oil-pan flange. It will have to come off, too.

A 10mm Allen wrench and short section of pipe work well for breaking loose head bolts.

Head should break loose from block with little effort *if* you removed *all* head bolts. Breaker bar in a center exhaust port (as shown here) works well to help lever the head off the block. But choose an intake port instead if you have a later-model emissions head because a breaker bar in an exhaust port could damage the sheet-metal inserts. If there is any resistance, stop! Double-check for an overlooked head bolt. Check that you removed two bolts at front cover.

Lift head straight up off block so it clears timing-chain guides. Set cylinder head aside, but be careful. Gasket surface of aluminum head is easily damaged.

L20B has two engine-to-bellhousing supports. Remove them to allow access to oil pan.

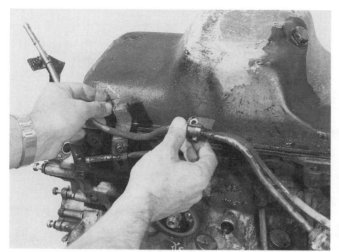

Fuel pipes come off before pan.

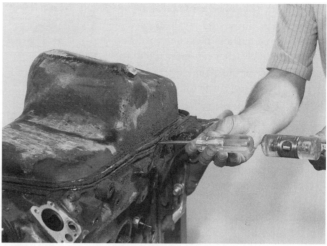

Remove all bolts and oil-pan-flange support, then break loose pan from block. Drive screwdriver between pan and block. Do this gradually in several places being careful not to bend flange. Lift off pan and set aside. Use pan for storing pan bolts and other hardware from bottom end of engine.

Remove its two bolts, then oil-pump pickup.

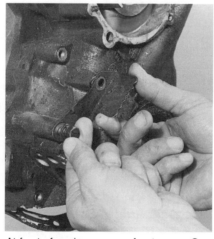

At front of engine, remove front cover. One front-cover bolt also retains timing pointer. A second bolt secures pointer to cover.

Break loose cover by carefully tapping against its back side.

Now for the oil pan: Remove all pan bolts. There should be an L-shaped load-spreader plate that fits against the oil-pan flange at the right-rear corner of the pan. Set it aside and remove the pan. Break the pan loose by whacking one of its bottom corners with a large, soft mallet, or carefully work around between the pan flange and block with a screwdriver and hammer. Don't drive the screwdriver all the way in and pry in one location to break the pan loose. You will bend the oil-pan flange needlessly.

Oil-Pump Pickup—With the oil pan out of the way and the bottom end of the engine in clear view, remove the two oil-pump-pickup bolts and lock washers and remove the pickup. This keeps the oil pickup from getting bent if the engine tilts down on its bottom face. The pickup has to come off anyway.

Front Cover—If you already removed the oil-pump/distributor drive, now remove the front-cover bolts—the timing pointer will still be under the right bottom bolt—and the front cover. If you didn't remove the oil-pump/distributor drive, do it now before attempting to remove the front cover.

Break the cover loose from the block by tapping against the backside of the distributor-mounting boss with a soft mallet or a wood block. It should pop right off. If it doesn't, double-check that all bolts are out.

As you've probably realized by now, there are 6mm and 8mm front-cover bolts of various lengths. Store these bolts and their washers in a separate container marked **FRONT COVER** to avoid mass confusion at assembly time.

The distributor adapter is bolted to the front cover. If you decide to remove the adapter for cleaning and gasket replacement, be sure to match-mark its relationship to the front cover *beforehand*. Otherwise, distributor timing will be lost at assembly time.

Timing Chain—You should now have full view of the timing chain, its two guides, drive sprocket and tensioner. You'll also have a clear view of the oil-pump/distributor-drive gear and crank-

Chain-tensioner pulls out of housing with preload spring. Remove it and timing chain.

Remove two bolts, then timing-chain-tensioner housing.

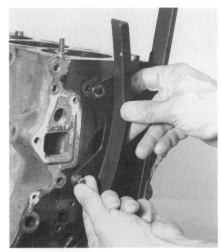

Remove chain guides.

shaft oil slinger. Keep all cam-drive components together as you remove them.

Start by removing the chain-tensioner rubbing shoe and its preload spring. Just pull the shoe and spring from its housing that's bolted to the front face of the engine block.

The chain is next. It should be draped over one of the guides and routed around its drive sprocket. Disengage it from the sprocket and remove it. Slip the oil slinger off the crank nose.

Unbolt the rest of the timing-chain components: tensioner housing and two guides. Each is retained with two bolts.

PISTON & ROD REMOVAL

Turn your attention to the bottom end. The piston-and-connecting-rod assemblies are next. First, make arrangements for turning the crankshaft. The crank journal for each piston-and-rod assembly should be rotated to bottom-center—BC—before removing each connecting rod and its piston.

The easiest way of doing this is to reinstall the crank-pulley bolt and washer loosely. All that's needed to turn the crank is a 26mm socket on the bolt head and a breaker bar.

Remove Ridge—Because the top piston rings don't travel all the way to the top of its bore at TC, there's a small length of unworn bore covered with carbon buildup at the top of each cylinder. This is the *ridge*.

Remove the ridge before you attempt to remove the piston-and-rod assemblies,

Grooves on tensioner shoe are not bad. Regardless, if engine needs to be rebuilt, replace tensioner and chain guides.

particularly if the pistons may be reusable. The ring lands can be damaged if the pistons are forced up and out of their bores over the ridge. However, if you're sure you won't be reusing the original pistons, go ahead and force them out. Use a long punch or bar that will reach up under the piston domes from the bottom end. *Don't hammer on the connecting rods.*

Fortunately, L-series engine blocks wear very well, so there's a good chance that most of what appears to be the ridge will simply be carbon. This carbon buildup can be easily scraped away with a screwdriver. Just be careful that you don't gouge or scratch the bore surface below the ridge. If you weren't planning on reboring, you may have to regardless if

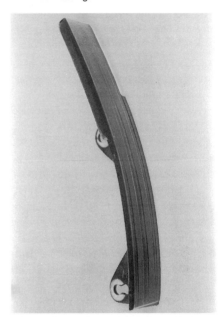

Like tensioner shoe, slack-side guide is not badly grooved, but will be replaced to make sure everything up front is new.

Ridge reamer positioned for removing ridge: If ridge at top of bore is pronounced, it must be removed to avoid damaging pistons as they are removed. It's unlikely that you'll have to do this because L-series Nissan/Datsun blocks are tough.

Before removing connecting-rod caps, check rods and caps for numbers immediately adjacent to their parting line. If not numbered, mark both rod and cap before removing nuts. Use numbers or prick-punch marks that correspond to cylinder number.

Lift off cap and bearing and set aside.

To protect bearing journal from rod-bolt threads during rod-and-piston removal, slip thread protectors or short sections of fuel hose over rod bolts. Never overlook this: rod bolts are very hard, cranks are very soft!

this happens. If a piston is in the way, turn the crank to move it down its bore.

After the ridge in one bore is cleaned up, you'll be able to judge how bad the ridge is. If you can hook a fingernail under the ridge, it's excessive. You'll have to remove all the ridges to ensure that you won't damage the pistons. This is where mixed emotions creep in. If the ridge is bad, bore wear is significant. This being the case, the block probably needs to be rebored—meaning new pistons. So damaging the pistons on removal is not a concern. They'll be "tossed" anyway.

If you're in a dilemma about this, simply run each piston down to BC and check bore wear using the procedure beginning on page 64.

If you elect to remove the bore ridges, you'll need a *ridge reamer.* This tool has a cutter mounted in a fixture that can be adjusted to fit the bore. A socket and handle or wrench from your toolbox is all you'll need to rotate the tool.

When removing a ridge, cut the ridge *only to match the worn bore.* Remove any more material and you may have to rebore the block whether it needs it or not. Also, when going from bore to bore, you may need to rotate the crankshaft to move a piston down its bore to create room for the ridge reamer.

Connecting-Rod Numbering—Now you can get on with the piston-and-rod removal process. Rotate the block upside down to expose the bottom end if the

engine is mounted on an engine stand. Lay it on its on its side if you are working on a bench.

Before removing or loosening any connecting-rod caps, make certain each rod and cap is numbered. Connecting rods and their caps are machined as an assembly. Any mixup here will spell trouble or extra expense when it comes time to assemble your engine. Nissan stamps the numbers during manufacturing (usually!). Number the rods 1 through 4 or 1 through 6, depending on your engine, from front to rear. Matching numbers should be on the machined flat that runs across the parting line on the right side of the connecting rod and cap.

For rods and caps, use a set of small number dies or punches. Mark any rod or cap that is not already marked on the machined flat on the right side—the side next to the oil-filter mount—next to its parting line. If you don't have number punches, use *prick-punch* marks corresponding to the cylinder number. Or, use an electric engraver. It eliminates the need to hit the rod or cap you're marking. Again, make double-sure all rods and caps are marked before they are removed.

You'll have to turn the crankshaft to gain access to the rods. Mark two rods, turn the crank and do two more. Turn it once again to get the final two if you're working with a six-cylinder engine.

Check Side Clearance—Also, before removing the rods and pistons, check con-

necting-rod side clearance—the distance between the side of the rod and the crank. Use feeler gages to check this clearance—it should not exceed 0.024 in. (0.6mm). Half of the maximum side clearance, or 0.012 in. (0.3mm), is desirable. Although unlikely, the connecting rod should be replaced if maximum clearance is exceeded.

Remove Rods & Pistons—When removing a piston, rotate the crankshaft so the piston is at BC. You'll have better access than if it were at TC. Anywhere in between may cause the rod to hang up between the crank and the bottom of the cylinder.

Complete each piston-and-connecting rod removal before moving on to the next. After removing the two rod-bolt nuts, remove the cap. If it's tight, pull on the cap and tap the side of it with a mallet. It should pop loose.

After the cap is off, slip something over the rod bolts to protect the crankshaft bearing journal. A bare connecting-rod bolt banging or dragging against the bearing journal will surely damage it. Use a short section of 5/16-in. fuel-line hose over each bolt. A 2 in. length is about right. Or stop by your local auto-parts store. They may have complimentary plastic sleeves made just for this purpose.

Not only will covering the rod bolts protect the rod-bearing journals, it can also keep the connecting-rod bolts in place. If the rod bolts are loose in the rod like they were in the L20B shown, the hoses or

Coax piston out of bore by pushing against rod with butt end of hammer handle.

Be ready to catch piston as it falls from bore.

Refit cap and bearing halves to rod for better inspection. Loosely secure with nuts.

sleeves keeps them from falling out. Rod bolts should always be installed in their original positions. Not only do they retain the cap, they also position it to the connecting rod. Consequently, interchanging rod bolts has the same effect as interchanging rods and caps.

Push the piston and rod out the top of its bore by pushing against the underside of the piston. The butt-end of a hammer handle or a short section of broomstick handle works well. Guide the connecting rod into the bore while being ready to catch the piston when it pops out the other end. Once the piston starts moving, it'll come out fast.

Before removing the next piston, remove the sleeves from the rod bolts and install the cap and nuts loosely *with the two bearing-insert halves in place.* Now you can remove the other piston-and-connecting-rod assemblies.

Rod Bearings Tell a Story—Don't throw away the old rod bearings just yet. They will save you the expense of farming out much of the inspection work because a bearing's wear pattern is an accurate measure of connecting-rod condition. This also applies to the crankshaft. To keep the crankshaft bearings in order, tape each half together with some masking tape and record which journal the pair went with. Scribe the bearing number and its position on the backside of the inserts. These worn parts that normally get tossed in the trash as soon as they are removed will be valuable later on in the inspection and

Break loose main-bearing cap bolts.

reconditioning stages.

CRANKSHAFT REMOVAL

Before you remove the crankshaft, check to see if it spins freely. Turn it by hand. If it turns freely, great. Chances are the crankshaft and its main-bearing bores in the block are straight. You can confirm this by inspecting the main bearings once the crank is out. If there is no uneven wear, you can be certain the block and crank are straight.

Main-Bearing-Cap Removal—Position the engine block upside down. Start crankshaft removal by loosening all main-bearing-cap bolts. Once broken loose, they are easy to back out all the way. Set

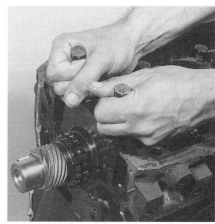

Work main cap from its register by using bolts loosely inserted into cap as handles.

all but two of the bolts aside. You're about to put these two to good use.

Because Nissan/Datsun L-series engine blocks are of the *deep-skirt* design—the block extends below the center line of the crankshaft—and the main-bearing caps fit tight in their *registers,* you'll have to use a little finesse to remove the caps.

To remove all but the center and rear main-bearing caps, insert two bolts back into each cap, but don't thread them into the block. Start with the number-l cap. Using the bolts as handles, rock the cap back and forth while lifting as you work it out of its register. You can lift with the bolts if you force their heads toward one another as you lift. Set the cap aside with

It's easier to remove oil-pump gear and crank sprocket before crank is out of engine. This is easily done by driving each item off with hammer and wood block.

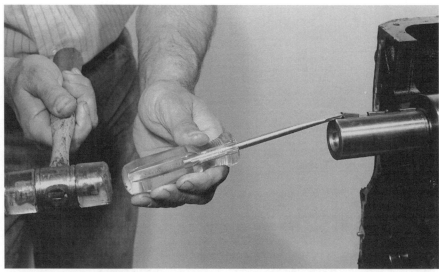

Rotate Woodruff keys from slots by tapping against front edges with screwdriver and mallet. Don't misplace keys.

Remove center main cap by threading long front-cover bolt into center of cap, then lever against underside of bolt head. Short 2x4 is used as fulcrum.

Flex your muscles and lift crank straight up out of block.

Rear main seal will come out with crankshaft. Remove it and discard.

its bearing-insert half, then turn your attention to the crankshaft nose.

Remove Oil-Pump/Distributor Gear & Crank Sprocket—The oil-pump/distributor gear and crank sprocket could have been removed before the front main-bearing cap, but it's an easier job with the cap out of the way. The photos illustrate.

Round up a chunk of wood similar to the 2x4 pictured. You can use it to pry against with a small bar or large screwdriver to start the gear and sprocket off. Or just drive them all the way off using a hammer or mallet with the wood block against the gear or sprocket. You can readily see how much better access is with the

front main-bearing cap off.

Finish Removing Main Caps—Finish removing all but the center and rear main-bearing caps. Store the bearing inserts with their caps. Round up one of the long front-cover bolts. It'll be used for *pulling* the center and rear caps. Nissan has a special puller for this, but improvising with a 2x4, a pry bar and the front-cover bolt is actually faster. Besides, who needs the additional expense?

The center and rear caps can't be rocked back and forth as you did with the other main-bearing caps. The center cap supports the crankshaft thrust-bearing insert, so it fits snugly between the crankshaft thrust faces. The rear cap is extra-wide and tight as it houses the rear main bearing and rear-main and cap-to-block seals.

Thread the front-cover bolt into the threaded hole provided in the bottom of the center cap. Rotate the crankshaft so the 2x4 will stand up on its edge alongside the crank and on the main webs, as shown. Using the block as a fulcrum, hook under the bolt head with the pry bar and pry the cap from the block.

Use the same setup to remove the rear cap, but lay the 2x4 flat against the bottom surface of the block. You'll have to pry it a bit farther than the center cap because of the long cap-to-block seals.

Keys—There are three *Woodruff keys* in the nose of the crankshaft: cam-drive-sprocket, oil-pump/distributor-drive-gear and crank-pulley keys. Unless there is obvious damage, leave them in place. They fit tightly in their keyways, so there is no danger of losing them. If you have to

Except for center bearing, top main-bearing halves are removed by simply rotating sideways from their bores.

Remove two screws, oil-breather breather and screen from block. Soak screen in solvent to clean.

Force one end of center bearing insert down, then remove from bore by grasping free end.

remove them, use a mallet and screwdriver or punch, as shown. Tap the keys out of their grooves. If the crank has to be ground, then remove the keys before sending it to the machine shop.

Remove Crankshaft—If you're ready to flex your muscles, lift the crankshaft from the block. In the case of a six-cylinder, flexing your muscles is a mild statement. It has two additional throws. There's not much problem lifting at the nose end. But there isn't a natural *handle* at the rear of the crankshaft. You can provide a finger hold by threading a flywheel bolt into the flywheel flange. A finger in the transmission pilot hole is another way to get a grip at the rear of the crankshaft. If lifting the rear is still a problem, loop a short section of rope around the rear crankshaft throw and tie a firm knot in it.

Lift the crankshaft straight up and out of the block. The rear-main seal will come with the crank as it's a full-circle lip-type seal. Just pull it off the flywheel flange and

INSPECT MAIN BEARINGS
Before tossing out the main-bearing inserts, inspect them; they'll tell a story. Bearing inserts are made from plated copper-lead alloy or lead-based babbitt both on a steel backing or shell. If your engine drove a lot of accessories, such as power steering and air conditioning, the front top bearing insert should be worn more than the others. This is due to the higher vertical load put on the crankshaft and bearing by drive-belt tension. Don't be concerned. Wear like this is normal because of the way the crankshaft is loaded. For the same reason, wear may also show up on the bottom of the center bearing.

If the bearing inserts are the copper-lead type, a copper color will show evenly through the tin plating. This makes it easy to distinguish wear because of the contrasting colors of the tin and copper. As for the lead-base inserts, it's more difficult to see wear because of the similar colors of the lead and tin.

You should be concerned about uneven wear from front to back on the total circumference of the bearing (top and bottom), scratches in the bearing surface and wiped bearing surface-bearing material displaced in the direction of crankshaft rotation because of metal-to-metal contact.

The first condition indicates that the bearing journal is tapered diameter is not constant from one end to the other, causing uneven bearing and journal loading and uneven wear.

Scratches in the bearing surface indicate that foreign material in the oil passed between the bearing and crank journal. This is usually caused by a clogged oil filter. Dirty oil bypassed the oil filter and recirculated through the engine.

A wiped bearing surface is usually caused by the journal not receiving adequate lubrication. This can be caused by periodic loss of oil pressure from a low oil level in the crankcase, a clogged oil passage or a malfunctioning oil pump.

If you find uneven wear, scratching or scoring on the bearings, look for the cause of that problem during component inspection. Also, a problem with the bearing may be symptomatic of a similar problem with the crankshaft. Consequently, you should pay particular attention to the crank journals that had bearing damage to see if there is a corresponding problem with the crankshaft.

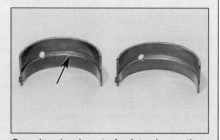

Save bearing inserts for later inspection. Note small oil hole (arrow) in insert at left that feeds chain tensioner.

discard it. Some main-bearing halves may stick to the crank as well.

Always be very careful when handling the crank out of the block. Dropping it on one end on a cement floor is enough to bend it.

Remove the cylinder-block main-bearing-insert halves. Simply rotate them sideways front-to-back or back-to-front out of

their bearing bores. Store each with its mating insert and main cap. The center-bearing insert can't be rotated because of its thrust flanges. So force the end opposite the end having the locating tab down using a screwdriver so the opposite end projects above the block. Lift the insert from the block.

Oil-Breather Baffle & Screen—While

Oil-pressure sending unit can be removed with adjustable wrench. A special socket for this is available at auto parts stores.

To remove main-oil-gallery plugs from block, drill and tap hole in center of each plug. Use 13/64-in. drill for 1/4-20 bolt. Run bolt into plug, clamp onto bolt head with Vise-Grip pliers, and lever out plug. If you're going to use pipe plugs later, now is the time to tap holes.

you're looking into the bottom end of the block, remove the oil-breather baffle and screen. You'll find them opposite the oil-pump pickup mounting boss between the number-3 and -4 main-bearing webs on four-cylinder engines and between the number-4 and -5 webs on sixes.

The baffle that retains the screen is held in place with two Phillips-head screws. After removing the screws and baffle, pull the screen from its pocket in the block.

Oil-Pressure Sending Unit—About all that's left in the block to remove are the oil-pressure sender and the water-jacket and oil-gallery plugs. Start with the easiest—the oil-pressure sender.

You'll find the oil-pressure sender installed in the block immediately beside the oil-filter mounting boss. There are two types of senders: idiot-light and gauge types. Special sockets are available for removing the idiot-light senders, but a Crescent wrench can be used, as shown.

Removing a gauge-type sender can present a problem. There's a hex on the sender's threaded nipple, but a sender will sometimes thread so far into the block that there isn't enough room left for a wrench. You can clamp onto the rolled flange at the base of the sender canister with a pair of Vise-Grip pliers. Once the threads are

broken loose, remove the pliers and unthread the sender by hand.

Oil-Gallery Plugs—Oil-gallery plugs are 13mm (slightly larger than 0.5 in.) diameter steel "slugs." These are driven into counterbores in the ends of the main oil gallery that runs the length of the block. The plugs are visible at the front and rear faces of the block. Plug removal is so difficult that many engine rebuilders don't bother removing them. I do because I want the main oil gallery in my newly rebuilt engine to be as clean as possible. Whether or not you remove these plugs is up to you. Base your judgment on how dirty and worn the engine is after reading the following.

Remove one oil-gallery plug by drilling and tapping a hole in its center. Tap size should be slightly less than plug diameter—3/8 in. or 10mm works fine. Run a bolt with compatible threads into the plug, clamp on the bolt head with Vise-Grip pliers, then lever against the pliers with a bar or screwdriver to pull the plug out.

You can remove the plug at the opposite end of the oil gallery using the same method. Or, if you have a steel rod that will reach the plug through the open end

of the oil gallery, simply drive out the remaining plug.

Find oil-gallery-plug replacements now so you'll have them at assembly time. Order new plugs from your Nissan dealer—they probably won't have them in stock.

A better method of plugging the main oil gallery is to tap the block to accept 1/4- or 3/8-in. socket-head pipe plugs. The plug that installs in the front should be shortened so it will not project into the number-1 main-bearing oil passage. This would block oil going to the front main. In addition, the plug must install below the front face of the block so it doesn't interfere with the fit of the front cover or chain tensioner.

If you opt for the pipe plugs, tap the block now rather than at assembly time so metal chips that result from cutting the threads will be flushed from the oil gallery. You'll need a 1/4- or 3/8-in. NPT (National Pipe Thread) tap and two 1/4- or 3/8-in. NPT socket-head plugs.

CAUTION: Don't try to tap the block and install the plugs at assembly time because the metal chips can cost you a crank and bearings if they get into the oil. Don't cheat because it will cost you!

CHAPTER FIVE

Parts Identification & Interchange

Block is easily identified with numbers stamped on pad at right rear. Engine designation is stamped there along with serial number. This is obviously an L20B.

You will find numbers in many locations on a Nissan/Datsun. They are on the chassis, body, engine, transmission, differential housing, instrument panel and numerous other places. You won't need them all; only those related to the engine.

Depending on what items you'll be looking for, you'll need one or all of the following: engine number, vehicle identification number (VIN) and numbers from the car identification plate. Use these when shopping for new parts at your Nissan dealer, and for used parts at the junkyard, swap meet/flea market or advertised in the paper.

The engine number is on the right side of the engine block, immediately above the starter. The VIN can be found on '69 and later models at the base of the windshield at the left side. The car identification plate is in the engine compartment, usually on the firewall.

It can he a real timesaver and money-saver to know which parts from one engine will interchange with those from another, especially if your engine needs a major part. For example, will an L20B crank work in an L16, or will an L26 head work on an L28? Assuming that certain parts interchange, the next problem is identifying them. With that problem solved, you can shop for used parts knowing your options, rather than playing Russian Roulette.

So, your first step is to identify which

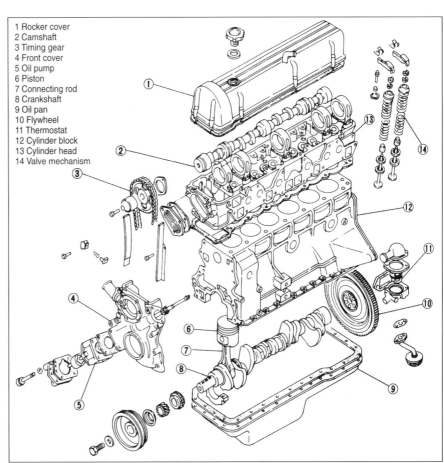

1 Rocker cover
2 Camshaft
3 Timing gear
4 Front cover
5 Oil pump
6 Piston
7 Connecting rod
8 Crankshaft
9 Oil pan
10 Flywheel
11 Thermostat
12 Cylinder block
13 Cylinder head
14 Valve mechanism

Nissan/Datsun L-series engines have a high degree of parts interchangeability. However don't assume that a part will interchange from one L-series engine to another, particularly crankshafts, connecting rods or pistons. Do so and metal-to-metal contact may result. Be careful with cylinder heads, too, even when interchanging between engines of the same displacement. A too-high or too-low compression ratio may result. Drawing courtesy Nissan.

engine you have. You must know the year, engine model and serial number.

IDENTIFICATION

Which Engine Do You Have?—To start from ground zero, I'll assume that you don't know which engine you have. It will either be a four- or six-cylinder engine. If your Nissan/Datsun is *rear-wheel drive* and the engine has an *overhead cam* and four cylinders, it will be an L13, L14, L16, L18 or L20B. If it has six cylinders, it's an L20A, L24, L26, L28, L28E, or L28ET. The L28 with E and ET suffixes designate fuel injection and fuel injection with turbo-

charging, respectively.

Note: If the engine was exported to the United States in a standard production car, it won't be an L13, L14 or L20A. These engines weren't built for the U.S. market.

You'll find the engine numbers stamped on one of two machined pads at the right side of the engine block toward the rear, directly below the deck surface. One pad is immediately above the starter motor, close to the rear face of the block. Record that number. On it is the *engine model number.* While you're at it, also record the number that's on the adjacent

ENGINE APPLICATIONS

Engine	1966	1967	1968	1969	1970	1971	1972	1973	1974	1975	1976	1977	1978	1979	1980	1981	1982	1983	1984
L13			510	510															
L14					510	510	510												
L16			510	510	510	510	510	510											
					521	521	521	620											
L18								610	610										
									620										
									710										
L20A	CEDRIC	CEDRIC	CEDRIC	CEDRIC	CEDRIC	CEDRIC	CEDRIC	CEDRIC											
L20B										610	610								
										710	710	710	510	510	510				
										620	620	620	620	620	720				
												200SX	200SX	200SX					
L24					240Z	240Z	240Z	240Z											
										810	810	810	810	810	810	810	810	810	810
L26									260Z	260Z									
L28										280Z	280Z	280Z	280Z	280ZX	280ZX	280ZX	280ZX	280ZX	
L28ET																280ZX	280ZX	280ZX	

Beginning and ending with sixes, L-series engine had numerous applications over its 18-year life span.

pad. It's the *engine serial number*. It will tell the parts man the sequence in which the engine was built. This number is important, particularly if changes were made in mid-model year or if service bulletins were issued that may affect part(s) used. It can also tell you if an engine you are considering swapping parts with was produced before or after yours. If the serial number is higher, the engine is newer and vice versa.

So, if L20B is stamped on the side of the block, the engine is a four-cylinder L20B; it's as simple as that.

Now that you know which engine you have, let's look at and compare the major components that make up the L-series engines. With few exceptions, the L-series Nissan/Datsun engine has undergone little change. This holds true between four- and six-cylinder engines and engines with the same number of cylinders, but with different displacements. Let's start with the foundation of the engine, the cylinder block.

CYLINDER BLOCK

All L-series blocks are cast iron. Basic dimensions of the L-series engines have remained surprisingly similar over the years, even though displacements have been increased by bore and/or stroke changes.

Bore Spacing—All L-series engines of the same number of cylinders have the same *bore spacing*—distance between bore centers. Bore spacing of four-cylinder blocks is 3.780 in. (96mm) between cylinders 1-2 and 3-4, and 3.858 in. (98mm) between cylinders 2-3. For six-cylinder engines, bore spacing is 3.799 in.

(96.5mm) between cylinders 1-2, 2-3, 4 and 5-6, and 3.858 in. (98mm) between cylinders 3-4. Center cylinders are spaced farther apart to allow for a wider center main-bearing web. Because the center crankshaft main bearing controls crankshaft thrust, a wider bearing and, consequently, a wider web are required.

Deck Height & Overall Block Height—*Deck height* is the distance between the crankshaft main-bearing-bore center and the block deck. *Overall block height* is the distance from the oil-pan rails to the deck. Overall block height is more than deck height because L-series-block skirts extend below the main-bearing-bore center to improve block rigidity. Except for the L20B, all L-series cylinder blocks have 8.1830 in. (207.85mm) deck height and 10.469 in. (265.9mm) overall height

L20B dimensions were increased by 0.771 in. (19.583mm) to give a 8.954 in. (227.45mm) deck height and 11.240 in. (285.5mm) overall block height.

L20B deck height was increased to accommodate the longer crank stroke. Increasing crankshaft stroke causes the pistons to operate proportionally higher in the bores, providing that connecting-rod *length* and piston *compression height* or *pin height* is maintained, pages 56 and 58. In some other engines, stroke has been increased without increasing deck height by reducing piston compression height or connecting-rod length. However, in the L20B, only the rod length was *increased*.

Cam-Sprocket Oiler—For whatever reason, only L-series fours have cam-sprocket oilers at the block. Immediately

---

VISUAL IDENTIFICATION IS IMPORTANT
Regardless of how many identification numbers you've armed yourself with, the final determining factor is a part's physical features. So, before you set off to find a crankshaft, cylinder head, block or whatever, measure all critical dimensions and record them. If possible, take along the part you want to replace. Another option is to take photographs. Don't forget a tape measure, 6-in. rule and vernier calipers for doing the measuring.

Examples: If you are looking for a crankshaft, measure its main- and connecting-rod bearing journals. For a connecting rod, you should have its big- and small-end diameters, and its center-to-center length-distance between big- and small-end bores. The tough item to check is a cylinder head. Measuring valve sizes, comparing port

shapes, and counting combustion chambers is easy, but determining combustion-chamber volume is not. You would need access to cc'ing equipment—a burette and a 4-in.-square piece of glass or clear plastic with a hole in the center. Then, you'd have to take it along on your shopping trip. For this one, I have a better idea.

Although crude, you can check combustion-chamber volume by filling a combustion chamber—valves in place—with clay. Force the clay into every nook and cranny of the combustion chamber, then scrape it flush with the head-gasket surface. The hunk of clay you dig out exactly represents the combustion-chamber volume. Take the clay along in a plastic bag for checking combustion-chamber volume of that unknown cylinder head.

CYLINDER-BLOCK SPECIFICATIONS mm (in.)				
Engine	Cylinder Bore*	Deck Height	Overall Height#	Main-Bearing Housing Bore Diameter
L13	83 (3.268)	207.85 (8.1830)	265.9 (10.469)	58.66—58.67 (2.3094—2.3099)
L14	83 (3.268)	207.85 (8.1830)	265.9 (10.469)	58.66—58.67 (2.3094—2.3099)
L16	83 (3.268)	207.85 (8.1830)	265.9 (10.469)	58.66—58.67 (2.3094—2.3099)
L18	85 (3.346)	207.85 (8.1830)	265.9 (10.469)	58.66—58.67 (2.3094—2.3099)
L20s	85 (3.346)	227.45 (8.954)	285.5 (11.240)	63.61—63.68 (2.5043—2.5073)
L20A	78 (3.071)	207.85 (8.1830)	265.9 (10.469)	58.66—58.67 (2.3094—2.3099)
L24	83 (3.268)	207.85 (8.1830)	265.9 (10.469)	58.66—58.67 (2.3094—2.3099)
L26	83 (3.268)	207.85 (8.1830)	265.9 (10.469)	58.66—58.67 (2.3094—2.3099)
L28	86 (3.386)	207.85 (8.1830)	265.9 (10.469)	58.66—58.67 (2.3094—2.3099)

*2.0mm (0.080-in.) maximum overbore without sonic testing
Bottom of pan rails to deck surface

As you can see from chart, L-series block dimensions remained relatively unchanged from one engine to another, particularly main-bearing-bore size. Note "taller" L20B block.

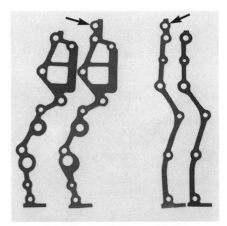

Front-cover gaskets show height difference between L20B and other L-series block—more than 3/4 in. Note additional Front-cover-bolt hole (arrows) at top of L20B gaskets.

above the front main bearing in the front face of the block, it's offset slightly to the right as viewed from the front. This oiler, page 68, is positioned so it sprays oil on top of the cam sprocket at the crank. All L-series engines have an oiler at the top. It's a hole in the front camshaft tower that directs oil onto the back of the cam sprocket.

Other Identifiers—The final things to watch for are cylinder-bore and main-bearing-bore diameters. Of the nine basic L-series engines, there are only four different bore sizes—a feature engine modifiers can utilize, as discussed in *How to Modify Your Nissan & Datsun OHC Engine.* And, except for the L20B, main-bearing-bore diameter is the same at 2.310 in. (58.67mm); L20B main-bearing bores are 2.506 in. (63.65mm).

Let's look at each block, beginning with the four cylinder L-series engines.
L13, 14, 16 & 18—Although these engines have different displacements, all but the L18 have the same bore size at 3.268 in. (83mm); the L18 has 3.346 in. (85mm) bores. Main-bearing-bore diameter, at 2.3096 in. (58.66mm), and deck heights are the same at 8.1830 in. (207.85mm).

L20B—Although basically the same design, the L20B cylinder block is unique. Both bore size and crankshaft stroke were increased to raise displacement from 1770cc of the L18 to 1952cc. Bore diameter was increased to 3.346 in. (85mm); stroke went up from 3.071 in. (78mm) to 3.386 in. (86mm).

Also, connecting-rod *center-to-center length*—distance between big- and small-end bores—was increased from 5.12 in. (130.05mm) to 5.75 in. (146.05mm). Because piston compression height was retained, block deck height was increased. Finally, to accommodate 0.0787 in. (2mm) larger main-bearing journals, bearing bores in the block were increased about 5mm to 2.506 in. (63.6mm).

Other than the obvious *L20B* stamped in the side of the block, you can easily identify an L20B block by looking at its front face. There is an additional front-cover bolt hole in the very top at *each* side. These two additional bolt holes, which are obvious because of being closely spaced to the "old" top front-cover bolt holes, were added to obtain the needed gasket-clamping force on the front cover. The front cover was lengthened to match the deck-height increase.

So, because it is unique, the L20B cannot be interchanged with other L-series blocks. Consequently, if you have an L20B engine, you'll have to use an L20B block. But, you can replace a complete L16 or L18 engine with an L20B or vice versa. Other than possibly having to use the oil pan from your original engine, the only problems you may encounter are throttle-linkage and exhaust hookups. Although these are relatively minor, plan to contend with them if you make the switch.

Will an L20B block fit in an early 510? Sure, just redrill the holes in the motor mounts where they fasten to the block. Mount the brackets about 3/8 in. higher on the block and you're in business.
L20A, 24, 26 & 28—Other than internal differences in the six-cylinder family, the only major difference in L-series six-cylinder blocks is bore size. Bore diameters are: L20A: 3.071 in. (78mm); L24 and L26: 3.268 in. (83mm); and L28: 3.386 in. (86mm).
L24 Oil Dipstick—A minor difference between L24 Z-car and Maxima blocks is that the Maxima oil dipstick is forward of, not to the rear of the oil filter. The original dipstick-tube boss remains, but is not drilled.
L28 Cylinder Webs—Although it does not affect interchangeability, early L28 blocks are cast with the front three and back three cylinders *Siamesed.* Webs are cast between them to increase cylinder stability. Beginning in 1981, the L28ET (turbo engine) webs are slit to improve coolant circulation. As of model year 1982, all L28 webs are slit.

Unlike early L28 block, Turbo block has water-passage slots in webs that Siamese front three and rear three cylinders. Early L28 cylinders are not Siamesed, allowing free flow of water between cylinders (arrow). Photo by Frank Honsowetz.

Typical L-series crankshaft: Forged with cross-drilled connecting-rod bearing journals. Six-cylinder cranks are not counterweighted.

Nap-Z engine block will accept L-series head if engine-stamping pads (arrow) are ground flush with normal surface of block. Otherwise, exhaust manifold interferes with pads.

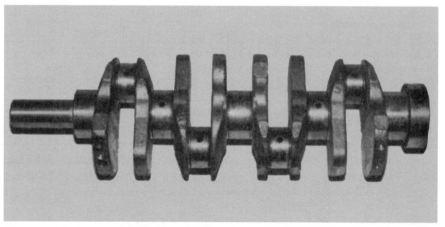

Fully counterbalanced L20B crank is as tough as they come. Rather than four counterweights, this one has eight. Photo by Frank Honsowetz.

CRANKSHAFT

All L-series crankshafts are forged steel. The fours have five main bearings; sixes have seven. Each connecting rod has its own *throw*, or rod-bearing journal. Almost all L-series crankshafts are *fully counterweighted*—two counterweights are used opposite each connecting-rod throw rather than one to compensate for the weight of the throw and the majority of the connecting rod. Those that are not fully counterweighted are *partially counterweighted*. These include the Ll3, L14, late L16 and early L20B fours and all of the sixes. Counterweighting is considered a necessity when building a racing engine, particularly one that will be used at high rpm.

Otherwise, a partially counterweighted crankshaft is OK.

With two exceptions, all main- and connecting-rod-bearing journals are the same diameters, regardless of number of cylinders, at 2.163 in. (54.94mm) and 1.967 in. (49.97mm), respectively. L20B main-bearing journals are larger at 2.360 in. (59.94mm). For some strange reason, probably to reduce friction and increase mileage, the 1982 and '83 Maxima L24 connecting-rod-bearing-journal diameters were reduced to 1.768 in. (44.91mm). Other than these few changes, stroke instead of bore was usually increased to increase engine displacement.

As you can see from the chart, of the

nine L-series engines, there are seven different strokes: five for four-cylinder engines and three for the sixes. You might think something is wrong because five and three add up to eight, not seven. The reason for this is the L16 and L24 share the same 2.902 in. (73.7mm) stroke. They also have the same 3.268 in. (83mm) bore size. Other L-series engines with the same stroke are the L26 and L28 at 3.110 in. (79mm).

CONNECTING RODS

As with other L-series engine parts, there is a wide range of interchangeability between connecting rods. To start with, all L-series rods are forged steel. Also, the

CRANKSHAFT SPECIFICATIONS
mm (m.)

Engine	Stroke	Main Bearing Journal Diameter	Oil Clearance	Connecting-Rod Journal Diameter	Oil Clearance
L13	59.9 (2.358)	54.942—54.955 (2.1631—2.1636)	0.033—0.081 (0.0013—0.0032)	49.961-49.974 (1.9670-1.9675)	0.025-0.066 (0.0010-0.0026)
L14	66.0 (2.598)	54.942—54.955 (2.1631—2.1636)	0.033—0.081 (0.0013—0.0032)	49.961-49.974 (1.9670-1.9675)	0.025-0.066 (0.0010-0.0026)
L16	73.3 (2.886)	54.942—54.955 (2.1631—2.1636)	0.033—0.081 (0.0013—0.0032)	49.961-49.974 (1.9670-1.9675)	0.025-0.066 (0.0010-0.0026)
L18	78.0 (3.071)	54.942—54.955 (2.1631—2.1636)	0.033—0.081 (0.0013—0.0032)	49.961-49.974 (1.9670-1.9675)	0.025-0.066 (0.0010-0.0026)
L20B	86.0 (3.386)	59.942—59.955 (2.3600—2.3604)	0.033—0.081 (0.0013—0.0032)	49.961-49.974 (1.9670-1.9675)	0.025-0.066 (0.0010-0.0026)
L20A	69.7 (2.744)	54.942—54.955 (2.1631—2.1636)	0.033—0.081 (0.0013—0.0032)	49.961-49.974 (1.9670-1.9675)	0.025-0.066 (0.0010-0.0026)
L24	73.7 (2.902)	54.935—54.955 (2.1628—2.1636)	0.033—0.081 (0.0013—0.0032)	49.961-49.974 (1.9670-1.9675)*	0.025-0.066 (0.0010-0.0026)
L26	79.0 (3.110)	54.935—54.955 (2.1628—2.1636)	0.033—0.081 (0.0013—0.0032)	49.961-49.974 (1.9670-1.9675)	0.025-0.066 (0.0010-0.0026)
L28	79.0 (3.110)	54.935—54.955 (2.1628—2.1636)	0.033—0.081 (0.0013—0.0032)	49.961-49.974 (1.9670-1.9675)	0.025-0.066 (0.0010-0.0026)

*82-84 Maxima, 44.911mm (1.765-in.) rod journal
Main & rod undersizes 0.25mm (0.010)
                    0.50mm (0.020)
                    0.75mm (0.030)

Except for stroke, L-series crankshaft bearing-journal dimensions have virtually gone unchanged. Exceptions are the L20B crank with larger main-bearing journals and the Maxima L24 crank with small rod-bearing journals.

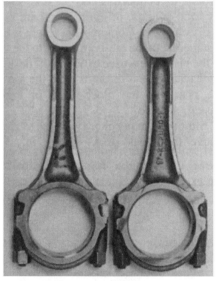

Longer L20B connecting rod beside pre-1981 5-1/4-in.-long L24 rod: Both rods use 9mm bolts.

CONNECTING-ROD SPECIFICATIONS
mm (in.)

Engine	Rod-bolt Size	Center-to-center Length	Big-end Diameter	Small-end Diameter
L13	8mm	139.9 (5.508)	53.00—53.01 (2.0866—2.0871)	20.965—20.970 (0.8254—0.8256)
L14	8mm	133.0 (5.236)	53.00—53.01 (2.0866—2.0871)	20.965—20.970 (0.8254—0.8256)
L16	To 3/72, 8mm From 4/72, 9mm	133.0 (5.240)	53.00—53.01 (2.0866—2.0871)	20.965—20.970 (0.8254—0.8256)
L18	8mm	130.2 (5.132)	53.00—53.01 (2.0866—2.0871)	20.965—20.970 (0.8254—0.8256)
L20B	9mm	145.9 (5.750)	53.00—53.01 (2.0866—2.0871)	20.965—20.970 (0.8254—0.8256)
L20A	8mm	128.0 (5.039)	53.00—53.01 (2.0866—2.0871)	19.96—19.97 (0.7858—0.7862)
L24	To 6/81, 9mm From 7/81, 8mm	133.0 (5.240)	53.00—53.01~ (2.0866—2.0871)	20.965—20.970 (0.8254—0.8256)
L26	8mm	130.2 (5.132)	53.00—53.01 (2.0866—2.0871)	20.965—20.970 (0.8254—0.8256)
L28	8mm	130.2 (5.132)	53.00—53.01 (2.0866—2.0871)	20.965—20.970 (0.8254—0.8256)

*82-84 Maxima, 47.95mm (1.888 in.) big-end diameter
#82-84 Maxima, 19.97mm (0.786 in.) small-end diameter

Noteworthy is connecting rod for '82-83 Maxima L24. For some reason, smaller big and small ends are used.

basic design is the same for all L-series original-production rods, regardless of engine application. For example, all have *pressed pins*. The piston pins are retained in the small end of the rod with an interference fit. At the *big end* (crankshaft-journal end) the bearing cap is retained with bolts and nuts.

Major differences crop up when comparing connecting-rod center-to-center lengths. For example, the seven L-series engines exported to the United States use three rod lengths: 5.13 in. (130.2mm) for the L18, L26 and L28; 5.24 in.(133.0mm) for the L14, L16 and L24; and 5.75 in. (145.9mm) for the L20B. Finally, the L20A and L13 engines add two more center-to-center lengths at 5.04 in. (128.0mm) and 5.51 in. (140.0mm), respectively.

With exception of the 1982-84 L24 Maxima (810) engine, big- and small-end bores are the same: 2.086 in. (53.0mm) at the big end and 0.825 in. (20.9mm) at the small end. The smaller 1982-84 Maxima engine big- and small-end bores are 1.888 in. (47.9mm) and 0.786 in. (19.9mm), respectively.

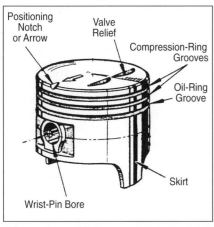

When talking with your engine machinist, it helps to know piston terminology.

Three 85mm (3.347-in.) bore-size cast pistons: Two at left are for L20B. Piston at right is for LZ20E Naps-Z engine. Lower pin height of L-20E piston makes it desirable for use in aftermarket and turbocharged L20B. Photo by Frank Honsowetz.

Finally, two bearing-cap-bolt sizes were used in the L-series engines: 8mm and 9mm. Those using the 8mm bolt include the L13, L14, L16 (through March 1972), L20A and L24 Maxima engine. Engines using the 9mm bolt include the L20B, L16 (starting April 1972), L18, L24 (except for Maxima engine), L26 and L28.

PISTONS

All production L-series engines use three-ring, cast-aluminum pistons with skirts to stabilize the pistons in their bores. The first two piston rings, counting from the top

down, are compression rings; third is the oil ring. The piston-pin bore is offset 0.040 in. (1.00mm) to the right, or *thrust side* of the piston, to reduce engine noise from *piston slap*. Piston slap is caused by the piston skirt striking the bore during the power stroke. Offsetting the piston pin reduces the noise by causing the piston to be pressed against the bore before the air/fuel charge is ignited.

Major differences in L-series pistons are *diameter, compression height, pin-bore size* and *dish volume*. Piston diameter is self explanatory: Different piston diame-

ters were required to match different bore sizes of the L-series engines.

Compression height is not quite so simple. To compensate for different crankshaft strokes or connecting-rod lengths, *compression heights* or *pin heights*, are normally changed. Compression height is the distance from the pin-bore center to the top of the piston. It is used to obtain the desired *deck clearance*—distance from the top of the piston to the block deck or head-gasket, surface.

Although the piston may extend slightly above the block deck—0.001 in., for

Application	Nissan part number	Bore size inch/mm	Pin height inch/mm	Piston dish volume (cc)	Nissan Ring Set part number
L16	12010—23002	3.268/83	1.50/38.1	7.01cc	12033—23000
L16 + 1mm	12010—22006	3.308/84	1.50/38.1	7.01cc	12038—A3500
L24	12010—E3111	3.268/83	1.50/38.1	—0—	12033—E3100
L24 + 1mm	12010—E3116	3.308/84	1.50/38.1	—0—	12038—E3116
L24 Option	12010—H2711	3.268/83	1.50/38.1	—0—	12033—E3100
L18	12010—U2001	3.347/85	1.50/38.1	4.36cc	12033—A8702
L18 + 1mm	12010—A8706	3.386/86	1.50/38.1	4.36cc	12038—A8702
L18 Option	12010—A8720	3.347/85	1.50/38.1	—0—	12033—A8775
L20B	12010—U6001	3.347/85	1.50/38.1	11.36cc	12010—U6001
L20B + 1mm	12010—U6006	3.386/86	1.50/38.1	11.36cc	12038—U6001
L28	12010—Y4111	3.386/86	1.50/38.1	10.9cc	12033—N4200
L28 + 1mm	12010—Y4116	3.425/87	1.50/38.1	10.9cc	12038—N4200
L28 Turbo	12010—P9012	3.386/86	1.50/38.1	10.9cc	12033—P9010
L28 Turbo + 1mm	12010—P9017	3.425/87	1.50/38.1	10.9cc	12038—P9010
L28 (after 7/80)	12010—P7912	3.386/86	1.50/38.1	—0—	12033—P7910
L28 + 1 mm (after 7/80)	12010—P7917	3.425/87	1.50/38.1	—0—	12038—P7910

NISSAN CAST PISTONS

When choosing pistons, refer to chart. Chart courtesy Frank Honsowetz.

example—clearance is required to prevent the piston from striking the cylinder head at the top of the compression and power strokes. Therefore, most engine designs move the pin up or down in the piston to compensate for crankshaft-stroke and/or connecting-rod-length changes. However, such is *not* the case with the L-series engines. Remarkably, pin height has remained at 1.50 in. (38.1mm). This and the many common bore sizes are a tremendous advantage when swapping cranks or trying to come up with the desired compression ratio. Frank Honsowetz explains this process in detail in his book *How to Modify Your Nissan & Datsun OHC Engine*.

As you may have concluded from the connecting-rod discussion, except for the 1982-83 L24 Maxima engine, all L-series engines use the same 0.8266-in. (21mm) diameter piston pin. L24 Maxima pistons use a smaller 0.7876-in. (20mm) pin.

Here's where things get complicated. Some L-series pistons are flat on top; others are *dished* (recessed at the top to reduce compression with a given cylinder head). Dish volume, specified in cubic centimeters (cc's), ranges from zero for flat-top pistons to a maximum of 11.36cc for L20B pistons. If you're going to do any piston or cylinder-head swapping from one engine to another, dish volume is a variable you must consider to avoid achieving an undesirable—too high or too low—compression ratio.

Direct-oiling setup routes oil to center of cam through bearing journal. Note grooved journal. Oil exits cam at squirt hole in lobes (arrows).

L-series Piston Volumes	
Engine	**Dish Volume (cc)**
L13	N/A
L14	N/A
L16	7.01
L18	4.36
L20B	11.36
L20A	N/A
L24	0
L26	N/A
L28*	10.9
L28ET	10.9
*Zero dish volume after 7-80.	

You must also consider cylinder-head combustion-chamber volume when doing piston or cylinder-head swapping. See page 61 for more about this.

CYLINDER HEAD & VALVE TRAIN

No big surprises here: In case you were

wondering, all L-series cylinder heads and their valve trains are basically the same. To start with, all heads are cast aluminum with a single overhead cam. There are two valves and one spark plug per cylinder. Intake and exhaust ports are all on the left side because these are *non-crossflow heads*. Let's look at cylinder head and valve-train design up top.

Cam & Rocker Arms—The camshaft is supported by four cam towers on four-cylinder engines or five on-six-cylinder engines. Valve-train oiling is where you'll find one variation.

Sixes built from March 1977, and all fours, oil the cam and rockers through the cam. Camshafts for this type of lubrication are drilled lengthwise so oil is fed to a squirt hole in each cam lobe. Oil is supplied to the cam from the second and fourth cam bearings for fours and the second and fifth cam bearings for sixes.

On sixes built up to March 1977, a spray bar provides lubrication for the cam lobes and rockers. These cams are not drilled. Running parallel to the cam immediately to its right, the spray bar is fitted to number-2 and -4 cam towers. Oil is routed to the spray bar from an oil gallery in the head and up through the cam towers. One hole adjacent to each cam lobe sprays oil on that lobe and rocker.

CAUTION: When installing a cam in a non-spray-bar six-cylinder head, check that the cam is drilled for lobe and rocker-arm lubrication. Also, the back end of the cam must be plugged. Otherwise, your engine will have a huge internal oil leak, low oil pressure and no lubrication to the cam lobes and rocker arms.

Can you install a drilled (internally oiled) camshaft in an engine that also has a spraybar? Sure, you can use both oiling methods at the same time with no problem.

Under each cam lobe is a forged-steel rocker arm. At the right, each rocker rests on a pivot—adjustable screw-type on most engines and non-adjustable hydraulic-type on '83 L28s. Each rocker opens its valve at its tip end. At the center of each rocker is a pad that the cam lobe wipes against. As it rotates, the rocker arm is operated, thereby opening and closing the valve.

L13s, 14s and early 16s used one-piece forged-steel rocker arms. These were later replaced with two-piece rockers. For

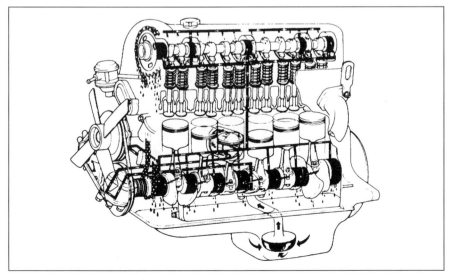

On sixes built prior to March '77, valve-train lubrication is by spray bar. Oil is routed to spray bar from number-2 and -4 cam towers. Drawing courtesy Nissan.

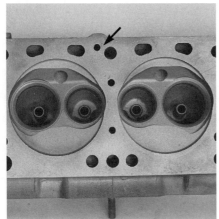

Combustion-chamber side of L20B cylinder head: Small hole (arrow) routes oil from block to cam bearings.

STANDARD VALVE SIZES
in. (mm)

Engine	Diameter		Length	
	Intake	Exhaust	Intake	Exhaust
L13	1.50/38	1.30/33	4.56/115.9	4.57/116.0
L16 early	1.50/38	1.30/33	4.56/115.9	4.57/116.0
L16 late	1.65/42	1.30/33	4.56/115.2	4.57/116.0
L18	1.65/42	1.30/33	4.53/115.2	4.57/116.0
L20A	1.50/38	1.30/33	4.36/110.7	4.36/110.7
L24 one 2-bbl	1.50/38	1.30/33	4.59/116.5	4.63/117.5
L24 up to 7-73	1.65/42	1.30/33	4.59/116.5	4.57/116.0
L24 after 8-76	1.65/42	1.38/35	4.59/116.5	4.57/116.0
L26	1.65/42	1.38/35	4.59/116.5	4.57/116.0
L20B	1.65/42	1.38/35	4.53/115.2	4.57/116.0
L28 up to 7-80	1.73/44	1.38/35	4.53/115.2	4.57/116.0
L28 as of 7-80	1.73/44	1.38/35	4.45/113.1	4.48/113.9

improved cam-lobe and rocker-arm wear, a cast-iron pad was brazed onto the forged-steel rocker arm.

Valves & Seats—Three intake-valve and two exhaust-valve sizes are used in L-series engines. Although most differences are slight, stem lengths vary. Valve-head diameters and stem lengths are shown in the above chart. Valve-stem diameter is the same for all engines, intake or exhaust, at 0.3134 in. (7.96mm).

Valve-seat inserts are used in the L-series heads simply because valves cannot operate directly on cast aluminum. Sintered-iron or bronze-alloy inserts are used under the intake valves and steel inserts are installed under the exhausts. The inserts are retained in counterbores with an interference fit.

Big Brother—Unfortunately, bronze-alloy inserts are not as durable as they should be. This came with the advent of the U.S. Environmental Protection Agency's (EPA) mandated elimination of tetraethyl lead. Tetraethyl lead—TEL—had major advantages over other gasoline additives in terms of valve durability and *anti-knock* benefits.

It's not uncommon to find an intake valve in an early-70s high-mileage L-series engine *sunk* deeply into the head. Consequently, bronze-alloy intake-valve inserts were phased out in favor of sintered-iron inserts. So, if you have a cylinder head with bronze inserts, replace them. They are easy to recognize. After polishing an area of a bronze-alloy insert

Early L20B head is easy to recognize by its semi-square-shaped exhaust ports.

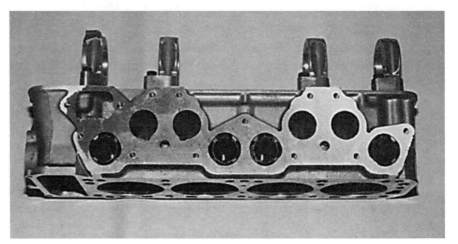

L20B emissions head features round exhaust ports and sheet-metal liners. Liners act as glow plugs to burn excess hydrocarbons in exhaust gas. Photo by Frank Honsowetz.

with sandpaper or emery cloth, the area has a copper look.

Exhaust Ports—Up until 1978 for four-cylinder engines and 1977 for sixes, L-series heads used "square" exhaust ports. You can see this by looking at the intake/exhaust-manifold mounting face. Cylinder heads used in following model years have round exhaust ports with cast-in sheet-metal inserts.

The size of the exhaust ports was reduced with the insert. The purpose of the metal inserts was to reduce emissions, not to increase horsepower. Because the inserts are not backed up by aluminum over most of their length, they get hot enough to glow in a manner similar to a model-airplane two-stroke-engine glow plug. The superheated inserts ignite unburned fuel as the combustion products exit the exhaust ports. The result is reduced hydrocarbon (HC) emissions.

Combustion Chamber—Beginning with the L13 and L16 engines in 1968 and ending with the L28 in 1983, L-series heads have had various combustion-chamber designs. This was particularly true in later years when reduced emissions was a major consideration.

Combustion-chamber design is affected by two variables: desired shape and volume. Combustion-chamber shape is a function of valve and spark-plug placement, and desired air/fuel-mixture flow. It is also influenced by chamber volume. Combustion-chamber volume is influenced mainly by desired compression ratio, which is *inversely* proportional to chamber volume. As chamber volume increases, the compression ratio drops and vice versa. This is the main consideration when interchanging L-series cylinder heads. Although four- and six-cylinder heads are interchangeable within the two groups, compression ratio can be changed significantly by changing the head.

As previously mentioned in the piston discussion, piston design combines with cylinder-head design to establish compression ratio. Although there's not much you can do to modify these designs, you can take advantage of them to keep or change your engine's compression ratio. This is particularly important in light of the lack of higher-octane gas. The option of using 100-octane gas to prevent detonation and the resulting engine damage was restricted years ago. Although improving over the '90s, 87-octane pump gas is normal and 92 is about the best you can find. This means 9.5:1 compression is a practical compression-ratio limit. Much higher

High-performance SSS cylinder head has small combustion chambers. Head is available from Nissan Motorsports. Photo by Frank Honsowetz.

compression and you will have to resort to drastic measures such as severely retarded ignition, richer air/fuel mixture and/or fuel additives. Let's look at how piston-dish and combustion-chamber volumes combine to affect compression.

Starting with a real-world situation, suppose an early 240Z cylinder head with a chamber volume of 42.5cc is installed on an L28 originally equipped with a 44.6cc head. The resulting compression will be over 10.0:1. And, assuming the head was milled a small amount, compression can easily exceed 11.0:1—too much for today's gasoline.

Although I recommend that you don't mess around with swapping a cylinder head from another engine, particularly if it has a different displacement, here's how to do it right. First, get a copy of *How to Modify Your Nissan & Datsun OHC Engine* by Frank Honsowetz. Swapping heads definitely falls under the modifications category. After you've read and understood what's in Frank's book, take your engine and head to a shop that specializes in modifying engines and knows how to cc an engine.

Calculating Compression Ratio—The process of cc'ing an engine involves measuring the combustion-chamber volume in the block and head to find *total clearance volume*. This is done with a piece of glass or clear plastic, and liquid from a chemist's burette. The resulting figures are then used to calculate the compression ratio that will result from the engine/cylinder head combination. It's much better to find out now that compression would be too high than after the

engine is together.

To find an engine's compression ratio, you need cylinder-head volume, piston-dish volume, volume created above the block by piston-deck clearance and compressed head-gasket thickness. This all adds up to total clearance volume.

One thing you can't measure with a burette is the volume created by compressed head-gasket thickness. From calculations, this volume is *about* 7.14cc when the gasket is compressed to 0.047 in. (1.2mm). If cylinder-head-chamber volume is 45.20cc and piston-dish volume is 11.36cc, total clearance is *about* 63.70cc. If *deck clearance* is zero, then this is close to total clearance volume. However, if the piston is below or above the deck, this will add or subtract clearance volume.

One more item is the volume on the outside of the piston, immediately above the top compression ring. Although minimal, it must also be considered. Fortunately, it, the effect of deck clearance and piston dish are obtained at once when cc'ing the assembled engine.

Once you've obtained your engine's total clearance volume (CV)—let's suppose it's 65.70cc—you'll need *swept volume* before you can calculate compression ratio (CR). Swept volume (SV) is the volume displaced by one piston as it travels from BC to TC. It's simply the displacement of one cylinder, or total displacement of the engine divided by the number of cylinders. If the engine is an L20B, swept volume is 1952cc divided by 4, or 488cc. The calculation is:

$$CR = (SV/CV) + 1 = (488cc/65.7cc) + 1$$
$$= 7.43 + 1 = 8.43:1$$

This compression is OK for today's gasoline. There's even a little safety margin, considering that 9.5:1 compression should be OK. However, let's see what happens if cylinder-head chamber volume is reduced 10cc. According to the formula, compression ratio is:

$$CR = (488cc/55.7cc) + 1 = 8.8 + 1 = 9.8:1$$

We're now getting in a range approaching the limit for street use. However, if the engine will be used for racing only and 100-octane gasoline is available, it's OK.

The bottom line is this: If you swap cylinder heads, use pistons with a different dish, or mill the cylinder head or block, calculate compression ratio first!

CHAPTER SIX

Shortblock Reconditioning

Reconditioning short block starts with removing all crud and gunk from block. Cast-iron block is lowered into hot tank for a good soaking in cleaning solution.

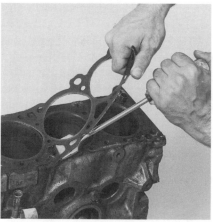

After checking gasket for signs of leakage, remove it from block deck surface. Gasket scraper is superior to putty knife or screwdriver for removing gasket material.

Most people have an inherent knack for taking things apart, so I'll assume you've had no real problems to this point. Problems usually occur during inspection, reconditioning and assembly. Unfortunately, these problems don't show up until the engine has been reinstalled and is running—or not running.

More often than not, goofs are due to insufficient information. Because of this, I've tried to include all of the information you'll need to inspect your engine and recondition it. So, if you apply this information with an abundance of common sense and a reasonable amount of care, your rebuilt engine should perform better than it did when new.

CYLINDER-BLOCK CLEANING & INSPECTION

One of the most important jobs you'll have to do is clean each engine component thoroughly. After you're tired of cleaning these parts, it's equally important that you keep them clean.

Head-Gasket Check—Before destroying the evidence, inspect the head gasket for leaks, both compression/combustion and coolant. Coolant leaks will show up as rust streaks on the block and/or head surfaces, even though the head is aluminum. Black or gray streaks radiating from a combustion chamber or cylinder indicate a combustion leak.

If you find a leak connecting a cylinder with a water passage, your engine was probably losing coolant because the cooling system was over-pressurized. On the other hand, a compression leak vented to the atmosphere or another cylinder will have shown up only if you performed a compression check *prior* to tearing down the engine. If you discover what looks like a leak, check the block and head surfaces for warpage or other imperfections in the area of the suspected leak after you clean them.

One type of leak to be particularly watchful for is a combustion leak connecting two cylinders. The block or cylinder head may be *notched*. Notching occurs when hot combustion gases remove metal as they flow back and forth between cylinders. The effect is like a cut from an oxy-acetylene torch.

An aluminum cylinder head is particularly susceptible to notching. Although more prevalent with a racing engine, notching can also occur with a street engine if it's operated a long time without correcting the leak. If a cylinder suffered a combustion leak, check for notching after cleaning the head. Notch damage can be repaired by welding and resurfacing the damaged surface.

Clean Block—The cleaning process can be handled several ways. The best way is

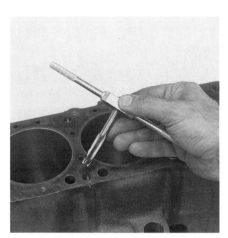

Threaded holes in block should he chased to ensure accurate bolt torquing at assembly. Note material removed from threads in "clean" block.

Light, water-dispersant oil temporarily protects iron and steel engine parts from rust. Get some.

to take the block to your local engine rebuild for *hot tanking* or *jet spraying*. Because your L-series Nissan/Datsun engine has an aluminum cylinder head, make sure he can clean aluminum parts.

Although the situation has changed rapidly because of the increased use of aluminum in engines, many engine rebuilders traditionally used a highly caustic soda that dissolves aluminum. Some may still do. So check first. Even though the block is cast iron, it's a good idea to have most of the other engine parts cleaned at the same time. This includes the aluminum cylinder head, front cover and cam cover. Many machine shops now use ovens to bake the parts so the grease is turned to ashes that flake off.

Other techniques you can employ to clean engine parts are steam cleaning, using spray-on engine cleaner at the local car wash or washing with a garden hose with cleaner, detergent and a scrub brush. Paint thinner or gasket remover can be used to soften gasket material. Gasket remover is strong stuff, so be careful not to get it on your skin. Regardless of the method used, concentrate on cleaning the block interior, particularly the oil galleries and bolt holes. Hook a rag on a wire and drag it through the oil galleries. Pipe cleaners are handy, too.

Many supermarkets carry nylon cof-

feepot brushes that are well suited to this job. Copper-bristled gun-bore brushes work well, too. Team these with carburetor cleaner and you'll be able to do an excellent cleaning job on the oiling system.

Be Tidy—The easiest way to ruin friendships and upset family members and neighbors is to be thoughtless and make a greasy mess. Find an out-of-the-way place to do your cleaning, then clean up the mess afterward. Do your scraping over a large piece of cardboard or newspaper. It will catch the big chunks of grease and gasket material. Fold or roll up the paper afterward and discard it to rid yourself of the major mess.

Washing off parts is messier still, with engine cleaner, dirty water and grease clumps flying everywhere. Remember, you'll be using some pretty strong soap and solvent that kills grass and stains driveways. So it's really best to take major engine parts to a rebuilder for cleaning. Save the manifolds and accessory hang-ons that don't generate such a mess for yourself.

Scrape Gaskets—Get the worst job out of the way by scraping all gasket surfaces. A gasket scraper is a tool specifically designed for this. Now is the time to invest in one. If you try the job with a putty knife or a screwdriver, then switch to a gasket scraper, you'll find out what I mean. You

could've saved skinned knuckles, a lost temper and loads of time.

Surfaces that need to be scraped are the cylinder deck, front cover, oil pan, intake manifold and oil pump. Don't stop with the block. While you're at it, scrape the head and exhaust manifold, too.

Chase Threads—After you think the block is as clean as it's going to get, *chase* the threaded holes. Run a tap the same size and pitch as the fastener into the threaded hole to clean it out. Just make absolutely sure you use the right tap. Threading the tap into the hole should offer no more resistance than running the bolt into the same hole.

Do the thread chasing with a *bottom tap,* not a *taper tap* used to start a thread. You'll be shocked at the amount of crud a tap extracts from the threads, even after you've done a "meticulous" job of cleaning. The thread-chasing procedure is particularly important for bolts that must be torqued accurately during assembly. The major ones are the main-bearing and cylinder-head bolt-hole threads.

Don't forget to clean stud threads, too. A wire brush will remove most deposits, but chase stud threads with the proper size *die* to be sure.

Clean Coolant Passages—After you've cleaned head- and main-bearing bolt-hole threads, go after the coolant passages. Remove any loose rust, deposits or core sand. Pay particular attention to the passages connecting the cylinder head to the block. This will ensure good coolant flow between the head and block. A round file works well for this job, but be careful of the head-gasket surface. A gouge in the wrong place can cause a head-gasket leak. Give the same treatment to the cylinder head.

Compressed Air—Compressed air is handy for forcing dirt out of hard-to-reach areas and for drying the block is. If you don't have an air compressor, a portable air tank with a blow gun will work just as well—until the pressure drops.

Prevent Rust—Controlling moisture becomes more of a problem as you clean more of the parts. Bearing-bore surfaces, cylinder bores, valve seats and other machined surfaces will rust from humidity in the air after old oil, grease and sludge is removed. So, prevent this by coating machined surfaces with a water-dispersing oil after cleaning or machining.

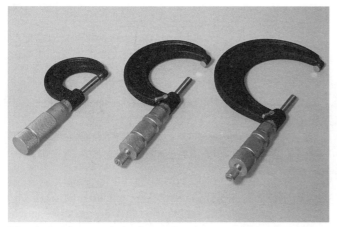

Micrometers are needed to inspect engine components. From left to right are 1—2-, 2—3- and 3—4-in. mikes. You'll also need set of telescoping gages.

Bore surfaces show little wear. Regardless, wear shows above original crosshatch and below ridge. As with most L-series blocks, this one didn't need to be rebored.

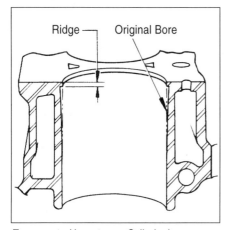

Exaggerated bore taper: Cylinder bore wears more at top of ring travel due to combustion-chamber pressures and minimal lubrication. This wear is called *taper*.

WD-40®, for instance, will do the job with a lot less fuss and mess than a squirt can of motor oil. More important, water-dispersant oil does what its name implies: It disperses water rather than trapping it underneath where it can rust the base metal. Whatever you do, don't leave a freshly machined surface unoiled or it will rust for sure.

BLOCK INSPECTION & RECONDITIONING

Inspecting the engine block to determine what must be done to restore it to tiptop condition is the first reconditioning step. To do a satisfactory inspection job, you'll need 3—4-in. inside and outside micrometers, a precision straightedge and feeler gages. A set of telescoping gages will eliminate the need for the inside mikes. You may not need the straightedge if the head

gasket checked out OK. If the original gasket didn't leak, the new one shouldn't either, if it's installed correctly.

Check Bore Wear—Cylinder-bore wear dictates whether the block needs boring or just honing. This, in turn, largely determines whether you have to install new pistons—no small investment. Fortunately for you, L-series engine bores have excellent wear qualities.

There are three common ways of checking bore wear. The best way is with a bore gage. Next accurate is the inside micrometer, or telescoping gage and outside mike. The last method involves using a piston ring and feeler gages to compare end-gap differences at different positions in the bore. End gap changes with bore wear—more wear, more gap. All of these methods will tell you what each bore's *taper* is.

Bore Taper—Cylinder walls don't wear the same from top to bottom. A bore wears more at the top and considerably less down the bore. This is commonly referred to as *taper wear*. Virtually no wear occurs in the bottom half of a bore. High pressure is exerted by the top compression ring against the bore during the power stroke. The pressure decreases rapidly as the piston travels down the bore from the top of its stroke, or top center (TC). This varying pressure is the major cause of bore taper. In addition, the bottom of a bore, which mainly stabilizes the piston, is better lubricated. This is evidenced by the shiny (worn) upper part of a bore—while the surface at the bottom retains its original crosshatch pattern (unworn).

Measuring Taper—Measure bore taper by comparing the distance across the bore diameter at the bottom versus that at the top, directly below the ridge.

Bores not only wear differently from top to bottom, they wear unevenly around their circumference. Measure across each bore in line with the crankshaft, then 90° to the crankshaft center line. Take several measurements in between and use the highest figure as maximum bore wear.

You won't be able to detect this difference in wear if you're measuring with feeler gages and a ring as opposed to a dial bore gage or micrometers. You'll only able to measure *average wear*. Don't be concerned, because your measurement will be close enough to determine if the block needs to be bored.

It's not practical to size each bore separately, in the event boring and honing are necessary. So, simply find the bore with the highest wear to determine if and how much all of the cylinders will have to bored.

One exception to this rule is when one cylinder is damaged or worn past the bore limit, but the others are OK. In this case, it may be less expensive to have that cylinder *sleeved* rather than junking the block. Sleeving is detailed on page 66.

Due to uneven bore wear, taper, or the difference between maximum and minimum bore wear, measuring may not tell you how much a cylinder must be bored to *clean it up*—expose new metal the full length of the bore. This is because uneven wear *shifts* a bore's centerline in the direction of maximum wear. Consequently, the bore must be restored to its original centerline. Here's an extreme example: If a

G2-G1 ΔG	TAPER
0.000	0.0000
0.001	0.0003
0.005	0.0016
0.010	0.0032
0.015	0.0048
0.020	0.0064
0.025	0.0080
0.030	0.0095
0.035	0.0111
0 040	0.0127
0.045	0.0143
0.050	0.0159
Approximate Taper = 0.30 X ΔG	

G2 - G1 is ring end-gap difference. Measure ring end gaps as described at right and determine bore taper from chart.

bore is worn 0.008 in. (0.202mm), and 0.005 in. of this wear is on one side of the cylinder, it must be bored 0.010 in. (0.254mm) oversize, or the first available oversize. It's foolish to have a block bored more than necessary except for piston and ring size availability.

Dial Bore Gage & Micrometer— When using a dial bore gage or micrometer to measure taper, measure the point of maximum wear immediately below the ridge. Because wear will be irregular, take several measurements around the bore to determine maximum wear. Determine taper by subtracting the measurement at the bottom of the bore from that at the top.

Ring & Feeler Gage—Although an indirect measurement and therefore less accurate, you can measure bore wear with a piston ring and feeler gage. Compare the difference between the circumferences of the worn and unworn sections of the bore.

Accuracy decreases the more irregularly a bore is worn. However, it is accurate enough to determine if you'll need to bore and install oversize pistons, or if you can get by with cleaning up the original pistons. honing the bore and installing *moly* rings.

To use the ring-and-feeler method, place a ring in the cylinder and compare ring end gaps. Measure the gap with the ring at the bottom of the bore, then at the top of the bore—immediately below the ridge. Use the same ring, used or new, and make sure it is square in the bore to get an accurate reading.

Least expensive tools for checking bore wear are an old piston ring and feeler gages. Ring is squared in bore, then gap is measured in two locations: near bottom of bore, and immediately below ridge. Find approximate taper by multiplying difference in gaps by 0.3.

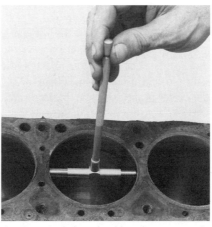

Another tool for checking bore wear is telescoping gage. Measure bore at top . . . .

To square the ring, push it down the bore with a bare piston—no rings. Measure the gap with feeler gages and record the results. After determining end-gap differences, use above chart to determine bore taper. *Taper is approximately 0.3 times ring end-gap difference.*

How Much Taper is Permissible?— To decide how much taper your engine can live with, you'll have to ask yourself how many *good miles* you want out of your engine. Do you want it to last another 10,000, 20,000, 40,000 . . . ?

If the bores are excessively tapered, new rings won't fix the problem. The rings will quickly fatigue and cease to seal properly as they expand and contract to conform to the irregular bore on every stroke. Consequently, they lose their *resiliency*, or *springiness*. This reduces ring-to-bore seal-

Piston is used for squaring ring farther down in bore.

. . . . then move down in bore to find taper. Gage is measured with 3–4-in. mike. See chart, page 55, for original bore sizes.

ing. Additionally, this ring expansion and contraction accelerates piston ring-land wear, further reducing bore sealing.

The story doesn't get any better. Because ring gap must be correct *at the bottom of a tapered bore*, the gap will be larger at the where compression and combustion pressures are highest. Consequently, there will be further leakage through the wider ring end gap. And end gap increases with wear as the miles pile on.

So, if you plan a "patch 'em up" job on your engine so it will go another 10,000, maybe 20,000 miles before it's right back where you started, you can get away with reringing a block having as much as 0.008 in. (0.200mm) taper. If you are using the ring-and-feeler-gage method, 0.006 in. (0.150mm) is the number.

If your object is to end up with a *truly*

Sleeve has just been installed. Top will be machined flush with block deck, then bored and honed to restore damaged cylinder to like-new condition.

SLEEVING AN ENGINE

A sleeve, or *liner,* is basically a portable cylinder, a cylinder insert. It is used to replace or restore a cracked, scored or otherwise damaged bore that can't be restored by boring and honing. The cost of sleeving a cylinder is minimal compared to purchasing a new or used engine block.

Typically, a sleeve is a cast-iron cylinder that is slightly longer than the cylinder when installed in the engine. It has a smaller ID than the original bore for finishing stock. Wall thickness is about 0.100 in. (2.54mm).

To install a sleeve, bore out the damaged cylinder to 0.003-in. (0.076mm) less than the sleeve OD. Rather than boring all the way to bottom of the bore, some machinists prefer to stop the cutter just short of the bottom to leave a step or shoulder for the sleeve to bottom against. The step and interference fit of the sleeve prevent it from shifting after the engine is back in operation.

Before installing the sleeve, warm the block with a torch, furnace or whatever, so the block will grow. At the same time, cool the sleeve to shrink it—a freezer works fine. The sleeve will almost drop into place. However, sleeve temperature will quickly rise to the same temperature as the block, assuming it's an interference fit. Then, press or drive the sleeve the rest of the way into the block. Seal it at the bottom. Some shops don't bother with heating and cooling. They just drive the sleeve all the way in.

Trim off any excess sleeve projecting from the top of the block, or deck, flush with this surface. Finally, bore and hone the sleeve to size, or so it matches the other cylinders.

rebuilt engine, bore the block if taper exceeds 0.004 in. (0.100mm)—no matter how you do the measuring.

Remember, bore taper gets worse with use, never better. It's best to start a rebuilt engine's life with a straight bore and new pistons for maximum longevity.

Piston-to-Bore Clearance—All this talk about whether or not to bore may turn out to be purely academic. The main reason for not boring is to avoid the cost of new pistons. This is a very real reason because a new piston with rings comes close to the cost of sleeving a cylinder.

If the pistons are damaged or worn to the point of being unusable, you'll have to purchase new ones whether the block needs to be bored or not. So, to make the final determination as to whether you should rebore—the pistons are the big expense— check piston-to-bore clearance. Refer to page 75 for other checks you should make before giving the pistons the final OK.

Two methods can be used for checking piston-to-bore clearance. The first is mathematical. Measure across the cylinder bores 90° to the crank centerline and approximately 2 in. (50mm) below the block's deck surface. Then measure the piston *that goes with the bore.* Measure across the thrust surfaces of the piston, or 90° to the wrist pin, and about 1/2-in. (13mm) below the center of the wrist pin. Measure both the block and the pistons at the same temperature—preferably normal room temperature, or 70F (21C). If the temperature of these components differs by much, your measurements will not be accurate.

Standard piston-to-bore clearance is 0.002 in. (0.050mm). Absolute maximum clearance, or the difference between your piston and bore measurements, should be no more than 0.009 in. (0.229mm).

Direct measurement of piston-to-bore clearance is the next method. Insert a piston-and-rod assembly—less rings—upside down *in its bore,* and with the wrist pin parallel to the crankshaft main-bearing bores. Check piston-to-bore clearance using selected feeler gages inserted between the *thrust face* of the piston and the bore. A piston's thrust face is the right skirt as you would view the piston from its top and the positioning notch or arrow pointing away from you.

Check piston-to-bore clearance with the piston pulled to the top of the bore so the piston skirts are flush or even with the block's deck surface. Positioning and checking the piston and bore in this manner ensures that the clearance you're checking is what the piston sees when it is correctly installed. For good measure, recheck the clearance with the piston skirts

about l-in. (0.04mm) below the deck.

There should be a light drag on the correct feeler gage as you pull it from between the piston and bore. To put a number on drag, it should be 0.5—3.5 lb. (0.22—1.6kg) when you're pulling the correct feeler gage. A fish scale wired to a feeler gage is a good way to check pulling force. Again, piston-to-bore clearance should no more than 0.009 in. (0.229mm).

Piston Knurling—There is a method used to take up clearance between a piston and its bore, called *knurling.* Depressions put in the piston thrust faces create raised projections. This effectively increases piston diameter and reduces bore clearance. The problem with knurling is it's *temporary.* The projections wear off quickly, putting the clearance right back where it was. Don't do it! Replace the pistons and bore the block if piston-to-bore clearance is excessive.

Glaze-Breaking—If bore taper is not excessive and the pistons are OK, you don't have to go to the expense of buying new pistons and boring the block. However, it is good practice to *break the glaze.* Glaze-breaking doesn't remove any appreciable material from the bore; it merely restores the honed finish for positive ring break-in and sealing.

If you are going to use plain or chrome rings, this operation is necessary. It is optional with moly rings, but desirable because of the ring break-in aspect. Again, glaze-breaking is not done to remove material, so a precision-type hone should not be used. This type of hone will try to remove the bore taper, increasing piston-to-bore clearance in the process. Rather, a spring-loaded or brush-type hone that *follows* the existing bore without changing its shape should be used for glaze-breaking.

BLOCK DECKING

Before sending the block off to be bored or honed, first check for any irregularities on the deck surface if the gasket showed signs of leakage. If you will have additional machining done on the block, you should have them all done in one visit.

Another, more important reason to check and correct the deck now is that many engine shops still use the old and reliable Van Norman type boring bar that locates off the block deck surface. So, if the deck surface is off relative to the main-bearing bores, the remachined bores will also be off if the irregularity is not corrected first.

The L-series engine is very rigid, so it's unlikely there will be any problem with the deck surface. If there is, it will be slight. With that in mind, don't remove any more material than necessary if the block needs resurfacing—only enough to clean up and true the deck. The reason for this is practical. Material removed from a block's deck has the same effect as removing it from the cylinder head—compression ratio increases. Increase compression ratio too much and you won't be able to find fuel to run your engine.

To check the deck surface for flatness, you'll need feeler gages and a precision straightedge. The straightedge should be as long as the deck. Check the deck with the straightedge positioned diagonally across both corners of the deck and lengthwise from side to side using your feeler gages. Make sure the deck is perfectly clean—free of all gasket material. Otherwise, you will get incorrect readings.

The normal deck surface should be within 0.002 in. (0.05mm). Maximum deck-surface flatness is 0.004 in. (0.10mm)—the largest gap between the straightedge and the deck. If deck irregularities are greater than this, the block should be decked, or resurfaced.

Cylinder Head—Give the same straightedge treatment to the cylinder head while you're at it. Its gasket surface should be within the same specs as the block: 0.004 in. (0.10mm) maximum. Make sure the head-gasket surface is totally free of old gasket material.

Main-Bearing Bores—If you borrowed the straightedge, make one more block check before returning it. Turn the block upside down. Lay the straightedge lengthwise in the main-bearing bores. Using your feeler gages, check that the main-bearing bores are in alignment. Go from one main-bearing web or saddle to the next. Check the gap between the straightedge and bearing bore at each web.

There shouldn't be more than 0.001-in. (0.25mm) clearance. More than this means that the main-bearing bores will have to be *align-bored* to restore them to the same center.

While you're looking at the main-bearing bores, check their condition. If a bore

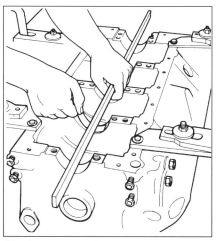

Check alignment of main-bearing bores with precision straightedge and feeler gage. A gap between the straightedge and bearing bore of 0.001 in. should not be exceeded. No, this isn't a Nissan/Datsun engine, but process is the same. Drawing courtesy Federal Mogul.

is out-of-round, this irregularity causes a varying oil clearance and uneven load distribution between the bearing and its journal. This results in uneven and accelerated bearing wear. Consequently, the bearing bore must be reconditioned.

A bearing bore that's too-large is even worse. An oversize bearing bore will let the bearing inserts move in their bore. The insert halves are not sufficiently *crushed* when the bearing cap is torqued. Crush is required to *force* the bearing to conform to its bore. It occurs because the outside circumference of the two bearing-insert halves is slightly larger than the ID of the bore. See the above drawing.

When a bearing half is placed in its bore, its ends project slightly above the parting surfaces of the bearing cap and connecting rod: This distance, or crush, should be 0-0.0012 in. (0-0.030mm) with one end of the insert flush with the cap parting surface. Consequently, when two bearing inserts are installed in their bore, the insert ends butt.

As the cap bolts are tightened, the two circumferences must become equal. The bearing shell compresses—is crushed—causing the bearing to assume the shape of its bore and clamping the inserts tightly in their bore. This tight fit and the tooth, or hone marks in the bearing bore, combine to prevent the bearing inserts from *spinning* or rotating in the bore rather than the bearing journal rotating in the bearing. Although unlikely with a main bearing—as opposed

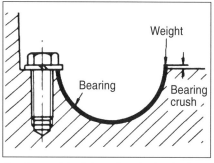

Bearing crush is distance insert extends above bearing bore at one end while other is flush with cap parting line. Crush locks bearing inserts in place, preventing them from spinning with bearing journal. Desired crush for main bearings is 0—0.0012 in. (0—0.030mm); 0.0006—0.0016 (0.015—0.040mm) for connecting rods. Drawing courtesy Nissan.

to a connecting-rod bearing—spin occurs when the force at the bearing journal that tries to rotate the bearing overcomes the force between the bearing and its housing. Consequently, if the bearing bore is too large, the bearing may move or spin.

To determine if a bearing has moved in its bore, look at its backside. Shiny spots on the back of the shell indicate movement. Again, movement may occur if the bearing bore is too large or the bearing-to-journal clearance is insufficient. If you discover any shiny spots, the block should be checked with a dial indicator, or better yet, a dial bore gage. A telescoping gage and micrometer can also be used for checking.

Check bearing crush with a new insert. Install a cap loosely and sideways opposite the side with the bearing-tab clearance notch so it overhangs the edge of the bearing bore. Wipe the bore clean. Install the bearing insert in the bore so it butts against the underside of the cap. Using your feeler gages, check the distance the opposite end of the insert projects above the opposite parting surface.

Bearing crush range: 0–0.0012 in. (0-0.030mm)

If a bearing bore needs to be remachined, all bearing bores must be align-bored with the bearing caps torqued in place. This will not only correct any sizing or shape problem with a bearing bore, it will ensure that all main bearings are on the same axis.

If you don't want to commit to new bearings yet, check bearing bores with a telescoping gage and micrometer. Torque the cap in place on the bearing bore you're checking.

Before toting block off to machine shop for boring and/or honing, install main-bearing caps. Torque bolts to spec to simulate block distortion of fully assembled block. Cylinder-head torque plate would be nice, but not critical.

If chain oiler is used, inspect it. This one was damaged by loose chain, but not so much that it couldn't be reused.

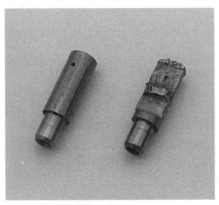

Chain oiler at right was severely damaged by loose chain. It was replaced by new oiler at left.

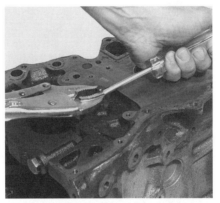

To remove chain oiler, clamp onto it with Vise-Grip pliers and pry out with screwdriver. Wait until assembly time to install new oiler.

Main-Bearing-Bore Diameter: 2.3094-2.3099 in. (58.66-58 67mm); 2.5043-2.5073 in (63.61-63.68mm) for L20B

Check for Cracks—Make a final check for cracks before declaring the block to be fit. Start by simply looking at it. This should reveal any obvious problems. However, you won't be able to see any hairline cracks. So you should have your block checked with the *Magnaflux®* or *Spotcheck®* process. You can have these checks made at any engine machine shop. Don't shrug off checking for cracks as unnecessary, particularly if your engine experienced mysterious oil- or coolant-loss problems.

Magnafluxing starts by setting up a magnetic field in the *ferrous* (iron or steel) piece being checked. Iron powder is then sprinkled over the magnetized area. The

particles (powder) are attracted to any cracks and appear as fine, white lines.

This process reveals small hairline cracks that, if left unattended, will likely result in many frustrations after the rebuild. Because machine shops have been "bitten" by cracks in blocks, cylinder heads, connecting rods and bolts, a good shop will automatically crack-check these parts *before* doing any expensive machine work or assembling the engine.

Most, but not all, cracks mean a block should be replaced. It depends on where the crack is. Generally, if a crack is in the skirt, below the water jacket at the side of the block, the block can be used. If it's into a water jacket or oil gallery, it's best to replace the block. If you run into this unfortunate situation, have your machinist

make a recommendation. Even if your block needs no machine work, take it in for Magnafluxing and be sure.

Spotchecking is similar to Magnafluxing, but uses a dye to reveal cracks in a part made of *any* material. Spotcheck kits consist of a *penetrant*—a liquid red dye—and a *developer*—a white powder. A cleaner is used to clean the area being checked.

The Spotcheck process goes like this: After the area to be checked is thoroughly cleaned, it is sprayed with penetrant and allowed to sit for a few minutes. This lets the penetrant creep into any cracks. The area is then cleaned again to remove the penetrant—it won't remove penetrant from cracks. After the area dries, it is sprayed with developer. If you've ever put white paint over wet red paint, you know what happens next. Cracks appear as bright-red lines.

Spotcheck, as is Magnaflux, is useful in checking the rods, head, pistons and crank. The major advantages of Spotcheck are its ability to check non-magnetic parts, such as aluminum pistons, its convenience, and relative low cost. Spotcheck is available from Magnaflux Corporation, 7300 West Lawrence Avenue, Chicago, IL 60656.

CYLINDER-BORE FINISHING
Plain Cast-Iron, Chrome or Moly Rings?—When you drop the block off to have it bored or honed, you should know what type of piston rings you intend to use. The machinist needs to know this because the final bore finish should be different for plain, chrome or moly rings. So, what type of rings should you use?

Chrome rings are especially suited for an engine that will inhale a lot of dust and dirt, such as a truck used on construction sites. Chrome is very tough and lasts longer than moly under these conditions. However, unless you have a similar situation, use moly rings. Under normal conditions, a moly ring will perform better that the chrome type, and requires virtually no break-in time. Plain cast-iron rings also break-in quickly, but they don't wear as well.

What's the Difference?—The advantage of a moly ring over its plain or chrome counterparts is its porous molybdenum facing—it carries more of its own oil. The facing has microscopic surface voids—little depressions carry oil similar to

If block will be decked, remove cylinder-head dowels. Otherwise, leave them in place so they won't get lost.

Freshly honed bores show classic cross-hatching.

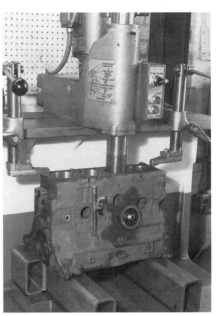

Pistons were worn out, so block was rebored to freshen bores. Major cost is replacing pistons, not the machine work.

Honing is necessary regardless of whether cylinders were rebored. Hand-held hone is being used here. Hone finish depends on type of rings that will be used.

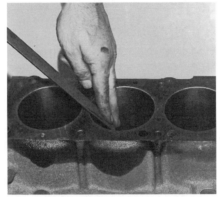

Square edge at top of bores is chamfered to provide lead-in for rings and pistons at assembly time.

the crosshatching of a honed cylinder bore.

In comparison, plain and chrome piston rings don't have these voids—at least not to the degree of the moly-faced ring. They depend more on bore crosshatching to supply bore lubrication. When the piston travels down the bore on its power stroke, the cylinder wall is exposed to burning fuel. Consequently, the oil on the wall is partially burned away, meaning the rings will not receive full lubrication during the return trip up the bore. This is not a problem with moly rings because they carry their own lubrication and are not directly exposed to combustion.

The reason for the different types of rings requiring different bore finishes should now be obvious. A chrome ring depends on a coarsely finished cylinder wall to retain lubricating oil. If plain or chrome rings are used, the bore should be finish-honed with a 280-grit stone. A 400-grit stone is good for moly rings. A 30° crosshatch is suitable for all ring types.

Install Main-Bearing Caps—Prior to delivering the block for boring and/or honing, install the main-bearing caps. Torque the main-bearing-cap bolts to specification, or 33—40 ft-lb (4.4—5.5 kg-m). This is necessary because the load from the main-cap bolts slightly distorts the bores. Therefore, the bores won't be the same shape before and after the bolts are torqued. The object of boring and honing the block with the main-cap bolts torqued to spec is to ensure that bore shape is close to what it should be when the engine is fully assembled and running—round.

Cylinder-head bolts are another source of bore distortion. But how can you bore or hone a block with the heads in place? Fear not, the dilemma has been solved. Some, but not many, engine shops use a *torque plate.* Because the torque plate had to be custom-made by the shop, you'll seldom find a shop with one for a Nissan/Datsun engine. It's a 2-inch-thick steel plate with clearance holes that cen-

ter on the bores. This provides access for a boring bar and hone. Like the main-bearing-cap bolts, the torque plate is installed and the head bolts are torqued to specification.

If the shop you choose does not use a torque plate, don't be overly concerned. One is not essential unless you are building an engine for all-out racing. Using a torque plate increases the machining cost due to the additional time required. Therefore, if you are on a tight budget, make some cost comparisons. Regardless of whether or not a torque plate is used, *do* install the main-bearing caps.

Chamfer Bores—After you have the block back from the machine shop, inspect the tops of the bores. The machinist should have filed or ground a small chamfer or bevel at the top of each bore after honing. This chamfer provides a lead-in for the pistons and rings when installing them. It also eliminates a sharp edge that will get hot in the combustion chamber, possibly causing preignition or detonation.

A 60°, 1/16-in.-wide chamfer is sufficient. Use a fine-tooth half- or full-round file for doing this job. Just hold the file at a 60° angle to the deck surface or 30° to the bore as you work around the top of each cylinder. Don't hit the bore surface with the end of the file. This will gouge a freshly honed bore.

Clean it Again—Even though the block *may have been* hot-tanked, jet-sprayed or

Clean block after all machine work is done to remove metal filings and other machining debris.

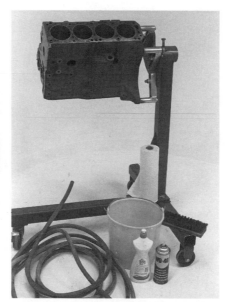

Even though block may have been cleaned at machine shop, scrub it again just to make sure it's clean. You'll need equipment similar to what's shown: hose, bucket, stiff bristle brush, detergent, paper towels and water-dispersant oil.

Oil passages are flushed with clean water to remove cleaning solution.

Before block can air-dry, coat it with water-dispersant oil to prevent rusting. Block can then be air-dried with compressed air.

whatever method your machinist uses for cleaning a block after honing, clean it *again*. If you're not convinced, wipe a white paper towel—not a cloth—through a bore as a quick check. It should come out absolutely spotless when the bores are declared clean.

Cloth leaves lint in the bores and will not dissolve in the oil. It'll end up in the engine's lubrication system. The same happens to paper lint, but it will dissolve and be filtered out by the oil filter.

This second cleaning removes machining residue, mainly potentially damaging grit left by the honing stones. If it isn't removed before the engine is assembled, your engine will "eat" a set of rings so fast it'll make your wallet ache. The damage doesn't stop with the rings. Grit will be circulated through your engine's oiling system and end up embedded in the crankshaft, connecting-rod and camshaft bearings, turning them into little grinding stones. Makes shivers go up your back, doesn't it?

So, even though the block may have been cleaned at the machine shop, enlist the use of the most cost-effective cylinder-

bore cleaning equipment known: a stiff-bristle brush, laundry detergent, a bucket, water hose and elbow grease. Applied generously, this will give you a super-clean block. Scrub and rinse the bores over and over.

Don't let water air-dry on freshly machined bore surfaces. They'll rust. Have a can of spray oil close at hand. Spray it on *before* you wipe a bore dry to protect against rust. CRC® or WD-40® displaces water rather than trapping it. If you have compressed air, use it to blow-dry the bores. Compressed air is fast, leaves no lint and will blow water out of little corners and holes.

Remember: Don't be afraid to use up a roll of white-paper towels for checking bore cleanliness. It's not unusual to have to scrub a bore four or five times before a paper towel comes out perfectly clean.

After you've dried the bores completely and they've all passed the white-towel test, spray them and *all* machined surfaces and oil passages generously with oil.

Although it will keep them rust-free while the block waits for assembly time, it will also make the oiled surfaces dust collectors. So, cover the block with a plastic trash bag. Seal the end of the bag. Stored it out of the way in a corner, under a bench or on an engine stand.

CRANKSHAFT

The crankshaft is the primary moving part in an engine. All of the other cylinder-block parts are devoted to turning, supporting or lubricating it. Because of the importance and loads imposed on the crankshaft, it is a very tough, high-quality component. As a result, it's rare that a crankshaft cannot be reused for a rebuild. One very rarely wears to the point of having to be replaced. What usually happens is the journals are damaged from a lack of lubrication or from poor lubrication—usually in the form of *very dirty oil*. This happens when the oil filter gets so loaded up with dirt that it is bypassed by the lubrication system.

The one thing that can render a crankshaft useless is mechanical damage resulting from another component breaking, such as a rod bolt. If this occurs at high rpm the crank and block will be heavily damaged, even if the engine is shut off immediately.

Crankshaft inspection starts with good look at bearing journals. This one obviously has trouble. Rod-bearing journal was scored when engine lost oil pressure.

Check bearing-journal diameter and roundness. Measure journal in one direction . . . .

. . . . then 90° to first measurement. If micrometer readings differ by 0.012 in. (0.03mm), journal is out-of-round. Regrinding or replacing is next step. Also check journal diameter from end to end.

Main & Connecting-Rod Journals— The most important crankshaft-inspection job involves making sure the bearing journals are round, their diameters don't vary over their length, and their surfaces are free of cracks, deep gouges or grooves. A cracked crankshaft *must* be replaced. The best way to check a crank for cracks is by Magnafluxing. Spotchecking is a good choice and your last resort is visual inspection. The cost of Magnafluxing and Spotchecking is minimal.

Remember: A broken crank will destroy your engine.

If a bearing journal is oval, or egg-shaped, it is *out-of-round*. This condition is more prevalent with rod journals than main-bearing journals. If a bearing-journal diameter gradually gets smaller from one end to the other, it is *tapered*.

Finally, the journals should be free from any nicks or scoring that could damage bearings. Don't get excited by a small groove in a journal. It's not going to hurt anything as long as the journal is OK in all other respects. Pay special attention to the edges of each oil hole in the rod and main journals. Sharp edges protruding above the normal journal surface can cut grooves in the bearing inserts, wrecking the bearing and spoiling your rebuild. Eliminate any sharp edges by chamfering them with a small round file.

Surface Finish—Look at surface finish first. Any rough bearing journals must be reground regardless of taper or out-of-roundness. Your sense of feel is better than your eyesight, so run the end of a fingernail over the length of each journal. If it feels too rough, it is.

If you find a rough bearing journal, a regrinding job is in order. If you're in luck, the standard 0.0098, 0.0197, 0.0295- or 0.0394 in. (0.25, 0.50, 0.75 or 1.00mm) regrind job will clean up all of the main- or rod-journal surfaces. I say *surfaces* because if one journal has to be ground, all rod or main journals should be ground the same. You don't want one odd-size bearing because bearings are sold in sets. The additional cost of machining all main or rod journals is slight. The major expense is the initial setup cost.

Therefore, if 0.010 in. is removed from the standard bearing journals, 0.010-in. *undersize* bearings will be required. Undersize refers to the journal diameter. The amount of undersize is the difference between the journal diameter after it is reground and the nominal, or average specified standard-size journal. Example: If the nominal specified diameter for main journals is 2.1634 in. (54.950mm) and they are reground to 2.1534 in. (54.696mm), the crank is 0.010-in. (0.25mm) undersize on the mains.

While you're checking bearing journals, look carefully at the thrust faces at each end of the center main-bearing journal. Be particularly attentive if your engine is backed up by a manual transmission. The thrust load resulting from the clutch being released forces the crankshaft forward and is resisted by the rear thrust surface of the crankshaft. If this load is maintained because of improperly adjust-ed clutch linkage as evidenced by badly worn clutch release fingers, excessive thrust-surface wear can result.

Check the crankshaft thrust surfaces by measuring the distance between the two surfaces. Or make the check by installing the crank in the block with its new bearings, page 118. To make direct measurements, you'll need a telescoping gage and a 1—2 in. micrometer, or an old or new bearing insert, feeler gages, and a micrometer. The distance between crankshaft thrust faces is 1.260 in. (32mm). If the maximum end play, page 120, is exceeded, you'll have to replace the crankshaft or have it reconditioned. Other dimensions and tolerances for crankshaft checking are in the table, page 57.

Out-of-Round—To check for out-of-round or tapered journals, you need a 1—2-in or 2—3-in. outside micrometer and an idea of what you're looking for. If a journal is round, it will be described by a diameter. This diameter can be read directly from your micrometer at any location around the journal. If it is out-of-round, you will be looking for the *major* and *minor* dimension of an ellipse. The minor dimension can be found by measuring around the journal in several locations. Major and minor dimensions will occur about 90° from each other. The difference between these two figures is the journal's out-of-round, or: Major Dimension - Minor Dimension = Out-of-Round.

Start with the connecting-rod journals when doing your checking. They are the most likely to suffer from this out-of-round condition. Connecting-rod journals are highly loaded at top center. With this in mind, check each journal in at least a couple of locations fore and aft on the journal. The standard allowable out-of-round is 0.0004 in. (0.01mm); maximum is 0.012 in. (0.03mm). Remember, if you find one journal out of spec, the crankshaft should be reground.

Taper—Journal taper causes uneven bearing wear more than an out-of-round journal. This is due to uneven bearing loads over the length of the bearing journal. As a journal tapers, it concentrates its load on the less-worn part or larger diameter of the journal. So, when a crank with excessively tapered journals is reinstalled with new bearings, high bearing load and wear occurs.

Taper is specified in so many tenths of thousandths-of-an-inch per inch or hundredths-of-a-millimeter per millimeter. This means your micrometer readings will vary by this amount when taken one inch (or one millimeter) from each other *in the same plane*—the mike is moved straight along the journal being measured and not rotated.

For connecting-rod journals, standard maximum journal taper is 0.0004 in./in. (0.010mm/mm); maximum allowable taper is 0.0012 in./in. (0.030mm/mm). Remember, if one journal is not within spec, all the other rod journals should be reground as well.

Crank Kits—If your crankshaft needs to be reground, consider trading it in for a *crank kit*. You'll be getting someone else's reground crankshaft.

A crank kit consists of a freshly reground or reconditioned crankshaft *and* new main and connecting-rod bearings. Consider taking this approach rather than having your crankshaft reground *and* buying new bearings. You'll end up saving some money. Just make sure that good-quality bearings accompany the crank before making your final decision.

After Grinding—Check your crankshaft carefully if you've had it reground—or the one from the kit. The factory spends a lot of time on quality control because mistakes *do* occur, so don't skip rechecking the crank after it's been reground.

Other than journal diameter, two problems to look for are sharp edges around

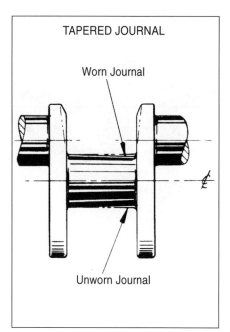

TAPERED JOURNAL

Worn Journal

Unworn Journal

Tapered journal is bigger at one end than at other. This will cause uneven bearing load and excessive wear.

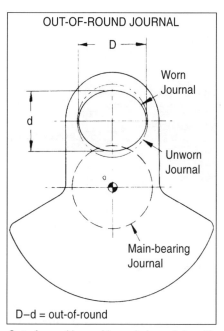

OUT-OF-ROUND JOURNAL

D

d

Worn Journal

Unworn Journal

Main-bearing Journal

D−d = out-of-round

Out-of-round journal is oval-shaped. As with tapered journal, this will cause excessive bearing wear.

Measure width of thrust bearing . . .

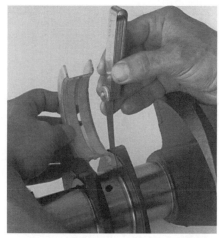

. . . then use bearing and feeler gages to determine distance between crankshaft thrust faces.

the oil holes and wrong shoulder, or fillet, radii at the ends of the journals. All oil holes should be chamfered—smoothed edges—to prevent bearing damage. As for the radius, it should go completely around each journal—where the journal meets the throw. If there is a sharp corner rather than a radius, it will weaken the crankshaft. A sharp corner is a likely place for a fatigue crack to start. A radius that's too large is great for crankshaft strength, but bad news for the bearing. The large radius will cause the bearing to *edge-ride*. The journal radius will interfere with the edge of the bearing.

Use the accompanying sketch to make a *checking template* for checking journal radius. Make it from cardboard or thin sheet metal. Journal radius should not exceed 0.100 in. (2.54mm). If a fillet radius isn't right, return the crankshaft to be corrected. Otherwise, it could spell trouble.

Smooth & Clean Surfaces?—A newly reground crankshaft should have its bearing journals checked for roughness—just like you checked your old crankshaft. Rather than using your finger, drag the edge of a penny the length of the journal. If the penny leaves a trail of copper, the

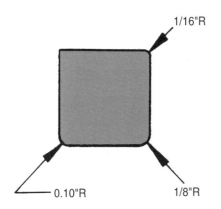

Make template using this as a pattern to check fillet radii. Too big a radius will interfere with bearings, too small a radius will weaken crankshaft.

If you find dings such as these in journal fillets of a reground crank, don't worry. Regrinders use blunt punch and hammer to straighten crank by striking in fillet area! Just make sure metal isn't raised. Photo by Frank Honsowetz.

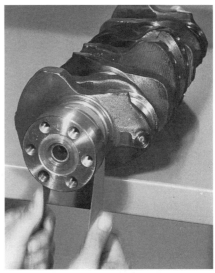

Use strip of emery cloth to polish crank journals. Polish evenly. Work around each journal to ensure finish is even.

journal is too rough. If this is the case, consider smoothing the journals yourself rather than going through the hassle of getting it redone. More often than not, you'll end up with a better job and avoid the frustration usually associated with getting the job done over. Also, if your original crankshaft checks out OK in all departments, give it the same treatment. This will put a *tooth* on the highly polished journal and oil-seal surface. It will also remove varnish buildup.

Regardless of whether the bearing journals are newly reground and need to be smoothed or are original, polish them with 400-grit emery cloth or 600-grit wet-or-dry sandpaper lubricated with 10W oil. A 1-in. wide strip a couple of feet long should be enough to do all of the bearing-main and rear-main-seal surfaces. If you want to get fancy, cut the strip long enough to fit around the journal and secure the two ends to each other with adhesive tape. Then, wrap the strip with a 3-ft length of 1/4-in. cotton rope and use this to rotate the strip with even pressure.

Wrap the cloth around the journal as far as possible. Lightly work it back and forth as you gradually move around the journal. Keep track of where you start on a journal so you can give it an even finish all around. If you concentrate in one spot too long or use too much pressure, you'll remove material unevenly. The object isn't to remove material but to give the journal a clean, smooth surface.

Be careful with the oil-seal surface. Don't do too good a job. Polish it just enough to remove any varnish or to smooth any nicks or burrs. Some oil is required between the seal and the crankshaft for lubrication. A highly polished surface will seal *too* completely. The result will be seal failure and a big rear-main leak.

Crankshaft Runout—This is how much *bend* there is in a crankshaft. *Runout* is determined by rotating the crank between two centers and reading runout at the center main-bearing journal with a dial indicator. The indicator must be positioned 90° to the journal to get an accurate reading. As the crankshaft is rotated, the indicator reading will change if the crankshaft is bent.

To do a runout check, you'll need a dial indicator with a tip extension and a way to mount the indicator. A magnetic-base mount works fine. The tip extension lets you position the indicator so a crank throw won't interfere with it as you rotate the crankshaft.

Start by setting the crankshaft in the block with only the top halves of the front and rear bearing inserts in place. Oil the bearings before you install the crank. To measure runout or bend, mount the indicator base to the block with the indicator positioned 90° to the journal. Position the tip so it won't interfere with the oil hole in the journal as the crank is rotated.

Rotate the crank until you find the low-est indicated reading, then zero the indicator. You can now turn the crankshaft and read runout directly. Turn the crank a few times to make sure the readings repeat.

A dial-indicator reading is a *total indicator reading* (TIR). Actual bend is half TIR. Therefore, Runout = TIR X 1/2. Maximum allowable runout is 0.0039 in. (0. 10mm), but for best results runout should be less than 0.0020 in. (0.05mm) for all L-series engines. If a crankshaft exceeds the maximum limit, it should be reground or traded in for a crank kit.

Installation Checking Method—To do a real-world crankshaft-bend check, install the crank in the block using *oiled new bearings*. Torque the caps to specification, page 120. If the crank can be rotated freely by hand, consider it OK. Any loads induced by what runout there is will be minor compared to the inertial and power-producing loads normally applied to the journals and bearings when the engine is running. I suggest this method of checking because crankshaft runout usually isn't a problem with a "tired" engine that just needs to be rebuilt. If you decide to use this approach, follow the procedure for crank installation, page 115.

Cleaning and Inspecting Crankshaft—When cleaning a crankshaft, it is very important to concentrate on the oil holes. Get them *clean*. Even if you had the crank "tanked," drag a strip of cloth through the oil holes using a piece of wire. Soak the

Bright line (arrow) is groove worn in crank by rear main seal. Give seal surface same polishing treatment as bearing journals.

After grinding, professional polishing setup spins crank while abrasive strip runs against journal. Photo by Frank Honsowetz.

Crank runout can be checked on V-blocks or in block with front and rear bearing inserts installed. Runout is checked with dial indicator set against center main. Runout less than 0.0020 in. (0.05mm) is acceptable. You can also check crank runout by placing the crank in a block that contains only two bearing halves—one at each end. Leave out the other block bearing shell shelves. Use a dial indicator as shown in this photo. Works great! Photo by Frank Honsowetz.

rag in carburetor cleaner or lacquer thinner and run it through each oil hole several times. To do the best job, a copper-bristle, 22-caliber gun-bore brush works great. You may have used one of these for cleaning the oil galleries in the block. So by all means, use it if you have one. If you don't have a 22-caliber gun-bore brush, buy one.

Pilot Bushing—With a manual transmission, a pilot bushing will be installed in the end of the crank at the flywheel flange. It supports the forward end of the transmission input shaft that pilots into it, thus the name *pilot bushing*.

Visually check the bushing bore for damage. If you have an old transmission input shaft, insert it into the bushing and check for lateral play by trying to move the shaft side to side. If there is noticeable movement, the bushing should be replaced. Make a more accurate check with a vernier caliper or a telescoping gage and micrometer. The bushing's bore should be no larger than 0.634 in. (16.1mm).

If your engine has a lot of miles on it and the pilot bushing has never been replaced, don't bother checking it—replace it. The cost is minimal. And it's a lot easier to do it now rather than after you've installed the engine.

You can use one of two methods to remove the pilot bushing: a slide-hammer puller, or a chisel and hammer. The slide-hammer jaws hook against the back of the pilot bushing. A heavy slide handle is im-

pacted against the opposite end of the shaft to knock the bushing free from its bore. If you are like most and don't have a slide hammer, a small chisel and hammer will work fine. Split the bushing, being careful not to damage the bore in the end of the crankshaft. You may have to split the length of the bushing on both sides to eliminate the press fit.

Regardless of which method you use, note how deep the bushing was positioned in the crank. The new bushing

should be installed at the same depth, or 0.177—0.197 in. (4.5—5.0mm) from the face of the flywheel flange.

Prior to installing the new bushing, soak it in oil. The bushing is made from Oilite, a bronze alloy that is self-lubricating. Soaking the bushing gives it additional lubrication. Also apply a light film of grease to the bushing bore in the crankshaft to ease installation.

Align the bushing with the crank bore and tap it into place. If you don't have a

Although crank is installed in block, you can inspect, remove and replace pilot bushing on bench. Checking is being done with vernier calipers.

If bushing is bigger than 0.634 in. (16.1mm) replace it. Split bushing with chisel, collapse, then pull out. Be careful not to damage counterbore in crankshaft.

Painful way of removing rings is with thumbs. Using ring expander is much easier.

bushing driver of the correct size, don't worry. You can use a brass mallet and thick-wall tube or pipe that matches the outer diameter of the bushing. This will prevent damage to the bushing or its bore while installing it. A socket works well for this if you don't mind pounding on it.

When starting to drive in the bushing, go easy at first. Be careful not to cock the bushing. Once it is started straight, it should go the rest of the way. If it cocks in the bore, stop and remove the bushing, then start over. Drive the bushing in until it is positioned correctly: 0.177—0.197 in. (4.5—5.0mm) from the flywheel flange to the bushing.

PISTONS & CONNECTING RODS

Replace Pistons?—If the block must be rebored for one reason or another, you'll have to replace the pistons. However, if you find that most of the pistons should be replaced, then the block should have been bored in the first place. Pistons are the major expense, so you may as well give your engine a fresh start with new pistons and *straight* bores. Also, the engine's durability will be as good or better than new, depending on the care you take during the rebuild.

CHECKING PISTONS

If your engine doesn't need to be rebored, your next step is to check the pistons to determine if are reusable *before disassembling them from the rods.* Start by removing the old rings.

Be careful not to scratch the pistons when removing the rings. A *ring expander* will help prevent this. Remove the top ring first, then the second followed by the oil ring, all up over the piston. If you do this by hand, make sure the ends of the rings don't gouge the piston. For convenience, support the rod so the piston doesn't flip-flop while you're trying to remove the rings. Clamp the rod *lightly* in a vise with the bottom of the piston against the top of the vise. If you don't have a vise, clamp the rod to the edge of your workbench with a C-clamp—again not too tightly.

Four items should be checked before a piston is given the OK: general damage to the dome, skirt or ring lands; ring-groove wear; piston-skirt and pin-bore wear. If any prove unsatisfactory, replace the piston.

General Damage—Not-so-obvious damage can render a piston unusable: skirt scuffing or scoring, skirt collapse, ring-land damage and dome burning. Obvious damage can occur from a valve dropping into a cylinder.

Scuffing and scoring is caused by lack of lubrication, excessively high operating temperatures or a bent connecting rod. All cause high pressure or temperature between the piston and cylinder wall. If there are visible scuffing or scoring marks-deep linear scratches in the direction of piston travel—replace the piston. Scuffing usually comes from the engine being overheated. Heat causes the piston to expand, reducing piston-to-bore clearance. When engine heat becomes excessive, the pis-

tons *attempt* to expand larger than their bores! This causes high skirt-to-bore pressure and friction, resulting in scuffed or collapsed piston skirts.

If the piston-skirt thrust face has an *asymmetrical* wear pattern, a twisted or bent connecting rod is the likely culprit. The connecting rod should be checked using the procedure described on page 79. If you think that one rod may be bent or twisted, have all of the rods checked. Most engine machine shops check connecting-rod alignment as part of their normal engine-building routine. However, if you are on a tight budget, the piston-skirt wear pattern should tell you if the rods are straight or not.

Damage to a piston's dome usually comes in the form of material removed as a result of being overheated from preignition. The edges of the dome will be rounded off or *porous*—spongy-looking. Some areas may show the effects of high heat concentration. To get a good look at the dome, remove any carbon deposits. A good tool for this is a worn screwdriver with rounded corners at its tip. The normal toolbox is usually well equipped with these. When scraping, be careful not to damage the piston by digging into the aluminum. Never use a sharp or hard tool like a chisel or gasket scraper.

Detonation—explosion of the fuel charge—breaks or distorts ring lands from impact loads. Severe detonation can blow a hole through a piston dome. This condition will be obvious. To check for not-

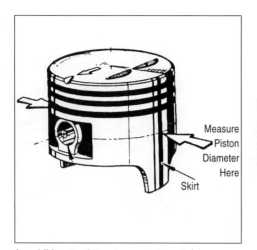

In addition to piston terms, note notch or arrow in piston top. Either one indicates front of piston which must point to front of engine when installed.

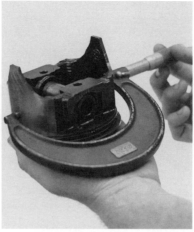

To determine piston wear, measure across thrust faces, as shown. Distance across skirts should be about 0.0005-in. (0.013mm) more at bottom of skirt.

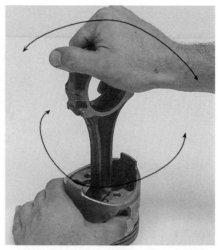

Check piston pin-to-bore clearance by holding piston firmly with thumbs over pin ends. Then, twist and rock rod in directions shown (arrows). If movement is felt at pin ends, clearance is excessive.

so-obvious damage, check the top ring land—it receives the brunt of the impact. If it's not damaged, the others should be OK.

Broken ring lands are readily visible, but a bent one may not be, particularly without a ring in the groove to use as reference. Reinstall a ring in the top groove and use a feeler gage that fits snugly between the ring and groove. Slide the ring and feeler gage around the groove to check for any ring side-clearance change that may indicate a distorted ring land. The top ring land is also the one that gets worn when an engine inhales dirt. This wear will be on the top surface of the ring land and even all the way around.

Piston-Skirt Diameter—It's micrometer time again. Mike each piston skirt 90° to its wrist pin and in the plane of the wrist-pin axis. Mike the piston skirt again, but at its widest point—it'll be farther down on the skirt. Compare the two figures. The second measurement should be at least 0.0005 in. more. If it's not, the skirt is partially collapsed and the piston should be replaced. This would have shown up as a knocking sound when the engine was still running, particularly during warmup.

Skirt collapse is usually accompanied by heavy scoring or scuff marks on the skirt: A sure sign the engine was severely overheated at one time. If a piston with these symptoms were to be reinstalled, you'd have a very noisy engine that would eventually experience total piston collapse.

Piston scuffing or scoring occurs when

an engine overheats. The piston tries to expand more than its bore. If the engine gets too hot, the piston skirts squeeze out the oil cushion between the skirts and their bore. Not only do the skirts make metal-to-metal contact with the bore, scuffing or scoring them, the skirts are overstressed—they are bent or broken. After the piston returns to its normal temperature, piston-bore clearance will be excessive and the engine will be noisy.

If you haven't already done so, mike the pistons to see how they "measure up." Measure across the skirt of each piston, about 1/2 in. (13mm) below the wrist-pin center. It should be about 0.0005 in. (0.013mm) *less* than that measured across the bottom of the skirt.

Wrist-Pin Bore Wear—Measuring pin-bore wear requires disassembling the piston and rod. Standard pin-bore clearance is about 0.0003 in. (0.008mm) with 0.0007 in. (0.018mm) wear limit. Standard pin diameter is 0.8265—0.8267 in . (20.993—20.998mm) with a pin-bore diameter of 0.8268—0.8271 in. (21.001—21.008mm). A practical and easier way of doing this is to *feel for wear*.

Excess clearance can be detected by trying to wiggle or rotating the connecting rod 90° to its normal direction or rotation. First, clean each piston with solvent. Oil that will "mask" excess clearance between the piston and pin should be removed. Otherwise, it will give the impression that piston-to-rod clearance is OK, even though it may not be.

Now, with the piston and rod *at room*

temperature, try wiggling the rod sideways while holding the piston firmly upside down on a flat surface. Then, try rotating it. If you feel any movement, the pin bore is worn beyond its limit and the piston should be replaced. Otherwise, it's OK.

After you use this method to check for pin-bore wear, make sure you lubricate the pin and its bore. Lay the piston on one side and run a bead of oil around the end of the pin. Do this a couple of times. After the oil soaks in, turn the piston over and do the same to the other end of the pin.

If you don't lubricate the pin, you'll run the risk of ruining some pistons during engine run-in. The wrist pin and its bore are highly loaded. Consequently, if they are not lubricated when you first run your engine, the aluminum pin bore will gall, causing the piston to seize on the pin. Lubricate the pin now so you don't overlook it later on.

Clean Ring Grooves—I saved the ring-groove cleaning job until last because it is tough and time-consuming. So, if some or all of the pistons didn't pass your previous test, you've avoided a lot of unnecessary work.

You'll need something to clean the ring grooves without damaging them. A special tool for doing just this is appropriately called a *ring-groove cleaner*. Prices vary widely, depending on tool quality. A ring-groove cleaner fits around the piston and pilots in the groove it is cleaning. An adjustable scraper fits in the groove and

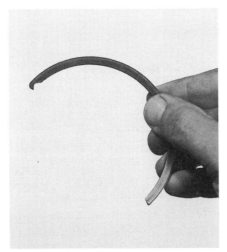

Inexpensive but effective, broken and ground ring is used for cleaning piston-ring grooves.

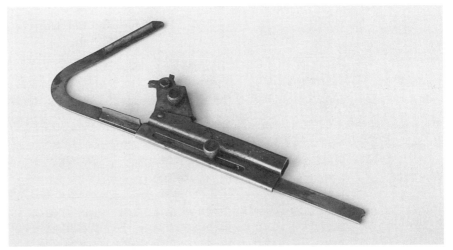

Ring-groove cleaner is much quicker to use than broken ring.

cleans carbon and sludge deposits from the groove as the tool is rotated around the piston.

If you would rather not make a purchase like this for a one-time use, clean the grooves with the broken end of a piston ring. It will take a little more time and you'll have to be careful, but it will clean just as well.

After you've broken an old ring in half, file the end of the ring like that shown above. Wrap tape around the ring so you don't cut your fingers on it. To make this job easier, regardless of the groove-cleaning tool you're using, soak the pistons in water overnight. Turn them upside down in a pan of water so the water covers all three ring grooves. This softens the carbon deposits.

Note: Do not remove any metal or scratch the grooves; just remove the deposits. Be particularly careful to avoid removing metal from the side surfaces of the grooves; these are the surfaces against which the rings seal.

Measuring Ring-Groove Wear— Again, chances are if a ring groove is worn or damaged it will be the top one. It's the groove that gets the most load and the least oil. So, start with the top compression-ring groove. This doesn't mean you shouldn't check the other ring grooves if the top one is OK. Unforeseen things can happen, so check them all. Look at the grooves first. Any wear will have formed a *step* on the lower portion of the ring land. The height of the step shows up as additional ring *side clearance*. The length of the step projecting from the back wall

of the groove is the ring *back clearance*.

Side clearance between one side of the ring and a ring land is measured with a ring and feeler gage. Insert the feeler gage in the groove with a ring as shown. If ring-groove width is excessive, proper ring-to-piston sealing is not possible. And the additional action of the ring moving up and down in the groove will accelerate wear.

Compression-Ring Grooves— On a typical L-series engine, compression-ring grooves should be no wider than 0.082 in. (2.14mm). New "2mm" compression rings measure 0.078 in. (1.98mm) wide. Subtracting these two numbers, side clearance should not exceed 0.005 in. (0.1mm). Ideally, ring side clearance is about half of that at 0.0025 in. (0.064mm). Refer to the chart, page 78, for your engine's specifications.

You are presented with a dilemma because side clearance should be measured with a new ring in the groove. It's foolish to lay out money for a new set of rings for checking your old pistons until you've determined that they are OK to reuse. You could use an old ring for checking, but it is likely worn, too. So, more than actual side clearance will show up if ring wear is not accounted for. To get around this problem, mike the old ring and *subtract* this amount from 0.078 in. (1.98mm), the minimum width of a new compression ring. Add this figure to 0.004 in. (0.10mm) for the maximum allowable *checking clearance.* I'll use the term *checking clearance* rather than *side clearance* because the gage thickness may not be

Ring-groove side clearance can be checked with old ring and feeler gages. Typically, 0.0025 in. (0.064mm) side clearance is ideal.

the actual side clearance with a new ring. If the old ring measured 0.076 in., it is 0.002 in. (0.05mm) undersize. Consequently, the maximum checking clearance is now 0.00X in., but will yield a 0.00X in. side clearance with a *minimum-width* new ring. In formula form, this looks like:

Maximum checking clearance
= 0.00X + (0.0XX - 0.0XX) or:
Maximum checking clearance in inches
=0.00X + (0.0XX - checking-ring width in inches)

To check side clearance, insert the edge of the ring in the groove with the checking-clearance feeler gage alongside *between the ring and the side of the ring groove*. If the ring and gage won't fit, the compression-ring grooves may be OK. To confirm this, find a gage that fits with the ring in the groove. Make sure the ring is

STOCK RINGS & PISTONS
inches (mm)

Engine	Groove width (nominal) Top	2nd	Oil	Ring width (nominal) Top	2nd	*Side clearance Top	2nd	Ring end gap Top	2nd	Oil
L13	0.08 (2.0)	0.08 (2.0)	0.16 (4.0)	0.0787 (2.0)	0.0787 (2.0)	0.0016-0.0031 (0.040-0.080)	0.0012-0.0028 (0.0030-0.070)	0.0098-0.0157 (0.25-0.40)	0.0059-0.0118 (0.15-0.30)	0.0118-0.0354 (0.30-0.90)
L16	0.08 (2.0)	0.08 (2.0)	0.16 (4.0)	0.0787 (2.0)	0.0787 (2.0)	0.0018-0.0031 (0.045-0.080)	0.0012-0.0027 (0.030-0.070)	0.0098-0.0157 (0.25-0.40)	0.0059-0.0118 (0.15-0.30)	0.0118-0.0354 (0.30-0.90)
L18	0.08 (2.0)	0.08 (2.0)	0.16 (4.0)	0.0787 (2.0)	0.0787 (2.0)	0.0018-0.0031 (0.045-0.080)	0.0012-0.0027 (0.030-0.070)	0.0138-0.0217 (0.35-0.55)	0.0118-0.0197 (0.30-0.50)	0.0118-0.0354 (0.30-0.90)
L20A	0.08 (2.0)	0.10 (2.5)	0.16 (4.0)	0.0984 (2.5)	0.0984 (2.5)	0.0016-0.0031 (0.040-0.078)	0.0012-0.0027 (0.030-0.068)	0.008-0.014 (0.20-0.035)	0.006-0.011 (0.14-0.29)	0.006-0.011 (0.14-0.29)
L20B	0.08 (2.0)	0.08 (2.0)	0.16 (4.0)	0.0783 (2.0)	0.0783 (2.0)	0.0016-0.0029 (0.040-0.073)	0.0012-0.0028 (0.030-0.070)	0.0098-0.0157 (0.25-0.40)	0.0118-0.0197 (0.30-0.50)	0.0118-0.0354 (0.30-0.90)
L24	0.08 (2.0)	0.08 (2.0)	0.16 (4.0)	0.0778 (1.977)	0.0778 (1.977)	0.0018-0.0031 (0.045-0.080)	0.0012-0.0028 (0.030-0.070)	0.0091-0.0150 (0.23-0.38)	0.0059-0.0118 (0.15-0.030)	0.0059-0.0118 (0.15-0.30)
L26	0.08 (2.0)	0.08 (2.0)	0.16 (4.0)	0.0778 (1.977)	0.0778 (1.977)	0.0018-0.0031 (0.045-0.080)	0.0012-0.0028 (0.030-0.070)	0.0091-0.0150 (0.23-0.38)	0.0059-0.0118 (0.15-0.30)	0.0059-0.0118 (0.15-0.30)
L28	0.08 (2.0)	0.08 (2.0)	0.16 (4.0)	0.0778 (1.977)	0.0778 (1.977)	0.0016-0.0029 (0.040-0.073)	0.0012-0.0025 (0.030-0.063)	0.0098-0.0157 (0.25-0.40)	0.0059-0.0118 (0.15-0.30)	0.0118-0.0354 (0.30-0.90)

maximum side clearance: 0.039 (1.0)

not up on the step when checking side clearance. Slide the ring and gage completely around the piston in the groove. Check for any clearance variations. This will verify that the land is free from distortion or uneven wear. The gage should slide the full circumference without binding. Check both compression-ring grooves using this method.

Oil-Ring Grooves—Oil-ring grooves are typically 0.1575 in. (4mm) wide. The real test is a snug-fitting oil ring. Here's that old problem again. You don't yet have a new set of rings to check with. Fortunately, oil rings and their grooves are well lubricated and aren't heavily loaded as are compression rings, particularly the top compression ring. Consequently, their wear is minimal. If they pass visual inspection, you can assume they are OK. To be positive, measure them. Do this by stacking two old compression rings together and mike their combined thickness.

As an example, if the combined thickness of two rings is 0.145 in. (0.368mm), and feeler-gage thickness to get maximum oil-ring-groove width is 0.020 in. (0.51mm), or 0.145 in. (0.368mm) minus 0.185 in. (4.7mm) = maximum allowable checking feeler-gage thickness of 0.020 in. (0.51mm).

Piston at left shows effects of bent or twisted connecting rod. Wear pattern is skewed from top right to bottom left. Wear pattern on piston at right is OK.

Maximum checking-gage thickness in inches = 0.185 in.—combined thickness of two compression rings in inches

If the oil-ring grooves in the pistons don't exceed this amount, you can be certain the rings will fit snugly in their grooves.

Now, use stacked rings with your feeler gage to check groove width as you did for checking the top two ring grooves.

Groove Inserts—If you find that the

cylinders don't need boring and the pistons are OK except for too much ring-groove wear, there is still hope. You can have your piston-ring grooves machined wider. To compensate for the additional width, *ring-groove inserts* are installed—they are usually 0.060 in. (1.52mm) wide and are installed beside the rings. In terms of cost, ridge-reaming and honing your block, machining your pistons in preparation for ring-groove inserts will cost 50—60 percent of a rebore and new pistons. Use new piston rings, regardless of which way you go. In this case, durability is directly related to cost. You can expect approximately half the life from an engine with inserted pistons compared to one that's been rebored and given new pistons.

CONNECTING RODS
Inspecting connecting rods involves checking three areas for: out-of-round or enlarged bearing bores, beams that are twisted or bent and damaged rod-cap bolts.

Now's when the old bearing inserts come in handy. If a rod bearing shows uneven wear from side to side—opposite sides on top and bottom bearing halves—the piston on that rod has wear spots offset from its thrust face and the rod's

With assembly in rod-alignment-checking fixture, piston is rocked in one direction . . .

. . . then in other direction. If big- and small-end bores are not perfectly parallel to one another, misalignment is indicated on gage.

crankshaft bearing journal was not *tapered,* the rod is bent. This will *side-load* the bearing. Take the piston-and-rod assembly or assemblies to an engine machine shop for accurate checking and straightening if this condition is found.

Connecting-Rod Straightness—A bent or twisted connecting rod will cause asymmetrical piston-skirt wear. The pistons shown in the nearby photo how a piston skirt wears with a bent or twisted rod compared to how one wears with a straight rod. If you find this condition, have the piston-and-rod assembly checked at an engine machine shop. They'll straighten the rod, if necessary.

Check Big End—Bearing condition also indicates whether the bearing bore—big end—of the rod needs to be *reconditioned* or remachined.

When a rod is reconditioned, the bearing bore is first checked with a special dial indicator to determine its shape—round, out-of-round or oversize. This is similar to what you did with the main-bearing journals. Check the condition of the bearing inserts. Their wear patterns should be even and their backside should be free from shiny spots.

A connecting-rod bearing bore must be round and it must crush its bearing inserts the right amount: 0.0006—0.0016 in. (0.015—0.040mm) when they are installed. Out-of-round connecting-rod bores must be reconditioned. This check is critical with connecting rods because they are considerably more likely to be

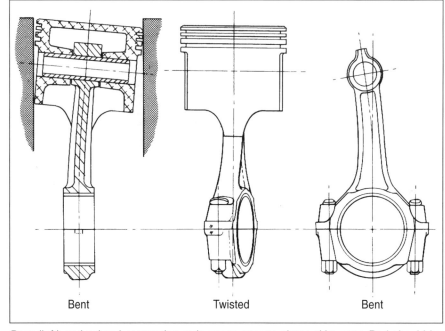

| Bent | Twisted | Bent |

Bent (left) and twisted connecting rods cause uneven piston-skirt wear. Rod should be straightened or replaced. Rod at right will not affect skirt wear.

"out of spec" than main-bearing bores.

Connecting-Rod Bearing Crush: 0.0006-0.0016 in. (0.015—0.040mm)

To determine if a bearing has been moving in its bore, look at its backside. Shiny spots on the back of the shell indicate movement. If this happened, either the bearing bore is too large or bearing-to-journal clearance is insufficient. If you discover any shiny spots, the rod(s) need to be checked with a dial indicator that's part

of an engine builder's connecting-rod conditioning hone. In a pinch, a telescoping gage and micrometer can also be used for checking. Recondition the rod(s) as necessary.

When a connecting rod is reconditioned, some material is precision-ground from the bearing-cap mating surfaces. Next, the cap is reinstalled on the rod, bolts are torqued to spec and the bore is honed to the specified diameter. Honing corrects the bearing-bore diameter and

Big end of connecting rod can be checked with telescoping gage and micrometers. Except for '82-83 L24 Maxima rod, big end should measure 2.0866—2.0871 in. (53.00—53.01mm). Maxima rod should measure 1.888 in. (47.95mm).

Measure across cap parting line, too. This measurement can be high if measurements in other positions "around the clock" are OK.

Here's how your engine machinist checks rods. Torque nuts to low end of spec when checking and honing rod: 20 ft-lb for 8mm bolts, 33 ft-lb for 9mm bolts. If new bolts are to be used, install them before checking and honing.

Cap and rod parting faces are ground before rod is sized, or honed.

Rods are honed in two's to help keep them square to honing mandrel. Bearing bores are checked periodically during honing process.

If rods and pistons are to be separated, pin must be pushed out with press. Never drive out pin with a punch and hammer.

concentricity, and also restores the *tooth*, or surface of the bore. Tooth *grabs* the bearing insert to prevent it from spinning. **Rod Bolts**—Inspect the rod bolts very closely. Use a magnifying glass to give them the old "eagle eye." Even better, have them Magnafluxed or Spotchecked. Cracks will show up immediately using either of these methods. Replace a cracked bolt: If you don't, it will end up breaking and may destroy the engine. See photos, pages 8 and 9.

A last note about connecting rods. Rod-bearing bores were originally machined with *their caps torqued in place*, so they must be checked the same way. When you deliver them to a machine shop for checking and reconditioning after you've inspected the rod bolts, make sure

the correct cap is installed on each rod. Although the machine shop may remove the cap, torque the nuts to specification before making the delivery.

Side Clearance—Although you checked connecting-rod side clearance, recheck it if you changed rods or the crankshaft. Using old bearing inserts, loosely assemble the rod to its crank journal and check side clearance with feeler gages. Remember: Desired connecting-rod side clearance is 0.012 in. (0.3mm)—maximum is 0.024 in. (0.6mm).

DISASSEMBLING & ASSEMBLING PISTONS & CONNECTING RODS

Disassembling or assembling connecting rods and pistons is a job for an expert with

the proper equipment. If you are replacing the pistons, the rods and pistons must part company. Only one method can be used to do this correctly. The wrist pin must be *pressed*—not *driven*—out of the small end of the rod. It is held in place by a 0.0006—0.0014 in. (0.015—0.035mm) interference fit. A press with mandrels to back up the piston and bear on the pin is required.

You can assemble a connecting rod and piston one of two ways. The first is done by carefully reversing the disassembly

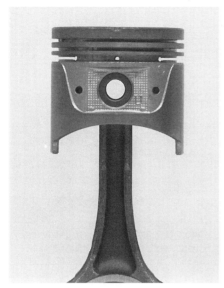

Note pin offset to right of piston, toward thrust side as installed in engine (to left as viewed). Because rods and pistons are directional they must be assembled one way; with piston notch toward front of engine, rod squirt hole to right—if used—and rod/cap numbers to left.

process. The other method, and the one I prefer, is the heating method. This is done by simply heating the small end of the connecting rod with a torch or a special electric heater. This expands the pin hole, allowing the pin to slide into place without need of a press. Pin and piston have to be fitted to the rod very quickly while the rod is hot, before the rod and pin approach the same temperature. Otherwise, the pin will be trapped by the interference fit before it's in position. A press will then be required to complete pin installation.

If you are assembling your own pistons and rods, be aware of the piston's location relative to its connecting rod. As installed in the engine, pistons usually have a notch at their front edge or an arrow stamped in the dome, either of which *must point to the front of the engine* when installed. Also, connecting-rod numbers *must face toward the distributor or left side,* of engine. The reasons for this are: The wrist pin is offset in the piston toward the *thrust side* of the cylinder bore about 0.040 in. (1mm). This reduces piston noise by preloading the piston against the cylinder-bore side that's opposite crankshaft rotation. Also, the connecting-rod squirt hole must point at the thrust side of the bore so the piston and bore will

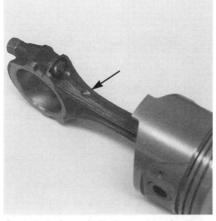

Squirt hole (arrow) oils thrust side of cylinder bore. It goes to right, opposite of connecting-rod number.

Oil-pump inspection begins by removing cover.

receive proper lubrication.

OIL PUMP & DRIVE SHAFT
Proper lubrication is necessary to the life of an engine. The oil pump is the heart of the lubrication system. Don't take any shortcuts. Check the oil pump for internal damage, such as grooving or scoring of the rotors and housing. Check clearances before declaring the pump reusable.

The oil pump is the best-lubricated engine component simply because all oil circulates through it. Unfortunately, the pump draws unfiltered oil *directly* from the oil sump or pan. Thus there is the potential for wear and damage, particularly with the L-series engine's cast-aluminum pump body.

Oil-Pump Damage—Damage occurs when particles suspended in the oil pass through the pickup screen and then the pump. This happens when some other

Instead of a press, I'm using heat to assemble rods and pistons. While torch preheats small ends of rods (left), pin is quickly slipped through and centered in piston and rod before it is grabbed by rod as it cools off rapidly.

Once bolts are out, tap off cover with soft mallet. Be careful not to let rotors fall out.

component is chewed up—such as a cam lobe and follower—or proper engine maintenance is not observed. Improper maintenance allows dirty oil to clog the filter, causing the pressure-relief valve to open and let oil *bypass* the filter. Large particles then circulate through the oil pump and engine. This can cause severe scoring and grooving of the oil-pump rotors and body—as well as bearing journals.

If this is the case with your engine, scoring and grooving will have shown up on components you've already inspected and reconditioned, or replaced. For example, an engine with heavily scuffed pistons and scored cylinder walls, badly worn camshaft lobes and rocker arms, or deeply grooved crankshaft bearing journals, will have circulated large amounts of debris through the oil pump. The oil-pump housing pictured on page 82 shows the damage resulting from a spun connecting-rod bearing.

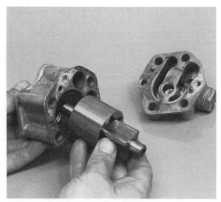

Slide rotors out of pump body.

Except for light scoring, rotor looks OK. Check for scoring by dragging fingernail lengthwise across rotors. It will catch on any grooves.

Unfortunately, aluminum housing is severely grooved. Pump should be replaced.

Oil-Pump Inspection—Inspect the pump internals. Remove the two bolts that thread into the underside of the pump cover through the pump-body flange. If the cover is stuck to the body, *lightly clamp* the pump housing between two wood blocks in a vise or to a bench with a C-clamp. The pump should be positioned so it is horizontal or the cap-end is up. Tap the underside of the pressure-relief-valve cap with a soft mallet to break the cover loose. Be careful that the rotors don't fall out when you remove the cover. If they fall on the floor, they could be damaged beyond use.

Unclamp the pump and, with your hands underneath, tip the cover-end down. The rotors should slide out. A quick look at the rotor and housing bore will give you an idea of pump condition. Grooving will be apparent, particularly in the aluminum pump-body bore. You'll be able to feel grooves by dragging a fingernail the length of the pump bore and rotors. If your fingernail goes "bumpity-bump," better get a new pump. However, if the grooves are slight, or non-existent, consider the pump OK in this department. Check its pressure-regulator valve next.

The pressure-regulator-valve assembly is in the pump cover. Check its operation by inserting a small screwdriver in the port nearest the valve. Try moving the valve in its bore by prying against its base. If the valve moves freely against its spring, it should be OK. The spring should move the valve back against its stop when you release it.

To remove the valve from the pump cover, temporarily install the cover to the pump body. Secure the cover with the two

Don't forget to check cover. Wear or heavy scoring between pump inlet and outlet means pump should be replaced.

Check pressure-relief valve by stroking with screwdriver. It should move freely and smoothly.

screws. Again, lightly clamp the pump between two wood blocks, then break the regulator cap loose. Once broken loose, you should be able to unthread the cap from the pump cover with little effort.

Be careful not to lose the brass washer and regulator spring when the cap is free of the cover. Set the spring, cap and its washer aside. After unclamping the pump, bump the pump against the palm of your hand with the valve bore aimed down. This should cause the valve to slide out. If not, remove the cover and push it out with a screwdriver.

Clean oil-pump components in carburetor cleaner, solvent or lacquer thinner. Remove any cover-to-body gasket material. Remember, you are working with soft aluminum. A steel scraper can easily damage these surfaces.

Slide the oil-pressure-regulator valve into its bore in the pump cover. With your

thumb over the end of the bore, tilt the cover back and forth. The valve should slide back and forth in the bore from its own weight. If it doesn't, check for nicks or burrs on the bore and valve surfaces. Smooth any irregularities with a small file. *Needle* files are great for this. Don't remove any more material than necessary. Recheck the operation of the valve.

After you're satisfied with the operation of the pressure-regulator valve, check the housing and rotor clearances. You'll need feeler gages for this job. Reinstall both rotors with their *index* or *dot* marks toward the pump body. This is the only way the inner rotor will install, but the outer rotor can be turned either way.

Oil-pump clearances are checked with feeler gages. Start with checking inner rotor-to-body clearance: It should not exceed 0.0197 in. (0.050mm). Rotor-tip clearance is next. Turn the rotors so an

To remove pressure-relief valve, remove cap, valve and spring. Temporarily install pump cover on housing, then lightly clamp pump in vise with soft jaws so you can break loose cap.

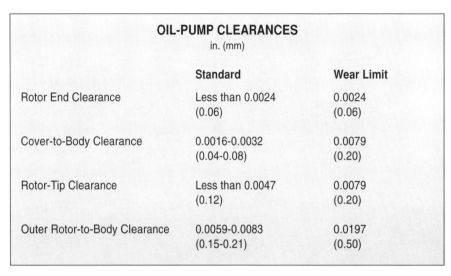

OIL-PUMP CLEARANCES in. (mm)		
	Standard	**Wear Limit**
Rotor End Clearance	Less than 0.0024 (0.06)	0.0024 (0.06)
Cover-to-Body Clearance	0.0016-0.0032 (0.04-0.08)	0.0079 (0.20)
Rotor-Tip Clearance	Less than 0.0047 (0.12)	0.0079 (0.20)
Outer Rotor-to-Body Clearance	0.0059-0.0083 (0.15-0.21)	0.0197 (0.50)

Valve should slide out. Clean it and all pump components.

After cleaning, check pump clearance. Install rotors with their marks toward housing. Ideally, rotor-to-housing clearance should not exceed 0.0083 in. (0.21mm).

inner- and outer-rotor tip are end to end. Measure tip clearance here. Maximum allowable tip clearance is 0.0079 in. (0.20mm). Check all four inner rotor tips in like manner.

The next two checks are made at the end of the pump: rotor-end and cover-to-body clearances. To make these checks, you'll need a small straightedge. With the rotors still in the pump body, lay the straightedge across the end of the rotors and pump body against the inner-rotor shaft.

First, check between the straightedge and the end of the rotors. This clearance should be less than 0.0024 in. (0.06mm). Don't worry if there is no clearance because the gasket will space the cover away from the rotor ends—assuming the

Rotor-tip clearance should be about 0.0047 in. (0.12mm).

Examples of rotor markings: Just make sure to install them toward housing. Obviously, this is no problem with inner rotor.

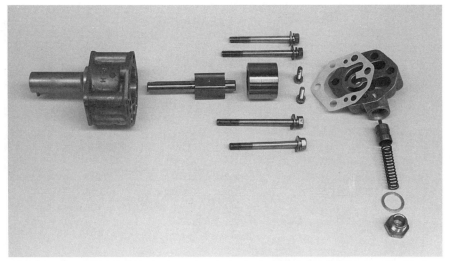

With a new gasket and all parts cleaned and checked, pump is ready to be reassembled.

After lightly oiling, slip rotors into housing.

Fit cover with new gasket to housing. Note alignment dowels.

Oil and install pressure-relief valve . . . then install spring.

Install valve cap with sealing washer. Push hard to compress spring.

next check proves OK. With the straight-edge in the same position, check between it and the pump body. Straightedge-to-pump-body clearance should not exceed 0.0012 in. (0.03mm).

If any clearance is not within specification, or the pump body or a rotor is damaged, the complete pump assembly must be replaced. The rotors and pump body are not serviced separately.

High-Volume Oil Pump—The pump for the 1981 280ZX Turbo is larger than the oil pumps for the other Datsun L-Series engines because it supplies oil for the turbocharger, as well as the engine. *A high-volume pump is not required by every engine.* Because it pumps more oil all of the time, the result is increased loads on the distributor and oil-pump drive gear. While the turbo pump is moderately priced and bolts right in to the other L-Series engines, it is not something to add to your engine unless it is specifically needed.

Assemble Pump—Make sure the parts are clean. Liberally coat the rotors with oil

and install them. Allen Osborne packs the pump with light grease such as Lubri-Plate®. He claims this makes the pump pick up prime much faster.

Fit the cover to the body with a new gasket. You'll find the gasket in the engine-gasket set. Make sure the outer rotor is installed correctly: index mark toward the pump body. Install the cover, using the inner-rotor shaft and dowels to align the cover to the pump body. The cover should "click" into place. Install the two pump-cover bolts and torque 5—7 ft-lb (0.7—0.9 kg-m).

The regulator-valve assembly is next. Oil the valve and slide it into its bore in the cover. With the regulator spring placed against the center of the valve, compress it with the cap and washer assembly. Carefully start threading the cap into the cover while compressing the spring. If there's any resistance, stop! Unthread the cap and start over. Don't crossthread the cap in the cover. This will ruin the threads in the pump cover. Torque the cap 29—36

ft-lb (4—5kg-m). As you did for loosening the cap, lightly clamp the pump to keep it from turning while tightening the cap.

CHAPTER SEVEN

Cylinder-Head Reconditioning

I saved cylinder-head teardown and inspection until now because once you start a head, you should continue working with it until the job is completed. This greatly reduces the possibility of losing or mixing pieces. Head reconditioning is a precise, tedious and dirty job requiring special tools and equipment.

It's best to limit your head work to removing and installing it unless you have the equipment *and* experience to do the job. You may do more harm than good if you attempt to do more. Leave the precision work to the specialist. It'll cost you no more for him to strip your head, too. While you're at it, farm out the job to an engine or cylinder-head shop—one that specializes in Datsun/Nissan engine work. This will ensure a better job. However, if you have access to some or all of the equipment, by all means do it yourself. You can then inspect all parts so you'll have an idea of what head work needs to be done.

Milling cylinder-head-gasket surface is standard cylinder-head-reconditioning operation.

DISASSEMBLY

The first cylinder-head-reconditioning step is to disassemble the head—tear it down. You'll need to remove the rocker arms, or cam followers, camshaft, valve springs, spring retainers, seals and the valves. This will give you access to each part. including the cylinder head, so it can be cleaned, inspected and reconditioned, or replaced, if necessary.

So the job won't be too messy, degrease the cylinder head. Either do the job with some spray degreaser and a water hose, or drop by your local car wash. Immediately afterward, spray the machined surfaces of ferrous-metal (iron or steel) parts with light oil so they won't rust.

When working with the cylinder head, don't forget that it's aluminum and is easily damaged. Be especially careful not to damage the head-gasket surface. One good gouge or scratch could mean an unnecessary resurfacing job or a blown head gasket after you have the engine back together again and running—a

depressing thought.

To protect the head-gasket surface during teardown, set the head on something soft. If the bench surface is wood, no need—unless it's full of nails. As you can see from the photos I used two 2x4s.

Remove Rocker Arms—The rocker arms, their springs and the camshaft are removed before any other valve-train parts. In the photos, I removed the rocker arms first, but it is possible to slide out the camshaft and then remove the rockers.

Start by removing each rocker *lash spring*. This is the mousetrap-type spring that hooks under a retaining spring at the lash adjuster and in the groove over the pivot end of the rocker. Lash springs prevent the rockers from bouncing around when they are momentarily unloaded by their cam lobes.

To remove the lash springs, lift each spring from its notch and over the end of the rocker. Unhook it from the retaining spring and set it aside. This is one valve-

Start removing rocker arms by lifting off lash springs. These are also called *mousetrap springs.*

train part you don't have to keep in order. But don't lose them. Store the lash springs where you'll be able to find them.

Now for the rockers: Choose one that's not loaded by the camshaft. You should be able to wiggle the rocker. The *toe* (pointed

Loosen jam nut and run rocker-arm pivot completely down.

Rotate cam so heel of lobe is against rocker before attempting to remove rocker arm.

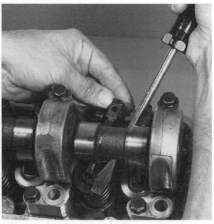

Using unmachined surface of cam as fulcrum, compress valve spring slightly by prying against spring retainer. Slip rocker arm off pivot.

end) of the cam lobe will be pointing away from the rocker. The heel (opposite the toe) will be toward the rocker.

Loosen the rocker-pivot/lash-adjuster locknut. You'll need a 14mm open-end wrench on the pivot and a 17mm open end on the locknut. Thread the rocker-arm pivot into the cylinder head as far as possible. You must hold the locknut to keep it from locking the pivot as you do this. This will give *almost* enough clearance to slip the rocker out from between the cam, rocker pivot and valve tip.

To get the additional clearance to slip the rocker off of its pivot, compress the valve spring slightly. Do this with a screwdriver. Pry under the camshaft and against the top of the spring retainer. Simultaneously, lift the rocker off of its pivot. Don't pry against a cam lobe; you'll damage it. Pry against the as-cast section between the two cam lobes as shown. Once you have the rocker off, store it so it can be reinstalled in its original position. Each rocker arm must be installed on the same cam lobe and pivot. Read on. I say more about this later.

Remove the remaining seven or 11 rockers using the same procedure. To unload a rocker, rotate the camshaft using an adjustable wrench or Vise-Grip pliers at the center of the cam until the toe is off of the rocker. When doing this, take care to prevent the camshaft from *walking* toward the back end of the cylinder head and out of its bearings. To ensure that this doesn't happen, loosely install the cam sprocket.
Keep Cam Followers in Order—
Each cam lobe and its rocker arm wears a

Keep rocker arms in order. At assembly time all valve-train parts should be remated with original parts, particularly rocker arms with their respective cam lobes.

little differently than the next one. So, if a used rocker is reinstalled with another lobe—new or old—the result may very well be a wiped lobe and rocker. New rocker arms can be installed with a used camshaft.

Keep the rockers in order by placing them in a labeled and compartmented container, like the egg carton shown. Or, label each rocker. Wrap masking tape around each one, making a flag. Label them **1, 2, 3** . . . from front to back.

Just as the rockers and cam lobes *wear-in* together, so do the rocker-arm tips and *lash pads* (slotted discs at the ends of the valves in the center of the spring retainers). Keep these pads with their respective rockers. To remove the lash pads, simply lift each one from the center of its spring retainer.

Lift lash caps from center of spring retainers. Store in order with rocker arms.

INSPECT CAMSHAFT

Before sliding the camshaft out of its bores, check to see if it turns freely. Use the sprocket on the end of the cam to turn it. If the cam turns without any resistance, the head is not warped nor is the cam bent. However, if the camshaft is difficult or impossible to turn by hand, one of these two problems exist—maybe both. More likely, though, it's the head.

Slide the cam from the head before you check for head warpage or cam straightness. Carefully guide it out the back of the head, being careful to avoid bumping a cam lobe into a bearing. Damage will result.

If the cam is hard to turn, use the procedure on page 91 to check for head warpage. If the cylinder head is OK, chances are the cam is not straight. This can be checked with a dial indicator while rotating the cam between two centers or

Remove thrust plate from front bearing tower. Cam can also be removed out rear of head unless head is on engine in vehicle.

Slide cam from head with care. Cam runs directly in cam towers, so be careful. Soft aluminum is easily damaged by harder cam lobes.

with two V-blocks under the two end bearing journals. Set the dial-indicator plunger against the center bearing journal of a six-cylinder, or against one of the two inboard bearing journals of a four-cylinder engine.

Zero the dial indicator after rotating the cam to get the *lowest* reading. Rotate it to get total indicator reading (TIR). Maximum TIR, or runout, for a six cylinder is 0.0039 in. (0.l0mm), and 0.0020 in. (0.05mm) for a four-cylinder. If this amount is exceeded, replace the camshaft

Inspect Cam Lobes—While you're looking at the cam, you might as well finish inspecting it. Start by checking the lobes.

A cam lobe and rocker wear gradually during their operating life. This wear can be slight. How much depends on how an engine is operated and, more importantly, how it is maintained. You must determine if its cam and rockers have worn so badly that they shouldn't be reused.

I'll say it right now: Using an old camshaft and rockers in a newly rebuilt engine is risky. It's not uncommon for a new cam and its rocker arms to fail during the first 100 miles of operation—or even before the car gets out of the driveway. Finally, if you lose track of the order of the rockers, toss them away and get new ones. The odds of getting 8 or 12 rockers back in the right order on 8 or 12 cam lobes are astronomical: 40,320 to 1 or 479,001,600 to 1! I recommend you go the full route and get a new cam; the rockers are the expensive part.

Check Camshaft First—When check-

Approximate lobe lift can be checked with vernier caliper. Measure from toe to heel, as shown. Then, measure 90° to this measurement to get approximate base-circle diameter. Subtract one from another to get lobe lift.

ing the cam and rockers. check the cam first. If it's bad, you'll have to replace the cam and the rockers, regardless of rocker-arm condition. Remember the second rule: *Never install used rockers on a new cam.*

To check the cam lobes and lobe lift, you'll need your trusty micrometers—vernier calipers are OK. Better yet, you can use a dial indicator. Maybe you made this diagnostic check prior to removing and tearing-down your engine. If you did and have already determined the condition of your cam, skip the balance of this section and continue on with stripping the head.

L-series lobe lift, not valve lift, should be 0.261 or 0.275 in. (6.65 or 7.00mm).

Although condition of lobes can be determined by simple visual check, accurate way to check lobe lift is with dial indicator. Indicator is zeroed when against lobe heel, then cam is rotated until maximum indicator reading is obtained. Reading is lobe lift.

Cam-lobe lift depends on the engine. If yours is an L13, an early single-carb L16, or L20, specified lobe lift is 0.0261 in. Otherwise, lobe lift should be 0.275 in. If it is 0.006 in. (0.15mm) less than specified, replace the cam.

The most accurate way of measuring lobe lift is with a dial indicator. To do this, leave or reinstall the cam in the head. Set up the indicator so its plunger is square to the lobe and, if it has one, out of line with the lobe oiling hole. Rotate the cam so the plunger is on the *heel* of the lobe—valve-closed position—and zero the dial. See the drawing, page 14, for an explanation of cam-lobe terms.

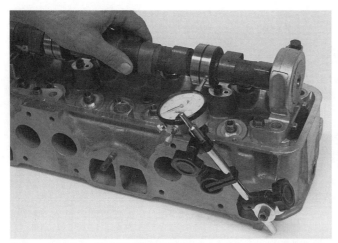

Cam runout (bend) is checked by supporting cam at ends and rotating while checking inner bearing journals with dial indicator. V-blocks can be used to support cam. Here, I've removed all but end cam towers for check.

Before compressing spring, break loose keepers by striking retainer with soft mallet. The sound of impact will change after keepers break loose from retainer. Adjust spring compressor only enough to release keepers and retainer.

Rotate the cam so the plunger is on the lobe *toe*—valve-open position. Observe the highest indicator reading. Continue rotating the cam to double-check your reading. The result is *actual lobe lift*. Again, if it's 0.006 in. (0.15mm) less than specified, replace the cam. If not, move to the next lobe and check it. Continue this until you've checked them all.

To use a mike or vernier caliper, take two measurements: First measure across the heel and toe, then 90° to this. The second measurement should equal the *base-circle* diameter—it defines the heel of the lobe. The difference between these two measurements will be *approximate lobe lift*.

Although using micrometers or vernier calipers is slightly less accurate than the dial-indicator method, one can be used to check cam-lobe *wear* rather than lift. The results from using mikes or verniers are even more inaccurate when checking high-performance camshafts. The reason is that the *ramp area* (transition area between the heel and toe) extends farther around the lobe. Consequently, it increases the base-circle measurement. This gives a false reduction in lobe lift when you subtract the larger-than-actual base-circle measurement from the heel-to-toe measurement. Not all is lost, however.

As I said in the preceding paragraph, you can use these results to determine lobe wear. Because cam lobes don't wear the same, measure all lobes and compare them. If "lobe lift" is within the 0.010 in.(0.25mm) wear limit, the cam is OK.

Otherwise, it should be replaced with a new or reground camshaft.

Besides measuring the lobes, also check the wear pattern on each. If there is any pitting, the cam should be replaced. Check for roughness by dragging a fingernail across each lobe nose. If a lobe is pitted or rough, a similar condition will probably show up on its mating rocker arm. Replace them both.

Measure Bearing Journals—Cam-bearing journals never seem to wear out. At least, I've never seen it happen. What is more likely to wear are the aluminum cam-bearing bores. Check them too, page 92. However, if you feel compelled to check the journals while your micrometer is handy, do it. Checking never hurt anything—and the key to building a good engine is to check and recheck. Cam-bearing journals should mike 1.8878—1.8883 in. (47.949—47.962mm).

Remove Valves—Before you remove the valves, make provisions to keep them in order. Use a yardstick or the bottom of a cardboard box with eight or 12 holes drilled or punched in it. Label the holes as to valve position. Or if you want to be super-safe, the same number of small boxes can be used to keep all valve parts segregated and together: valves, springs, retainers, keepers and *shims*. What appears to be a shim under each valve spring is a steel spring seat that prevents the valve spring or springs from galling the aluminum. Some L-series engines use two springs: inner and outer.

To remove the valves, you need a *valve-spring compressor*. Nothing else will do the job. Period. The compressor will compress the valve spring(s) and move the retainer down, relative to the valve tip. This allows the valve *keepers*—keys or whatever you want to call them—to be removed.

Although there are different types of compressors, the C-clamp type shown is the most common and easiest to use. One end of the compressor butts against the head of the valve while the other end fits over and around the spring retainer. When these ends are drawn together by the compressor mechanism, the valve spring is compressed, pulling the spring retainer down and away from the valve tip.

Before you use the compressor, break the retainers loose from their keepers so the compressor won't have to. First, place a small wood block under the head of the valve and a socket against the retainer. Then, strike the socket with a heavy, soft mallet to break the retainer loose. Be alert while doing this. It's possible that if the retainer is shocked hard enough, the spring will compress far enough so the keepers will pop out. Watch so you don't lose them.

Regardless of the type of compressor used, don't compress the springs more than necessary. Compress each spring only enough to expose the keepers so you can remove them with your fingers or a magnetic screwdriver. After you've removed the keepers, slowly release the compressor.

Once spring is compressed, retainers are removed from valve stem. Pencil magnet would have made this job easier. Release compressor and remove retainer and springs.

After removing valve, lift off outer spring seat.

Pry old valve-stem seals from top of valve guide . . . .

. . . . and remove inner spring seat.

As you remove each retainer, also remove the spring(s), spring seat(s) and valves. Store them as an assembly. If they are in good shape and don't require reconditioning or replacing they should he installed together.

Slide each valve from its guide and seal. All that's left are the valve-stem seals that are installed over the upper end of the valve guides. Remove these seals by prying them off with a screwdriver. You'll be replacing these seals with new ones.

CLEANUP & INSPECTION

Remove Gasket Material—Just as you did with the block deck, remove head-gasket material from the head. However, rather than using a gasket scraper, use gasket remover or paint remover. It's too easy to gouge the soft aluminum head with a hardened-steel gasket scraper. To assist in gasket removal, you can use a putty knife with extreme care. Be careful!

Clean all gasket surfaces: head-gasket, manifold and rocker-arm-cover sealing surfaces. Using a round file, carefully remove all deposits from the head-to-block water passages.

To make the next job easier, soak the head in water overnight. This will soften the carbon deposits, making them much easier to remove. Another trick: Slip an old intake and exhaust valve back into the head and on the seats while removing combustion-chamber carbon. This will keep the valve seats from getting gouged or scratched.

It's time to *misuse* a screwdriver. Get one that's already been misused or is badly worn, so you won't gouge the combustion chamber. Scrape the carbon deposits from the combustion chambers and exhaust and intake ports. When you're finished with one combustion chamber, transfer the valves to the next until all chambers are clean.

When cleaning a head with round exhaust ports and sheet-metal inserts, don't be concerned if the inserts are eroded or burned away. This won't adversely affect the performance of your engine. Besides, you can't replace them without replacing the head. And, high-performance engine builders typically remove the inserts to increase exhaust-port flow and engine power.

Before you invest any money in reconditioning the cylinder head, some checks must be made: cracks and warpage. This is particularly true if coolant, oil or combustion leaks were a problem.

Oil-Passage Cracks—Although not a common problem, it's not unusual for a crack to develop between a cylinder-head

Inspect gasket and gasket surface for leaks. Dark area between combustion chambers indicates combustion leak. Cause may have been head warpage.

Use blunt screwdriver to scrape carbon from combustion chambers and ports. Sharp steel tool can scratch and gouge softer aluminum.

oil passage and the water jacket. When this happens, oil leaks into the coolant when the engine is running because oil pressure is higher than coolant pressure. The reverse occurs when the engine is shut off. Coolant leaks into the oil as oil pressure drops to zero and coolant pressure actually increases for a short while.

If you suspect this to be a problem because of oil in the coolant and vice versa, have the cylinder head pressure-checked *before* you do anything else. The only way to fix the problem is to junk the head and replace it. Consequently, if you proceed with inspecting and reconditioning, and there is a crack in an oil passage, you may end up wasting a lot of your time and money.

If you only see coolant in the oil, but no oil in the coolant, it may be something as simple as the front cover has corroded through behind the water pump. This can happen if the engine has run for quite some time without any antifreeze in the cooling system to prevent corrosion.

Most cylinder-head-repair shops and many engine builders are set up to pressure-check Nissan/Datsun cylinder heads. Therefore, get on the phone and call around. The cost for this check is minimal and these people know what to look for.

However, if you insist, you can make the check yourself. To do it, you'll need a compressed-air source and a rubber-tipped blowgun.

To prepare the head for the pressure check, you'll have to seal all of the water-passage and oil-gallery outlets. Start by reinstalling the camshaft. Oil its bearing journals first. Use duct tape to seal the outlets that route coolant to the radiator and heater. If these surfaces are oily, clean them with lacquer thinner so the tape will stick.

Also, if you're working with a six-cylinder head that uses a spray bar, wipe the tube clean in the area of the spray holes. There is a hole opposite each cam lobe. Seal each hole by wrapping a narrow strip of duct tape over it and around the tube several times.

Position the head upside down on two short 2x4s so its deck surface is level. Fill the water jackets with water. Add some detergent to the water so air bubbles will be readily visible.

Using the blowgun, pressurize the oil gallery by inserting its tip into the head's oil-gallery inlet hole. It's at the center of the head. Look for air bubbles in the soapy water as you pressurize the oil passages. If bubbles appear, the head is junk.

Other Cracks—Unlike cracks in oil passages, other cylinder-head cracks can be found simply by visual inspection after the head is clean. This job is made considerably easier through the use of Spotcheck, page 68.

In addition to oil-passage cracks, there are others that can spell the end of a cylinder head: those between the valve seats, between a valve seat and a sparkplug hole, and in an exhaust port. It's possible that cracks in these areas can be repaired by welding. Check out the cost of the repair first; it may approach that of a new cylinder head.

A crack that can be repaired successfully, and at much less cost than that of a new cylinder head, is one in a valve seat. Not only does this repair have a high success rate, it is common. The reason for this is simple.

Aluminum cylinder heads, such as the L-series Nissan/Datsun, must use *valve-seat inserts*. Aluminum doesn't have the ability to withstand the heat and constant pounding of a valve opening and closing. To remedy this, the valve-seat area is counterbored to accept an insert: aluminum-bronze alloy or sintered-iron for the intake and steel for the exhaust. The insert is retained by an interference fit in the counterbore.

Therefore, if you find any cracks in the combustion chambers or exhaust ports—other than in the valve-seat inserts—I recommend that you replace the head. Turn to page 99 for replacing valve-seat inserts.

HEAD-SURFACE FLATNESS

A cylinder head is subjected to extreme loads from pressure and heat. In addition, an aluminum head is structurally weak compared to the cast-iron engine block. Therefore, it is highly susceptible to warping and cracking. Sometimes, all that's needed in an aluminum cylinder head is for the engine to overheat *once*.

Cracks, like the ones you just checked for, or severe warpage may result. The excessive mismatch between the block and head surfaces caused by this head warpage will, in turn, cause combustion or coolant leaks. Consequently, cylinder-head and block mating surfaces *must be flat*. If either isn't, that surface must be resurfaced, or milled.

CAUTION: ALUMINUM THREADS

When a steel bolt is threaded into aluminum, the softer aluminum threads are easily damaged. Common problems are crossthreading, overtightening and galling. Crossthreading is probably the number-one cause of damaging aluminum threads. However, if the threads are clean, the right size and reasonable care is taken starting the fastener in its hole, the chance of crossthreading is small.

When a fastener is overtightened, something has to give. In the case of a steel bolt in an aluminum head, the softer aluminum threads can be expected to give (strip).

Sometimes, aluminum threads strip even without crossthreading or over-tightening. This is a result of galling. It's common with spark plug threads. The problem is heat-expansion rates. When an aluminum head is hot, it grows several thousandths of an inch in all directions. Thus, the pressure between the spark-plug threads and those in the spark-plug hole increases. This forces the aluminum into voids in the spark-plug threads, locking the plug in its hole. When the plug is subsequently removed, its threads tear or gall the aluminum threads, particularly in the case of a hot engine. To protect against this, always use anti-seize compound on spark-plug threads; and don't change plugs on a hot engine.

How do you restore stripped threads? It can be done with a steel thread insert.

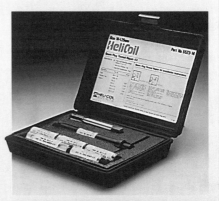

Damage to threads in aluminum head can be repaired with thread inserts. Shown is thread-repair kit from Heli-Coil®. Photo courtesy Heli-Coil Products Division, Mite Corp.

Thread inserts fall into three groups: steel-wire coil, threaded sleeve and locking threaded sleeve.

The procedures for installing inserts, sometimes called *thread savers*, differ. Basically, the old threads are drilled out, the hole is tapped oversize and the thread insert is installed. The new steel threads are actually stronger than the aluminum ones they replace. For this reason, race-car builders frequently install thread inserts in light-alloy components. It's a good preventive measure in any component that is removed and installed frequently.

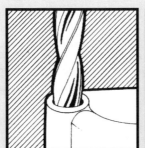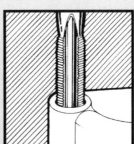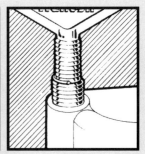

To repair threads, drill out old threads, retap to larger size, then install thread insert. Steel thread insert will now be stronger than original aluminum thread. Drawings courtesy Heli-Coil Products Division, Mite Corp.

Check the head-gasket surface with feeler gages and a *straightedge* that is at least as long as the cylinder head. Set the straightedge lengthwise and diagonally across the head in both directions. Check any clearance between the head and straightedge with your feeler gages. It is desirable to have no more than a 0.002 in. (0.05mm) variation in surface flatness. The absolute maximum variation is 0.004 in. (0.10mm) for both four- and six-cylinder heads.

If you found that the cylinder head must be milled, read this section before proceeding. You may need some extra parts after the head is milled. Or you may decide to purchase another head rather than machining the original one.

Cylinder-Head Milling—Be aware that two undesirable things happen when an L-series cylinder head *or* block deck is milled: compression ratio increases and cam-drive geometry changes.

The reason compression increases is simple: As material is removed from the bottom of the head, the combustion chambers get smaller. Refer to page 61 for how a reduction in clearance volume affects compression ratio.

Cam-drive geometry changes as the cylinder head moves down in relation to the crankshaft. Although slight, changing the fixed length of the cam-drive chain will result in the chain-tensioner extending farther from its bore to take up the slack it "reads" as chain wear. This retards the cam, assuming all other factors remain the same.

Nissan recommends that no more than a combined 0.008 in. (0.2mm) be removed from the block deck and head. So, if 0.002 in. (0.05mm) was removed from the block, no more than 0.008 - 0.002 = 0.006 in. (0.15mm) should be removed from the head.

Cam-Bearing Alignment—There is another complication with a warped cylinder head. Suppose the head cleans up with no problems: Great! But how about the alignment of the four or five cam-bearing bores?

Not only did the bottom of the head warp, so did the top—top and bottom surfaces remain parallel. Consequently, the cam towers are pulled out of alignment. And this problem is not corrected when the bottom of the head is milled—it gets worse. The warpage at the top of the head remains when the head is installed on the block. The top surface and the cam bearings are not pulled into alignment by the head bolts

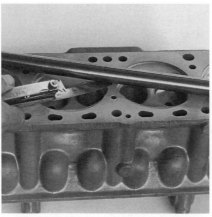

Don't even think about not checking head for warpage. Precision straightedge and feeler gages are required. Check lengthwise in several places across gasket surface, then diagonally across both corners as shown.

Telescoping gage and mikes are used to check cam-bearing bores. Standard bearing diameter is 1.8898—1.8904 in. (48.000—48.016mm).

as they are tightened, as was the case prior to milling the head. The result will be a cam that binds in its bearing bores.

To correct this problem, you'll have to do something that Nissan says not to do—remove the cam towers and cam bearings. This is done so the *top* of the head can be milled.

Nissan has a good reason for warning against removing the cam towers: They were align-bored after they were installed on the head. Therefore, if the towers are removed, then reinstalled out of alignment, the cam will bind and gall the bearings. And Nissan doesn't want to suggest that the bearing bores will align after they are reinstalled, even though each is positioned with two dowels. If you do remove the towers, Nissan insists that the cam-bearing bores be align-bored.

The paradox, of course, is that the cam towers are being removed so they can be put back into alignment. Engine builders do it every day without having to align-bore the bearings. Because they have considerable experience at doing this, I recommend that you take the head to an engine machinist who specializes in reconditioning L-series cylinder heads. Let him do the work. Just the same, let's take a look at how this work is done, starting with checking the cam-bearing bores.

Measure Cam-Bearings Bores—Use a 1—2-in. inside micrometer or a telescoping gage and a 1—2-in. outside micrometer. The bores should measure 1.8898—1.8904 in. (48.000—48.016mm). This gives a 0.0015—0.0026-in. (0.038—

0.067mm) oil clearance with 1.8878—1.8883-in. (47.949—47.962mm) cam-bearing journals.

If you find any bores that are 0.004-in. (0.10mm) larger than the cam-bearing journals, you'll have to replace the head. There are too many variables to expect a replacement cam-tower bearing bore to align with the existing bores. Encountering this problem is not likely because the cam bearings are well lubricated.

Mark Cam Towers—Cam towers must be reinstalled in their original positions. So you'll know where they go during assembly, mark each tower with a prick punch or number dies and a hammer. Mark each tower and the head at the tower base with a number of punch marks that correspond to the position of each tower; one punch mark for number-1, two punch marks for number-2, and so on.

Remove Cam Towers & Related Hardware—Remove the long and short bolts that secure the cam towers to the head. Notice how each tower stays with the head after the bolts are out. This is because of the tight-fitting dowels. To remove each tower, grasp it with two fingers and pull up. Use your other hand to hold the head down.

If you haven't already done so, unhook and remove the rocker-arm lash springs. Then, remove the rocker-arm pivots, pivot bushings and cam-tower dowels. Place a box-end wrench on each pivot bushing. Hit the end of the wrench with a lead or plastic mallet while you pull on the wrench. This will shock the bushing loose.

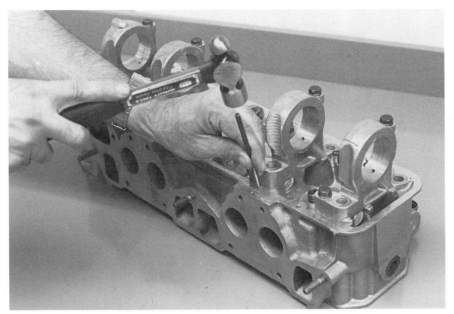

After marking, remove cam towers.

Before removing cam towers, mark them so each can be reinstalled in original position. Make marks with a prick punch, one punch mark for number-1, two punch marks for number-2 journal, and so on.

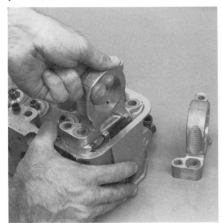

After bolts are out, work cam towers off locating dowels.

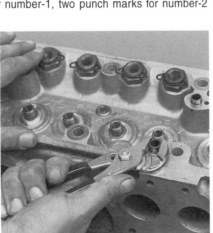

Remove all hardware from top of head if this side is to be milled. Remove dowels, taking care not to gall or score them.

Break stud bushings loose with box-end wrench and soft-faced mallet. First remove wire clips from bushings.

After all pivot bushings are out, remove the cam-tower dowels. Use Channel-lock pliers to work them out of their bores. Be careful not to gall the dowels.

Store the cam towers, their bolts and dowels, and the pivot bushings for safekeeping. They should be reinstalled immediately after the head is milled.

Cam-Tower shims—I hate to complicate things at this point, but there is another consideration. If the cam towers are installed directly to the top of the head after it is milled, the cam will move down in relation to the head. This changes rocker-arm *geometry,* and if the head is milled more than 0.020 in. (0.5lmm), you'll have

to restore that geometry. Read about rocker-arm geometry on page 108. One way to remedy this problem is to selectively install all new valve-lash caps. A less-expensive and easier way of doing this is to install special shims under each cam tower.

Known as *Head-Saver Shims,* cam-tower shims are used to restore the camshaft to near original position. Available in a 0.015 in. (0.38mm) thickness, they have the same shape as the base of the cam towers with holes for the locating dowels, bolts and the oil hole.

The top surface of the head should be milled so it cleans up its full length. An equal number of shims is then installed under each cam tower to within 0.015 in.,

but less than what was removed. This is particularly important with a six-cylinder head that has a single cam tower at its center and two others near its ends.

Install Pivot Bushings & Cam Towers—If you removed the hardware from the top of the cylinder head for any reason, reinstall it now. Start with the rocker-arm-pivot bushings. Lubricate the pivot-bushing threads, thread each bushing into place. Torque bushings 58—87 ft-lb (8—12 kg-m).

To install the cam towers, first install their locating dowels. Eight dowels are installed in four-cylinder heads and ten in sixes. Check each dowel for burrs that may have been put there when you removed

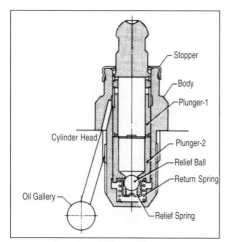

Hydraulic valve adjusters are used in '83 L24 Maxima and non-turbo L28. Check operation by working pivot—plunger—up and down with thumb. If plunger works freely, lash adjuster is OK. Otherwise, remove and replace. Drawing courtesy Nissan.

Cam towers can be reassembled to original height relative to deck surface after milling by installing Head-Saver shims. Head-Saver shims are made by several firms and are available through your auto-parts house or rebuilder.

Leveling head before milling head-gasket surface. Only light cut was required, so top side was not milled.

File smooth any rough spots off dowel, then position it over hole and tap into place until it bottoms in hole.

Install Head-Saver shims as required.

Using match marks as guide, install cam towers in original positions. Tap into place with soft mallet. After cleaning and oiling threads, install cam-bearing bolts finger tight.

them. File any burrs smooth. Install each dowel by holding it squarely over its hole with a thumb and forefinger and driving it into place with a light tap. You'll feel it stop when it reaches the bottom of its counterbore.

With all dowels driven in, install the shims, if necessary, and the cam towers. Arrange the towers so they'll match up with their index marks. Place the shim(s) for each cam tower on the head. Remember, an equal number of shims must be used under each tower. Also, if more than one shim per tower is required, or if the head is for a six-cylinder engine, you'll need more than one set of shims.

Now is a convenient time to check camshaft runout. Install only the front and rear cam towers, then turn to page 86 for

how to do this.

Install each cam tower by pushing it as far as possible onto its dowels. Using a soft mallet, lightly tap it the rest of the way. Don't tap in the center of the tower. Tap on the bolt bosses. Alternate between bosses to keep the tower moving down square until it bottoms on the head.

Install the cam-tower bolts; a long and short one for each tower. Lightly snug each bolt, but do not torque the tower bolts, yet. If you are absolutely sure the cam is straight and it has passed the inspection procedure starting on page 86, you can use the cam as a fixture to align the cam towers before tightening the bolts. Oil the cam-bearing bores and cam journals and install the camshaft. If the cam–bearing bores are in line, the cam

should rotate freely with one hand as you gradually tighten the tower bolts to 25—33 ft-lb (3.4—4.5 kg-m). If it doesn't, loosen the tower bolts, vertically strike the towers with a soft hammer, retighten the bolts and check again for ease of rotation. If this doesn't align the towers, the setup is not right. It will not "wear in." Bite the bullet and have the cam-bearing bores align-bored. Otherwise you risk destroying the cam and cam tower bearing surfaces.

VALVE GUIDES & VALVE STEMS

Valve-guide inspection and machining normally marks the beginning of hard-core, cylinder-head machine-shop work. This work includes valve, valve-guide and

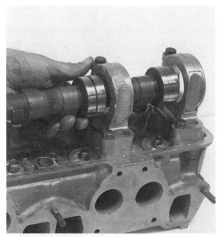

Oil bearings, then install cam and check for binding. Gradually tighten tower bolts checking cam rotation as you go. If cam binds, tap towers and recheck cam rotation. When cam rotates freely, final-torque bolts 25—33 ft-lb (34—45 N-m). Recheck cam rotation. Remove cam so it doesn't get damaged during valve-guide and seat work.

Experienced head rebuilders quickly check guide wear by the wiggle method. Valve is inserted in guide and wiggled up and down. Feel determines whether guides need work or not.

Next step up in guide-checking sophistication is measuring movement at valve head. Divide movement by 3 to get approximate stem-to-guide clearance.

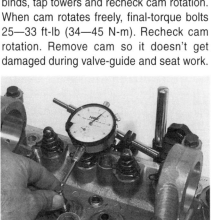

Wiggle movement can also be checked with dial indicator at tip end of valve.

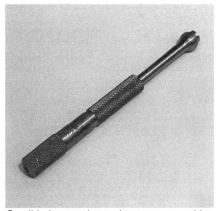

Small-hole gage is used to measure guides directly.

valve-seat reconditioning, and it requires special equipment and skills. If done incorrectly, it will ruin what would otherwise be a successful rebuild.

If a valve guide is badly worn, it won't *guide* the valve *squarely* onto its seat. The valve will wiggle and bounce from side to side before settling on the seat and closing. It may never close at high rpm, resulting in a compression loss. This condition doesn't improve with time. If not corrected, the seat eventually *beats out* and guide wear continues. Secondly, a worn guide allows excess oil to pass between the valve stem and guide, resulting in high oil consumption.

Let's look at reconditioning valves, valve seats and guides.

Checking Valve-Guide Wear—
Common methods of measuring valve-

guide wear include: *wiggling* the valve in the guide, with a dial indicator at the valve-stem tip, and with a *taper pilot,* or *ball-* or *small-hole gage* and a micrometer.

Wiggling a valve in its guide to determine guide wear requires a minimum amount of equipment. It's not the most accurate method, but it's good enough to determine whether the guides need attention. All you do is insert a valve in the guide—with its tip flush with the top of the guide—and wiggle the valve back and forth. Not very scientific, but this is the *first* method used by most engine rebuilders. They've developed a *feel* for how much wiggle is too much.

The first step up the "accuracy rung" is done by measuring *how much* the valve wiggles. Wiggle is measured at the valve head with the tip remaining flush with the

top end of the guide. Measure valve wiggle with a 6-in. machinist's scale or the depth-gage end of a vernier caliper. The amount of wiggle divided by three is the *approximate* stem-to-guide clearance in the direction of valve movement.

To check guide clearance with a dial indicator, install a valve in the guide. Mount the dial indicator 90° to the valve-stem tip in the direction you want to measure movement. It'll help to know that maximum wear occurs in the plane of the valve stem and the rocker-arm pivot. Move the valve about 1/8-in. off its seat and set the indicator tip—it should be a flat one—against the valve stem close to the top of the guide. Hold the stem away from the indicator and zero its dial. Push the tip end of the valve stem toward the dial indicator and read stem-to-guide clearance directly.

Using a taper pilot is the least-dependable way of determining guide wear. A taper pilot is a tapered pin, similar to that used to pilot stones for grinding valve seats, page 101. The pilot is inserted into the top or bottom end of the guide until it is snug. The diameter where the pilot stops is miked to determine guide diameter at that end of the guide. Measured diameter less the specified guide diameter is taken as the amount of guide wear—but it's not. The pilot measures the *minimum distance*

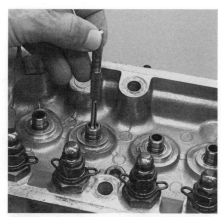

Expand ball gage while moving it up and down guide until slight drag is felt. Measure guides where they wear most—at top and bottom of guide.

Measure ball end with 1—2-in. mike to determine guide diameter. Stem-to-guide clearance of 0.004-in. (0.10mm) or more means guides are worn out.

of the guide rather than *maximum distance*. It's the maximum distance you are looking for, so don't use this method.

The most accurate method of determining guide wear is with a small-hole gage and micrometer. You'll need the C-gage for checking Nissan/Datsun guides. Unfortunately, small-hole gages are only sold in sets—cost is about $30. However, if you have access to one, or have decided to make the investment for a set of gages, here's how to use it.

Insert the ball end of the gage in the guide and expand it until it fits the guide with a *light drag*. The unworn section of a guide should measure 0.3150—0.3157 in. (8.008—8.018mm).

Check the guide bore at several places up and down and around the bore to locate maximum wear. After setting the gage, withdraw it and mike across the ball end. This is the exact distance across the guide-bore cross section at the point

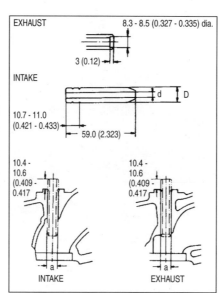

Intake- and exhaust-valve guides are shaped differently at bottom end. Check ends before installing. Also, they must come out top and go in top. Drawing courtesy Nissan.

you're checking. Subtract specified valve-stem diameter from this figure and you'll have maximum stem-to-guide clearance. Maximum wear will be found at the top and bottom of the guide. If the difference between maximum and minimum guide-bore wear, or *out-of-round*, exceeds 0.002 in. (0.05mm)—or 0.3177-in. (8.068mm) dia.—the guides should be reconditioned or replaced.

How Much Guide Clearance?—Maximum stem-to-guide clearance is 0.004 in. (0.10mm). Standard stem-to-guide clearance range is 0.0008—0.0021 in. (0.020—0.053mm) for intakes and 0.0016—0.0029 in. (0.040—0.073mm) for exhausts. The limit you set for guide wear should not be the maximum 0.004 in. (0.10mm) limit. It should be somewhere between the maximum figure and the *average* standard stem-to-guide clearance—an appropriate average of 0.0015 in. and 0.0020 in. for intakes and exhausts, respectively.

The number you decide on should be determined by the number of good miles you expect from your engine after the rebuild. By comparing the actual valve-guide clearance to the average standard clearance and the maximum wear limit, you can judge how many miles are left on the guides before the limit is exceeded. Or more importantly, you'll know when excess oil consumption and valve control will become a problem.

When deciding on a wear limit, keep

this in mind: As a valve stem and guide wear, they do so at an *increasing rate*. In other words, the more they are worn, the faster they wear. A guide and stem with 0.003 in. clearance may very well wear at twice the rate as one with 0.002-in. clearance. Consider the valve seats, too. A valve that is sloppy in its guide will wobble when closing, resulting in the seat getting beat out. Incidentally, valve-guide wear is higher in an engine used for stop-and-go driving, so all things considered, it takes good old horse sense when determining if it's time to recondition the guides.

Valve-Guide Reconditioning—You can restore valve guides by several different methods. These range from one I consider to be less than satisfactory to some that result in better-than-original valve guides In the order of increasing desirability knurling, new guides and guide inserts.

Guide Knurling—Knurling involves rolling a thread-like pattern into the existing guide to displace material. This reduces the guide's *effective ID,* making it smaller than the original guide. By effective diameter, I mean the diameter measured across the tops of the displaced material or *ridges* on one side, to the tops of the *ridges* on the other side. Because the valve guide is now effectively smaller, it must he reamed to standard size. This cuts off the ridges, or the tops of the spiral pattern created by knurling.

The problem with knurling is, it's the cheap way out. And as is usually the case, it's cheaper than it is effective. The reason it's ineffective is that the contact area between the guide and the valve stem is substantially reduced. The valve stem is now supported by the top of the knurled pattern only. This causes a proportionate increase in stem-to-guide contact pressure, causing increased stem and guide wear. Therefore, the problems caused by worn guides will not be cured, merely delayed. Don't use this method for reconditioning valve guides.

New Valve Guides—Installing new guides will restore the guides to as new condition—just as they were from the factory. This process involves removing the old valve guides, installing the new ones, then reaming the guides to size.

The old guides are pressed out the top of the head—from the combustion-chamber side toward the camshaft side. A stepped punch, a hammer or press and something to heat the head are needed for doing this job.

The punch should have two diameters: one that pilots in the guide and one that shoulders against it, but clears the head as the guide is driven or pressed out. A press will be required to install the new guides. Make the pilot diameter about 5/16 in., or 0.3125 in. (7.9mm); the large diameter should not exceed 7/16 in., or 0.4375 in. (11.1mm).

To make the job easier, heat the head to about 300F in an oven. Then support the head upside down so it's not on the cam towers. And make sure you leave room for the guides to come out. Use two 2x4s on edge or something similar. Wood is good because there will be little heat transfer from the aluminum—the head won't cool as fast.

Insert the punch in the first guide and drive or press it out. Reposition the supports as necessary and do this seven or 11 more times to complete the first half of the job.

After the head cools to room temperature—about 70F—ream the guide holes to 0.480 in. (12.2mm). This provides the necessary interference fit for the new *factory-service* valve guides. If using aftermarket guides, mike their OD. The holes should be reamed 0.0015 in. (0.04mm) smaller than the guides.

It's time to heat the head again. This time, heat it to 300—400F. After it's heated, support the head right-side up under the press ram—a press is needed to install the guides. Again, set it on some wood to slow cooling.

Sort the guides: exhaust and intake. Factory intake guides are tapered on the end opposite the lock ring. There may be no difference between aftermarket guides.

Lubricate the guide OD with anti-seize compound. Slip the guide over the stepped punch so the lock-ring end is against the punch shoulder. Press the guide into the head. When the lock ring bottoms against the top of the guide hole, stop. The guide is installed.

After all guides are installed, let the head cool. Finish guide installation by reaming them to size: 0.3150—0.3157 in. (8.000—8.018mm).

Valve-Guide Inserts—Valve-guide

Rather than replace guide, many rebuilders repair existing guides with thin-wall bronze inserts. To install insert, existing guide is first reamed oversize.

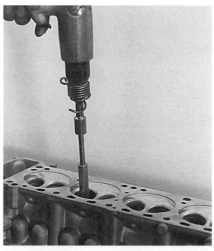

Insert is driven in from combustion-chamber side. If guide is replaced, it is driven out from chamber side with press or impact gun, as shown. In both cases, mandrel must be used. New guide is driven in from top side.

inserts can restore the guides to as-good-as or better-than-original condition, depending on the type used.

Inserts restore the guides to original condition. They are installed by driving them into place after machining the original guide to a diameter equal to the OD of the insert, less about 0.002 in. for an interference fit. This fit holds the new guide in place so it doesn't move up and down with the valve. After the guide is installed, it may or may not have to be reamed to size, depending on the way the insert is manufactured and installed.

Guide inserts come in two styles: *thread-in* and *press-in*. Thread-in inserts are similar to Heli-Coil replaceable threads except they are bronze and have a thread formed on their OD only.

To install the thread-type insert, the guide is threaded with a conventional tap. A sharp tap must be used or the guide insert will not seat completely when installed. As the engine accumulates miles, an insert that has not seated properly will increasingly shift up and down with the valve and pump oil into the combustion chamber. Consequently, this type of insert requires particular care during installation.

After tapping, the insert is threaded into the guide and expanded to lock it into place. This and the sharp tap ensures that there will be no insert movement. Expanding the insert also forces the back side of the insert into firm contact with the

After being driven in, thin-wall bronze inserts project from bottom end of guide. Excess is trimmed off after knurling.

original guide to ensure maximum exhaust valve stem-to-cylinder head heat transfer, or cooling. The guide is reamed to complete the installation.

The thin-wall bronze valve-guide insert is installed in a similar manner as the cast-iron insert. The existing guide is reamed oversize. Approximately 0.060-in. thick, it is installed with a special driver. Once in place, the guide is expanded and reamed to size using the *original* valve seat as a pilot to prevent *tilting* the valve guide. This should be done when reaming any type of guide. The guide is then trimmed flush with the original guide.

VALVE INSPECTION & RECONDITIONING

Now that the valve guides are in good shape, let's tend to the valves. You should

To lock inserts in place, knurling tool is run through them.

After knurling, inserts are reamed to size.

Begin valve-reconditioning process by cleaning. Thick coat of carbon on valve head hurts performance by restricting air flow and creates cold-start driveability problems.

Problem with this valve is obvious: Stem is bent. Such a valve must be replaced.

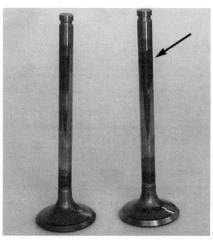

Dark portion at upper end of stem (arrow) indicates area of maximum wear. Valve at right has been faced.

have already checked them for obvious damage such as burnt heads and excessively worn stems.

Measure Valve-Stem Wear—All L-series engines use valves with nominal valve-stem diameters of 0.3139 in. (7.972mm) for the intakes and 0.3131 in. (7.952mm) for the exhausts. As you can see, the 0.0008 in. (0.020mm) smaller exhaust-valve stem gives the needed heat-expansion clearance. This allows intake- and exhaust-valve guide bores to be the same size.

Use the above figures as reference for checking stem wear. Or, compare the worn and unworn portion of each valve stem to determine exact wear. There's another point of high wear at the valve-head end, but maximum wear usually occurs at

the tip end of a valve.

You won't have any trouble recognizing this area. It is the bright-finish portion of the valve stem near the tip end. There's a sharp division between it and the matte finish unworn surface that extends to the tip. Maximum valve travel into its guide is represented by this division line. This is where a valve stops in its guide at its full-open position. If stem wear is significant, you'll be able to feel it by dragging a fingernail across this line.

You'll need a 1-in. micrometer to measure valve-stem wear. Measure the stem diameters immediately above and below the maximum-wear line. Subtract the two figures to determine stem wear.

Once you have a valve-stem-wear figure, you must decide if it's too much.

Again, this depends on the service you expect from your engine, if and how you reconditioned the guides, and a myriad of other questions. Arriving at an exact figure is virtually impossible.

If valves with more than 0.002 in. (0.05mm) wear are installed in guides that have more than the 0.004 in. (0.10mm) stem-to-guide-clearance limit; or if they are installed in guides reconditioned by knurling, the time spent on head work could've been saved by leaving the heads alone.

Knurling is a "patch 'em up" fix rather than a true rebuilding method. Think of it as wrapping tape around a radiator hose to repair a leak instead of replacing the hose. The problem is not cured, it's just delayed. On the other hand, new valves or used ones with no more than 0.001 in. (0.02mm) stem wear installed in guides reconditioned with bronze inserts should provide excellent service.

My suggestion is to use valves with no *more* than 0.002 in. (0.05mm) stem wear in new guide bores. Set this as your *absolute* minimum when deciding on which avenue to take when dealing with valve-stem and valve-guide wear. This should give you *at least half* the durability of new valves and guides.

Grind Valves—Assuming your valves checked OK, have them reconditioned. Grind their *faces*. The face is the surface on the valve head that contacts the valve seat. A perfect seal must exist at both valve faces and seats to seal each combustion chamber when its valves are closed. The face must center on the stem after it is ground. If not, the valve will not seal against its seat.

Valve faces are ground while the valve is rotated in a *collet-type chuck* against a fast-turning grinding wheel. The valve is held at a 45-1/2° angle to the wheel. The 1/2° interference provides a positive seal against the 45° valve seat.

As the valve face rotates by the collet chuck against the wheel's rotation, it is also oscillated across the face of the grinding wheel. Simultaneously, the valve and stone are bathed in cutting oil for cooling and to wash away the metal and abrasive particles. *Only* enough face material is removed to expose new metal on the valve face. If too much is removed, the valve's *margin* will be thinned excessively and the valve will have to be replaced.

Valve margin is the valve-head thickness at the OD of the valve face. A valve head with little or no margin has a knife-like edge and must be replaced. Otherwise, it's highly susceptible to burning, particularly if it's an exhaust valve. The minimum margin for an exhaust valve is 0.020 in. (0.5mm). Because an intake doesn't operate as hot as an exhaust valve, its margin can be as narrow as 0.015 in. (0.4mm).

After all the valves have been ground or replaced, they should be as good as new and ready for assembly into the cylinder heads. All you have to do is get the heads ready. It's now unnecessary to keep the valves in order because all original mating surfaces have been machined.

VALVE SEATS

Valve seats are reconditioned in a manner similar to the valves—by grinding. In some cases they are *cut* or machined with milling machine-type cutters.

However, before we get into reconditioning valve seats, let's look at something more involved—replacing a seat.

Because L-series cylinder heads are aluminum, valve-seat *inserts* must be used. Rings of sintered iron or aluminum-bronze inserts are used for intake-valve seats; steel is used under the exhaust valves. If an insert can't be reconditioned for some reason—cracked, excessively pitted or worn—it must be replaced.

Replacing valve seats is a job for a

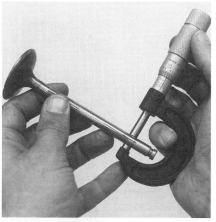

To check valve-stem wear, measure point of maximum wear . . .

. . . then compare to area that has no wear. Measure stem at several points to find maximum wear. No wear occurs immediately below keeper groove.

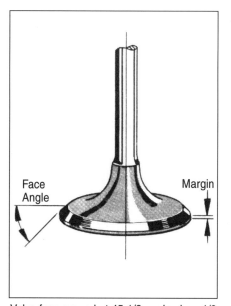

Valve face ground at 45-1/2 angle gives 1/2 interference with 45 seat to ensure positive sealing. Replace valve if margin is less than 0.015 in. (0.4mm) or 0.020 in. (0.8mm) for intakes or exhausts, respectively.

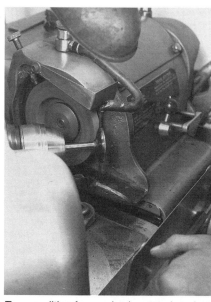

To recondition face, valve is rotated against spinning grinding stone as oil washes away metal and abrasive particles. Only enough material is removed to expose a uniform new surface.

cylinder-head or engine machine shop. Read on and you'll understand why.

Remove Seat—To replace a valve-seat insert, the first job is to remove the old one. Fortunately, intake-valve seats need to be replaced more often than the exhausts. Sintered-iron or aluminum-bronze inserts are relatively soft when compared to steel exhaust-valve seats. Steel exhaust-valve seats are very hard, making them hard to remove. They approach the hardness of the cutters used to remove them. Therefore, carbide cutters are essential.

The standard way of removing a valve-seat insert is to set up the cylinder head in a *seat-and-guide machine,* then machine or cut the seat out. Care has to be taken so only the seat is cut, not its aluminum counterbore. Consequently, the cutter can't be too large or run in too far. Once sufficient material is removed, the insert will collapse and it can then be removed.

One trick some engine rebuilders use to remove the hard exhaust-valve seats doesn't employ cutters. Instead, an electric welder is used to run a small weld bead around the seat. As the bead cools, it

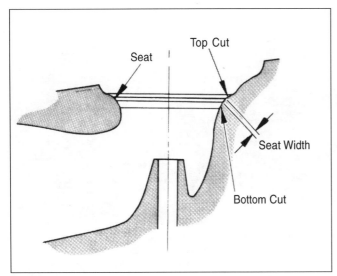

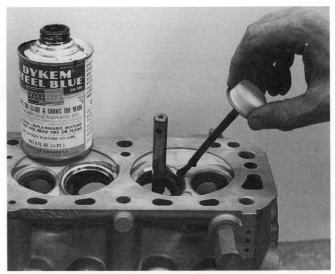

Three-angle valve job: Seats are ground to 45° angle, bottom cut to 60° and top cut 30°. Widths are 0.055—0.063 in. (1.4—1.6mm) for intakes and 0.071—0.079 in. (1.8—2.0mm) for exhausts. Wide exhaust-valve seat gives more valve-to-seat contact area for better heat transfer.

Machinist's blue is used to contrast freshly ground seat from other angles. Measuring seat width and diameters is much easier.

Replacement valve seat: If bronze-alloy intake-valve seats are used, replace them with sintered-iron or steel seats. Photo by Ron Sessions.

shrinks the seat and eliminates the press fit. The seat can then be lifted out!

Before the weld bead is applied, a protective coating must be applied to the combustion-chamber side to prevent weld spatter from sticking to the aluminum. Anti-spatter compound is available at welding-supply stores. Or, there's something that is much less expensive, works well and is readily available. It's Pam®. Pam can be picked up at the local grocery store. The head is simply sprayed to protect it before welding.

Back to using the cutter method of

removing a valve seat: If a seat-and-guide machine is not available, the same thing can be accomplished with a die grinder *if it's done very carefully.* The valve-seat counterbore must not be damaged.

Counterbore Size—Once the damaged seat is out, a new insert can be installed. This is where special equipment is a must. The counterbore must be sized so the seat insert will have the correct interference fit. Interference for intake valves is 0.0032—0.0044 in. (0.081—0.113mm); for exhausts, it's 0.0025—0.0038 in. (0.0025—0.0038mm).

To determine the proper counterbore diameter, measure valve seat-insert OD and subtract the specified interference fit. For example, if an intake valve-seat insert measures 1.792 in. (45.5mm), subtract the specified nominal interference of 0.0038 in. (0.097mm). Using these figures, 1.792-0.0038 in. = 1.754 in. (45.6mm). If the bore measures this, the insert can be installed. However, if the counterbore is damaged or enlarged, 0.020 in. (0.5mm) oversize inserts are available. The counterbore can be machined accordingly and the oversize seat installed.

As for how deep a counterbore should be, the answer is simple; same as the insert is thick. Counterbore depth will be about 0.0266 in. (6.7mm) for intakes and 0.293 in. (7.4mm) for exhausts. Machining a counterbore deeper should be unnecessary. Regardless, measure the insert and

counterbore to be sure.

If an insert counterbore needs to be machined, the cutter must pilot off the valve-guide bore. This is because the insert—and eventually the valve seat—must be concentric with the guide.

Install Valve-Seat Insert—A kitchen has all the equipment that's needed for installing a valve-seat insert. If you're thinking what I'm thinking, all you need is permission from the keeper of the kitchen. The only thing you may have trouble with is getting a six-cylinder head in and out of the oven.

Heat the cylinder head to about 350F in the oven. Don't let it exceed 390F. Heating to 350F expands the diameter of the counterbore, allowing the insert to drop into place. Another thing it will do is heat the cylinder head throughout and at the same rate. This lessens the chance of warping the head; a likely possibility if a torch is used.

If you must use a torch, prevent warpage by playing the flame over the entire head so temperature increases gradually. In addition, mark the head with 350F *temperature-indicating* crayon so you'll know when the head is up to temperature. When the rated temperature is reached—350F in this case—the crayon mark will melt.

Check at your local welding-supply store for temperature-indicating crayons. If they don't have what you need, write to:

Big Three Industries, Inc., 2901 Hamilton Boulevard, South Plainfield, NJ 07080. Ask them for a 350F Tempilstik®.

Besides heating the head, there's one more thing you can do—cool the valve-seat insert. Shrink its OD by placing the insert in the refrigerator freezer.

Once head and insert temperatures are stable, remove them from the oven and refrigerator and install the insert. *Make sure the valve seat is facing away from the combustion chamber before you drop the insert in place.* When the cylinder-head and insert temperatures converge, the interference fit will return, locking the insert in place.

Stake Insert—As insurance, mechanically lock the insert in place. Do this by *staking* it with a centerpunch. To stake an insert, centerpunch its OD in four places. The centerpunch marks should be centered on the parting line between the seat OD and insert counterbore. Arbitrarily choose a 12 o'clock position for the first stake. Centerpunch the insert three more times: at the 3:00, 6:00 and 9:00 o'clock positions. Once the insert is staked in place, proceed with *cutting the seats.*

RECONDITION VALVE SEATS

Valve-seat reconditioning equipment is special, expensive and requires skill and experience to operate. This is a job for the specialist and it's an essential part of every rebuild. Seat reconditioning is necessary if the guides were reconditioned or replaced. This is because the seats won't be *concentric* with the new guide bores—they won't have the same centers. Consequently, even though a valve seat may be in good condition, the guide won't allow the valve to seat fully when it's closed. Rather, it will be held off-center in relation to the seat. This is corrected when the seat is ground. A new valve-seat insert must also be ground.

A mandrel centered in the valve guide supports the valve-seat grinding stone or cutter. This is similar to the requirements for an insert-counterbore cutter.

Cutting Valve Seats—Valve seats are ground or machined using a manual, electric- or air-powered grinder, or hand- or machine-powered cutter alternating between three grinding stones or cutters with angles of 30°, 45° and 60°.

The critical angle, 45°, is the valve-seat

Valve-seat-grinding stone pilots on mandrel inserted into valve guide.

angle. If the 45° figure strikes you wrong, it's because the valve faces were ground to a 45° 30' angle. The 1/2° difference provides an edge-contact at the outer periphery of the valve face so the valve seals the first time it closes. Leakage due to poor seating can cause a warped valve, or a burned valve and seat.

The other two angles, 30° and 60°, are the *top cut* and the *bottom cut,* respectively. The 30° and 60° angles are important for low valve-lift airflow.

The 30° top cut on the combustion-chamber side trues and establishes the seat's outside diameter. The 60° bottom cut on the port side of the valve establishes seat ID, but more importantly, valve-seat width. Valve-seat OD should be ground approximately l/16 in. smaller than the valve-face OD. After the 30° top cut is made to establish seat OD, the valve seat is narrowed to the desired width with the 60° bottom cut.

Make intake valve-seat width 0.055—0.063 in. (1.4—1.6mm). Exhaust-valve seats should measure 0.071—0.079 in. (1.8—2.0mm) wide. The wider exhaust-valve seat makes for more valve-to-seat contact area to increase valve-to-head heat transfer. This, in turn, makes for cooler operating exhaust valves.

Tools that should be on hand to assist reconditioning, other than the actual grinding or machining equipment, are: a set of dividers, layout dye or machinist's blue and a 6-in. scale for setting the dividers for measuring seat OD. A special

Stone is placed over mandrel, then spun against seat with power tool to grind seat and top or bottom angles.

dial indicator for checking valve-seat concentricity is not necessary, but desirable. Bluing allows the seat to show up as a dark ring contrasted against the brightly finished top and bottom cuts. This makes the seat much easier to see and measure.

Hand-Lapping Valves—The process of manually grinding a valve face and its seat *together with lapping compound* is called *lapping.* Compound or paste is applied to the valve face, then the valve is oscillated in a circular motion while applying light pressure to the valve head.

I'm mentioning valve lapping in case you are aware of the process and think it is necessary for valve sealing. Generally speaking, if a valve face and its seat aren't ground correctly, lapping won't fix the problem, and if they are done right, lapping shouldn't be necessary for proper valve seating and sealing. So don't waste your time with lapping. A reputable rebuilder is your best guarantee for valves that seal.

If you do lap the valves, be sure to clean off *all* lapping compound when you are finished. Grinding compound and engines do not make good traveling companions. When you finish lapping each valve, mark it so you can put it back on the same seat.

Do They Seal?—Now that we are on the question of valve sealing, wouldn't it be nice to know if the valves will seal after you install the head on your engine? If one or more valves doesn't seal, now is the time to do something about it.

To determine if the valves will seal

Intake-valve seats are ground; exhausts are next.

Valve-seat concentricity and runout relative to guide is checked with runout gage.

Valve-seat runout and concentricity can be checked by lapping. Equipment is inexpensive. All that's needed is stick with suction cup and lapping paste. After applying paste to valve face, valve is rotated back and forth against seat with lapping stick. After lapping, keep valves in order.

when you first start your engine, start by installing the valves in the head. You can take two approaches to this. Do it now, then disassemble the heads for checking and setting up the valve springs. Or, complete the valve-spring checking and setting-up as outlined starting on page 103. Then assemble the valves in the heads and check them for sealing. Regardless of the route you take, here's how to check valve sealing.

With the valves and spark plugs installed, position the head upside down so the head-gasket surface is level. Using kerosene, fill each combustion chamber and check inside the ports for leaks. Use a penlight flashlight so you'll have a good view. If you don't see any moisture, consider the valves OK. Otherwise, note which valve(s) are leaking, then confer with your rebuilder to determine what the sealing problem is. Have him correct the problem.

A LESSON ABOUT VALVE SPRINGS

After the head and valves have been completely inspected and reconditioned, the valve springs are next. A valve-spring tester helps, but it's not absolutely necessary. However, it's helpful to understand what's involved in testing valve springs. Also, you should be familiar with some valve-spring terms and the importance of maintaining certain standards. Common terms are: *spring rate, free height, load at installed height, load at open height and solid height.*

Spring Rate—Spring rate usually isn't listed with valve-spring specifications. but it has a direct bearing on most of the other specifications. Also, it's one of the basic terms necessary to describe a spring's mechanical properties.

Spring rate governs the load exerted by a spring when it is compressed a given amount. Rate is usually expressed in so many pounds-per-inch of deflection. In terms of a valve spring, the more you compress it, the more it resists. A typical L-series valve-spring rate is 150 1b/in. for the outer spring. If it's compressed 1.00 in., it will exert 150 lb.

VALVE-SPRING SPECIFICATIONS			
Engine	Length In. (mm) Outer/Inner	Installed Ht @ Load In. @ lb (mm @ kg) Outer/Inner	Open Ht @ Load In. @ lb (mm @ kg) Outer/Inner	Out-of-Square Limit In. (mm) Outer/Inner
L13	1.89/None (48.1/None)	1.57 @ 68/None (40.0 @ 31/None)	1.18 @ 157/None (30.0 @ 71/None)	0.087/None (2.2/None)
L16	1.97/1.77 (50.0/44.8)	1.57 @ 47/1.38 @ 27 (40.0 @ 21/35.0 @ 12)	1.16 @ 108/0.96 @ 56 (29.5 @ 49/24.5 @ 25)	0.087/0.047 (2.2/1.2)
L18	1.97/1.77 (50.0/44.8)	1.57 @ 47/1.38 @ 27 (40.0 @ 21/35.0 @ 12)	1.16 @ 108/0.96 @ 56 (29.5 @ 49/24.5 @ 25)	0.087/0.047 (2.2/1.2)
L20A	2.05/1.97 (52.0/50.0)	1.53 @ 64/1.45 @ 29 (38.9 @ 29/36.9 @ 13)	1.21 @ 105/1.13 @ 47 (30.7 @ 48/28.7 @ 21)	0.087/0.047 (2.2/1.2)
L20B	1.97/1.77 (50.0/44.8)	1.57 @ 47/1.38 @ 27 (40.0 @ 21/35.0 @ 12)	1.16 @ 108/0.96 @ 56 (29.5 @ 49/24.5 @ 25)	0.087/0.047 (2.2/1.2)
L24 (Sing. Carb)	1.88/1.76 (47.8/44.8)	1.57 @ 37/1.38 @ 21 (40.0 @ 21/35.0 @ 12)	1.18 @ 95/0.98 @ 43 (30.0 @ 43/25.0 @ 19)	0.087/0.047 (2.2/1.2)
L24 (Twin Carb)	1.97/1.76 (50.0/44.8)	1.57 @ 47/1.38 @ 27 (40.0 @ 16/35.0 @ 10)	1.16 @ 108 0.96 @ 56 (29.5 @ 49/24.5 @ 25)	0.087/0.047 (2.2/1.2)
L26	1.97/1.76 (50.0/44.8)	1.57 @ 47/1.38 @ 27 (40.0 @ 21/35.0 @ 12)	1.16 @ 108/0.96 @ 56 (29.5 @ 49/24.5 @ 25)	0.087/0.047 (2.2/1.2)
L28	1.97/1.76 (50.0/44.8)	1.57 @ 47/1.38 @ 27 (40.0 @ 21/35.0 @ 12)	1.16 @ 108/0.96 @ 56 (29.5 @ 49/24.5 @ 25)	0.087/0.047 (2.2/1.2)

Certain spring loads are necessary to control valve-train inertia generated at high engine rpm. Increased spring loads are required just to close the valves, or keep them from *floating* when an engine is operated at high rpm. If a valve spring loses its rate, or *resiliency,* it is no longer capable of closing its valve at or near maximum-rated rpm. A spring that isn't compressed far enough when it is installed will have the same effect.

Free Height—Free height is the length of a valve spring at its unloaded height or length. If a spring's free height is too long or too short, the load exerted by the spring as installed in an engine will be incorrect because it will be compressed more or less by the spring retainer. Therefore, knowing what spring rate is in addition to free height gives you a clue as to why a spring does or doesn't meet its specifications.

Load at Installed Height—A spring's load at its installed height is a common spring specification. *Installed height* is spring height as installed in the cylinder head; measured with the valve closed. This is the distance from the cylinder-head spring seat to the underside of the spring retainer.

When a spring is compressed some amount, it requires a given force to do so. As mentioned previously, a typical valve-spring rate for an L-series engine is 150 lb/in. for the outer spring and 70 lb/in. for the inner spring. For example, if the outer spring is compressed 0.300 in. from its relaxed height—*free height*—to its installed height, it will have an installed load of 45.0 lb, or 150 lb/in. x 0.300 in. = 45.0 lb. This is typical of an outer spring.

The absolute minimum installed load is 10% less than the lower load limit, or 41 lb in this case. If a spring does not exceed or at least meet the minimum, it should be replaced. If your engine will be operated at its upper rpm limit, or is a high-performance model, make sure valve-spring load at least meets the *minimum* standard limit.

Load at Open Height—Another commonly listed specification is the load a spring exerts when the valve is fully open. Continuing the above example, if valve lift is 0.414 in., spring load is increased 150 lb/in. x 0.414 in. = 62.1 lb. Add the installed load of 45.0 lb to this amount and total spring load becomes 107.1 lb, typical

of an outer spring's *open load.*

Just as with the installed-height load, a spring must fall within the 10% minimum load limit or be replaced. In this case, the minimum is 96 lb. Again, consider what rpm your engine will be operated at when checking valve springs.

Solid Height—Solid height is the height of a coil spring when it is compressed so each coil touches the adjacent coil; it cannot be compressed any farther. The spring is said to *coil bind* or *go solid.*

Coil springs should never be compressed to their solid heights. If a valve spring were to reach solid height before its valve is fully opened, the load on the valve train would theoretically approach infinity. Before this could happen, the weakest component in the valve train would fail—something bends or breaks—probably a rocker arm.

Squareness—Valve-spring *squareness* is how straight a spring stands on a flat surface, or how much it *tilts.* How you look at valve-spring squareness depends on whether you are an optimist or a pessimist. In either case, it is desirable for a spring to be square so it loads the spring retainer evenly around its full circumference.

Uneven retainer loading increases stem and guide wear because the spring tries to force the valve sideways, or out-of-square—something you should minimize. You only need to check the outer spring for squareness.

INSPECT VALVE SPRINGS

Of the spring characteristics just discussed, the ones that should be checked are squareness, and installed and open spring loads. You must also make sure the spring doesn't reach its solid height.

Squareness—A flat surface, square and something to measure with are all that's required to check spring squareness. As pictured, setting the spring in the crotch of a carpenter's framing square works well. When you have the spring positioned, rotate it against the square to determine its maximum *tilt,* or gap from the top coil to the square. Measure this gap. If it exceeds 1/16 in. (1.6mm), replace the spring.

Spring Tester—As for the last two checks, a valve-spring tester is required. A spring tester allows you to compress a spring to its opened or installed height and read its load directly. Unless you've inher-

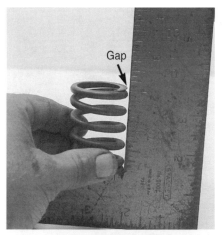

Check spring squareness. Rotate spring against corner of square until largest gap appears at top. If gap is 1/16 in. (1.6mm) or more, replace spring.

Quick spring check is to compare free height of springs. Spring at left has obviously sagged. It was on the exhaust valve.

ited an engine machine shop, chances are you don't have one of these expensive devices. The type pictured will eliminate a good portion of a $1000 bill.

Fortunately, there is a valve-spring tester that is within the average do-it-yourselfer's price range. Although not as convenient to use, all you'll need, in addition to the tester, is a vise and a pair of vernier calipers.

Clamp the spring and tester in the vise compress the spring to its installed or opened height—as measured with the calipers—and read spring load directly from the *pressure gauge.* A piston with a 1-square-in. surface area is used with a gage that is calibrated in psi, resulting in readings in pounds. Neat!

If your local auto-parts dealer or speed shop doesn't have such a tester, it is available from: C-2 Sales & Service, Box 70,

Check spring installed load by compressing to installed height. Shim as necessary to restore spring load, but check that spring does not bind by compressing to open height. Check inner springs and outers. Keep valves and shims in order.

Selma, OR 97538; or Goodson, 4500 West 6th Street, Winona, MN 55987.

The question is, "How do I check spring load if I don't have a spring tester?" The answer is simple: You don't!

Measure Free Height—Fortunately, a simple method can be used to determine if a spring can be reused: Compare its free height to what is specified. A spring that has been fatigued or overheated, usually from engine overheating, will *sag* or collapse somewhat. This is reflected in a spring's free height. A sagged spring's load is reduced in the installed and open position, or height.

Also, when a spring is removed from its cylinder head, it will not return to its original or specified free height. Use the valve-spring chart to determine what the free height of your springs should be, then measure them. Generally, a valve spring within 0.0625 in. (1.6mm) of its specified free height is acceptable to reuse.

Valve Spring—Replace or Not to Replace?—A typical small-displacement engine—compared to a big-displacement U.S.-built engine—must have valve springs

that are in good condition. The reason is simple. The typical V8 can be lugged at low rpm and still develop enough power to pull the vehicle. Valve float may never become a consideration. On the other hand, a small-displacement engine must be revved to higher rpm to develop the needed power in normal vehicle operation. This requires valve springs that are in top condition. Consequently, I replace any spring that is 1/16-in. shorter than its specified free height.

Whether or not you replace a spring should be based on what you'll be using your engine for and how far out of spec the spring is. If it's going to be used for puttering around town, you probably can get by with marginal springs. This is not the case, though, if the engine is to be constantly operated at or near peak rpm. Those slightly sagged springs will get progressively weaker. In turn, the valves with weak springs will float, limiting engine rpm to a lower speed than you can live with.

Shims—If your engine is to be used for severe service, the springs should be tested on a spring tester to determine if they can be corrected by *shimming*—placing a shim or *spacer* under the weak springs. This causes each spring to be compressed more at installed and open heights. Shim the outer springs only.

Beware: If not used carefully, shims can cause severe valve-train damage by forcing the spring to go solid, or *coil bind*. There's another problem to consider when using valve-spring shims. The springs were designed to be compressed a certain amount *continuously*. If this amount is exceeded, a shimmed spring will be overstressed, resulting in overworking, or fatiguing. The spring will quickly lose its load-producing capability, or resilience. So, if you have a questionable spring, replace it. When you shim a spring, attach the shim to the spring with some wire, string or whatever. If you don't and the shims get mixed up, you'll have to recheck the springs.

INSTALL VALVES

Now that the cylinder head, valves and springs have been inspected and/or reconditioned, you can get them all back together again—sort of like Humpty Dumpty. Except in this case, you won't need the

King's Horses or Men, just a valve-spring compressor and a ruler, plus some valve-spring shims—maybe. Yes, you may still have to install shims even though you didn't have to use them to restore spring load.

Valve-Spring Installed Height—One of the valve-spring loads you checked was at installed height. This, again, is the height the spring should be with the valve closed, and the spring, valve, retainer and shim(s) installed.

Note: *Shims used to correct spring load must be included in spring installed height.* Installed height *does not include the hardened-steel spring* seat that goes between the spring and cylinder-head spring pad; there's one for each inner and outer spring. Make sure every spring is at its correct installed height when installed. Otherwise, it won't achieve its specified installed or opened loads.

A valve stem projects out the top of its guide a certain amount when the valve is closed. How much the stem projects from its guide establishes the distance from the underside of the spring retainer—when installed on the stem—to the spring seat on the cylinder head. It should correspond to spring installed height. This distance changes as work is done on the valve seat and valve face. When material is removed from a valve face or seat, retainer-to-spring seat distance increases.

If your cylinder head's valve faces and seats were in good condition, only a small amount of material should've been removed to clean them up. This being the case, retainer-to-head distance shouldn't have been affected to any great degree. On the other hand, if additional work was done, this distance should be checked.

Spring Retainer-to-Spring Seat—Installed spring height can be checked by two methods: by trial-fitting the valve, or after installing the valve with its springs and shims.

To check installed height by trial-fitting the valves, simply insert each valve in its guide, then assemble the retainer and keepers on the stem *without the springs*. Lift up on the retainer to close the valve and to keep the retainer and keepers from falling down the stem. Now, measure seat-to-retainer distance. To get an accurate reading, lift up firmly on the retainer to force the valve against its seat and keep the retainer and keepers in place.

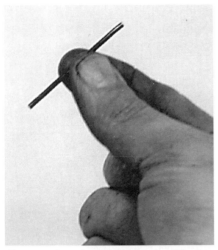

Short section of wire—coat hanger in this case—ground to correct length is handy for checking distance between spring seat and bottom side of spring retainer. Shim as necessary so spring will be compressed to correct height.

While lifting up firmly on spring retainer, insert checking wire between retainer and seat. Steel spring seat must be in place. Add shims at seat as necessary and recheck. Keep shims in order.

Valve, stem seal, inner and outer seats, spring, spring retainer and keepers ready to be installed in head. Some grease, oil and a spring compressor are all that's needed to do job.

Push stem seal over top of guides.

A telescoping gage or snap-gage and micrometers will give you the most accurate reading when making this measurement. However, you can do an adequate job with a 6-in. scale, providing you have a sharp eye. A neat trick is to cut, then file or and a short section of welding rod or heavy wire to the specified installed height of the spring. You can accurately check length with a micrometer. This will give you an accurate gage that, when placed between the spring seat and spring retainer, will show a gap the same thickness of the shim required to restore installed spring height. The shim that best fits between the rod, retainer and spring seat is the one to use.

If you don't have shims to check with, use feeler gages to determine shim thickness. Record this figure on a notepad so you'll have the information when it's time purchase the shims.

If you prefer measuring with a 6-in. ruler or telescoping gage and micrometer, subtract specified installed spring height from your retainer-to-spring-seat figure to determine shim thickness. For example, if you have a dimension of 1.610 in. 40.9mm) and specified installed height is 1.575 in. (40.9mm), shim thickness required to restore installed height is 1.610 - 1.575 in. = 0.035 in. (0.89mm). Though not a serious problem, adjustments can only be made in increments of 0.015 in.

(0.38mm).

Shims come 0.015, 0.030 and 0.060 in. thick. They can be stacked in varying combinations so you'll end up near the right overall thickness. Using the above example, a 0.030-in. shim must be used. This will bring the spring within 0.005 in. (0.12mm) of its specified installed height.

The second way to check seat-to-retainer distance varies from the first method only in that you install the spring, too. This means that you'll have to use the spring compressor to do so, but it does ensure that the reading will be accurate. You won't be able to use a *snap-gage* or anything between the retainer and the spring seat. One measuring device that works well here is a pair of vernier calipers. You can also use your less-accurate 6-in. scale. Measure the actual spring height by measuring from the spring pad to the top of the spring. Regardless of the method used, shim thickness is computed the same way—subtract *specified* installed spring height from the dimension you just measured. If the variation is less than 0.015 in., you don't need a shim.

When checking installed spring height, keep a record of the shims and their locations as you go along. Or better yet, line up the valves with their respective shims, springs and retainers over the valve stem in the exact order they will be installed in the head. You can just go down the line

when doing your assembly. Remember, you can mix up seals, retainers and keepers, but *springs, shims and valves must be installed in the position in which they were checked.*

After you've finished the installed-height check, use your list to purchase the necessary shims if you haven't already done so. Also, before installing the valves, make sure all parts are clean. Using your shim list, organize the shims with their valves.

Shims are sometimes color-coded according to their thickness. For example, V.S.I. uses the following color codes: black, 0.015 in.; silver, 0.030 in.; gold, 0.060 in.

Install Valves—Set the head on your workbench and organize the valves, springs and shims behind it in the order in which they will be installed. Start by installing all of the valve-stem seals. You'll find them in your gasket set. L-series engines use positive-sealing valve-stem

Apply grease to valve tip, dip stem in oil, . . .

. . . and slip valve into guide. Using a twisting motion, push valve through seal.

In this order, fit seats, shims (if used), springs and retainer over valve stem, then compress spring. Don't compress them more than necessary to install keepers.

Check that keepers (arrows) are firmly in place between valve tip and retainer.

If you removed rocker pivots, reinstall them. Run pivots all the way down. After all are installed, you can set rocker arms on pivots now or after cam is installed.

seals. To install each seal, position it over the end of the guide and push it on with your thumb. Do this seven or 11 more times. Now you're ready for the valves, springs and related hardware.

NOTE: If you are installing a high-lift camshaft, you must check to make certain that the bottom of the valve-spring retainer does not strike the top of the valve-stem seals at full lift. Allow at least 0.035-in (0.89mm) clearance.

To start the valve installation, coat the keeper groove with grease. This does two things: lubricates the stem tip so the valve will slip through its seal without causing damage, and holds the keepers to the valve while the spring compressor is being released.

With your oil can, shoot some oil into the guide bore and on the stem seal. put some on the valve stem, too. Now, slide the valve into its guide. When the tip

reaches the seal, rotate the valve and push it lightly through the seal. The keeper groove can tear the seal if you're not careful. Once the keeper groove is past the seal, push the valve closed. The seal will hold it there while you get the steel spring seats, springs and retainers and shims, if needed, installed.

Turn the head so the combustion-chamber side is facing you; don't lose track of which guides the valves and springs are mated to. Make sure the springs, retainers, keepers and spring compressor are close at hand. Now, position both springs over the stem and onto their seats. Fit the retainer over the stem and hold it there with one hand. With your other hand, fit the spring compressor over

the retainer and against the valve head. Check its adjustment so it doesn't over-compress the valve springs. Make sure the jaws of the compressor do not gouge the cam-cover-gasket or cam-tower mating surfaces.

Clamp down on the compressor no more than required for the retainer to clear the keeper groove. Fit two keepers into the groove, then slowly release the com-pressor. Guide the retainer over the keep-ers as you release the compressor so it doesn't nudge them out of their groove. When the compressor is released, set it aside and double-check that the keepers remained in the groove. If not, compress the spring and refit the keepers. Repeat this process until all valves are installed. When finished, lightly rap the retainer with a plastic hammer to ensure that the keep-ers have seated.

INSTALL ROCKER-ARM PIVOTS

If you removed the rocker-arm pivots, install them now. Make sure each is clean, particularly the threads. Also, run each jam nut all the way on.

Oil the threads, start the pivot in its bushing, then get out your speed handle and deep socket. Run the pivot into the jam nut.

After threading in the pivots, install the lash-spring retainers. One snaps in each rocker bushing; each goes in the groove immediately above the hex. Once they are in place, rotate the retainers so their ears point toward the valve springs.

Remember: If you are reusing the original cam, *the rockers and pivots must be reinstalled in their original positions*. If you don't do this, the cam and rockers will be wiped out. So, if you lost their order, they must be replaced. Also, *if a new cam is used, you must replace the rockers with new ones*. Rocker pivots can be reused and installed in any position on a new or used cam.

Slip the cylinder head into a plastic trash bag for now to keep it free of dust, dirt and moisture. You can get it back out when you're ready to install the camshaft and rocker arms.

INSPECT & INSTALL CAM

Before you install the cam, there are a few things to check first. Start by taking a final look at cam-lobe oiling. Then check camshaft end play.

Lubrication—If your cam is drilled for direct lobe lubrication, it should have a plug in the center of the rear cam journal. The sprocket bolt plugs the hole at the front. If the rear isn't plugged, you must install a plug. Otherwise, oil will pour from the back of the cam unrestricted and the engine won't develop oil pressure. It won't last long without oil.

If, however, your cylinder head is equipped with a spray bar, it's not necessary to have a cam that is drilled for direct lubrication. In fact, it's undesirable because this is more oil the pump has to circulate, possibly resulting in low oil pressure at high rpm. On the other hand, you must use a direct-lubricating cam if a spray bar isn't used.

If it's not possible or desirable to swap the direct-lubricating cam, you have another option. You can keep a direct-lubricating cam in a spray-bar head from robbing oil from the rest of the engine. Do his by plugging the oil holes in the bearing journals.

Drill and tap the holes for small socket-head setscrews. Run a bottoming tap in about 1/16 in. deeper than the setscrews are long. A piece of masking tape around the tap will tell you when the tap is in far enough. Check that the setscrews install below the bearing-journal surface. If they don't, remove them and run the tap in deeper.

Drill out the plug from the rear of the cam and flush the cam with solvent. You don't want metal chips caused by drilling and tapping to float around in the oil where they can do great damage, particularly between a cam lobe and rocker pad.

Now, you can install the setscrews. Put Loctite on their threads and run them in tight. Don't bother with replacing the plug at the rear of the cam.

Camshaft End Play—Three items affect camshaft end play: camshaft, cam sprocket and camshaft thrust plate. If any of these wear or are changed, end play can change.

To check end play, install the cam sprocket on the cam with the thrust plate in between. You can do this on the bench.

Install the sprocket bolt and washer or fuel-pump eccentric. Snug the bolt so the sprocket will be firm against the cam nose. Using feeler gages, check the gap between the thrust plate and the front cam-bearing journal. This gap, which translates into end play, should be 0.0031—0.0150 in. (0.08—0.38mm). Excessive end play is rare, but if it exists, replace the thrust plate.

Install Cam—If you haven't already installed the cam, get the cylinder head out of the bag and do it now. It should be as clean as it was before you bagged it up. To make cam installation easier, remove the sprocket from the cam.

Be careful of this one. If direct-oiling cam is used in direct-oiling head, make sure plug is in end of cam (arrow). Otherwise, oil will exit back of cam rather than lubricate valve train.

Check cam end play with feeler gages after temporarily installing thrust plate and sprocket on nose of cam. It should be 0.0031—0.0150 in. (0.08—0.38mm).

Oil cam bearings, then carefully install cam.

This is position cam-sprocket dowel should be in at TC; straight up and aligned with timing groove (arrow).

Although thread sizes are the same, cam-sprocket-bolt head is much smaller than one on crank-pulley bolt.

It's always a wise investment to install new sprockets with new chain, chain guides and tensioner.

If cam-drive components are new, install sprocket to cam with dowel in hole **1**. Note timing notch on sprocket hub aligned with thrust-plate groove (arrow). This sprocket is installed with dowel in hole **2** because performance cam is used. Advancing cam 4° from hole **1** to hole **2** moves power down in rpm range.

Using a paper towel, wipe the bearing journals and bearing bores to ensure that they are clean. Liberally lubricate the journals and bearings with GM's EOS or Ford's Engine Oil Conditioner.

Carefully insert the cam through the bearing bores. Don't bump the cam lobes into the bearings. The lobes are hard and the bearing bores are soft.

Install Thrust Plate—When the cam is in place, install the thrust plate. Note the timing mark on the thrust plate in the above photo. The mark installs to the front and on top. If you don't install it in this manner, you won't be able to time the camshaft to the engine. Using the two bolts and lock washers, secure the thrust plate to the number-1 cam tower. Torque the bolts 4—7 ft-lb (0.5—1.0 kg-m).

Install Cam Sprocket—The cam sprocket is installed now to keep the cam from moving longitudinally while the rocker arms are being installed. Should the cam move too far rearward after some rockers are installed, severe valve-train damage or personal injury could result.

Install the sprocket with its washer or fuel-pump eccentric. If you are replacing all cam-drive components, install the sprocket so number-1 dowel hole engages the cam-drive dowel. Otherwise, it does not matter because you'll probably have to remove the sprocket to retime the cam. The cam-timing process is discussed on page 131. Snug the bolt.

Install Rocker Arms—Now comes the tedious part of cylinder-head assembly—installing the rocker arms and checking rocker-arm *geometry*. Don't let that word scare you, just the consequences if it's not right.

ROCKER-ARM GEOMETRY

Geometry is only a fancy word for how a rocker arm, or more importantly, its cam-lobe pad sits in relation to the cam lobe. Some important things to know about rocker-arm geometry are how to change it and why it needs to be changed in the first place.

Let's review how a cam lobe opens the valve: As the cam lobe rotates and operates the rocker arm, which, in turn, opens and closes the valve, it wipes across the rocker-arm pad from its tip end to its pivot end. Where this wiped area or *contact patch* is in relation to the ends of the rocker pad is what we're interested in. *The rocker-arm contact patch must be centered—front to back—on the pad* for proper valve-train operation and cam, rocker-arm, valve and valve-guide durability. So you say, "If it was OK before the rebuild, why won't it be afterward?" The reason is that things have changed.

Remember the grinding you did on the valve seats and faces to recondition them? More or less, depending on how much grinding was done, the valve-stem tip now projects farther from the top of its guide. All things being the same, this will force the rocker arm closer to the cam lobe. But rocker arm-to-cam lobe clearance will be reduced.

To compensate, the rocker arm will have to be readjusted lower at its pivot end. As a result, the tip will now be higher and the pivot end lower, moving the contact patch toward the valve-tip end. Something has to be done to recenter the patch. Let's look at an opposite effect before looking at how to correct the problem.

If you installed a reground cam, material was removed from the cam lobes to expose new metal. However, this effectively increased rocker-to-lobe clearance. Thus, the pivot end of the rocker arm would have to be adjusted higher to reestablish the correct lash, or clearance. This moves the contact patch toward the pivot end of the rocker arm. Similar effects are encountered from milling the top of

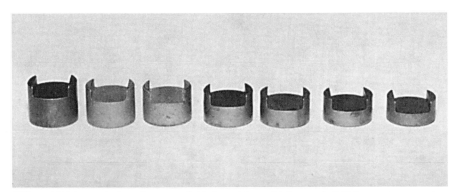

Different-thickness lash pads are available from Nissan Motorsports. Thicker pad moves wipe pattern toward rocker tip; thinner pad moves wipe pattern toward pivot. Using very tall lash pads (such as the four at left) requires using taller spring retainers that are available from Nissan. Photo by Frank Honsowetz.

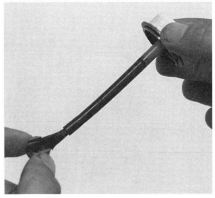

Apply machinist's blue to lash pad and rocker-arm wipe pad.

the head and shimming the cam towers.

A basic rule: **To center a cam-lobe contact patch, the rocker-arm end closest to the contact patch must be lowered and the other end raised.**
Lash Pads—Different-thickness *lash pads,* those funny looking slotted discs that install in the center of the valve-spring retainers between the valve tip and rocker arm, allow you to adjust rocker-arm geometry. For instance, if the tip extends farther out of its guide, forcing the valve-tip end of the rocker up, install a thinner lash pad to move it back down. And if the cam-lobe surface moves away from the rocker arm, for whatever reason, install a thicker lash pad.

Different-thickness lash pads are available from Nissan Motorsports and some aftermarket cam manufacturers. Those available from Nissan are 0.150 to 0.330 in. (3.85 to 8.5mm) thick in 0.010 in. (0.254mm) increments.

Now that you know that you can correct incorrect rocker-arm geometry, let's take a look at how to determine whether or not it needs to be corrected.

To check rocker geometry, you'll need some layout dye or a large black marker pen. You'll also need the assembly tools and materials used for installing rocker arms. This is because that is exactly what you have to do—install the rocker arms. You'll need moly grease, feeler gages and wrenches.

Find the lash caps and rocker arms. If you are installing the original rockers—

meaning you're installing the original cam—they must be installed in their original positions. However, you can put new rocker arms on any cam lobe, pivot or lash pad.

Install Rocker Arm—Work with each rocker arm one at a time. Using layout dye, coat the rocker-arm rub pad. Also coat the slotted side of the lash pad with dye. While you're waiting for the dye to dry, coat the cam lobes and rocker pivots with moly grease. Also lubricate the lash cap or *button* and the valve-tip end of the rocker you're checking first.

Install the lash cap, slotted side up, on its valve tip in the center of the valve-spring retainer. Double-check that the rocker pivot is threaded all the way in its bushing and the jam nut is up as far as it will go. You'll need all the available room to squeeze the rocker arm under the cam and onto its pivot and valve-stem tip.

Start by rotating the cam so the lobe heel is down and the toe is up. Doing this is easy for installing the first rocker, but it becomes increasingly difficult as rocker arms are installed. Then, to turn the cam, you'll need a socket and wrench on the sprocket bolt or an adjustable wrench on the *knobs*—two square bosses—at the center of the cam—for fours—or between the second and third bearing journal—for sixes. You'll also have to clamp the head to the bench to keep it from rolling over as you attempt to turn the cam. Support the head on two short 2x4s at the ends. Lightly clamp it immediately above one of the 2x4s.

Used rocker arm shows cam-lobe wipe pattern as it should be—centered on rocker wipe pad. This is what you should achieve with lash set to specifications and correct-thickness lash pad in place. Check rocker-arm geometry by first applying machinist's blue to wipe pad.

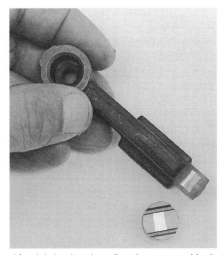

After lubricating, install rocker arm and lash pad, set lash, then rotate cam. Remove rocker arm and inspect. Wipe pattern at lash pad should look like this—centered. It should also be centered on cam-lobe wipe surface.

High-pressure lubricant such as molydisulphide (MoS$_2$) must be used to prelube cam. Most aftermarket cam manufacturers supply such lube with their cams. Lube cam lobes, rocker-arm tips, lash pads and rocker pivots.

If you are installing a new cam, also install all new rocker arms. Some Nissan/Datsun engine rebuilders don't do this. Don't make the same mistake.

Now, you're ready for the rocker arm. With a flat-tip screwdriver in one hand and the rocker arm in the other, fit the rocker under the cam lobe and place its valve end into the lash-cap slot. With the screwdriver, lever down on the valve-spring retainer, using the underside of the camshaft as a fulcrum. This should compress the valve spring and open the valve enough to allow you snap the pivot end of the rocker over the pivot by forcing it sideways with your thumb; see photo.

Set Valve Lash—Next on the list is setting valve lash. With the cam-lobe nose pointing away from the rocker arm, use a

Start by installing lash pads on their valves.

feeler gage between the heel of the lobe and the rocker rub pad. If it's an intake, set lash to 0.008 in. (0.20mm), set exhausts to 0.010 in. (0.25mm). Back the rocker pivot out with a 14mm open-end wrench until there's a slight drag on the gage. Snug the jam nut with one wrench while you hold the pivot with the other. You're now ready to wipe the pad.

Although you can determine whether a lobe is for an intake or exhaust valve by simply looking at the ports, the order for a four is E I I E E I I E; for a six, the order is E I I E I E E I E I I E.

Check Rocker-Arm Geometry— Using an adjustable wrench on the cam knobs or a socket on the sprocket bolt, rotate the cam two complete revolutions. Now, rotate the cam so the lobe points away from the rocker pad. Wipe the moly grease from both ends of the rocker pad so you can see the ends of the contact patch. If you're lucky, each end of the contact patch will be equidistant from its end of the pad. You can proceed with checking the next rocker arm. However, if it's closer to one end or the other, try a different lash pad.

If the contact patch is closer to the valve end of the pad, try the next thinnest pad. To change pads, you'll have to remove the rocker arm, re-dye it and the new lash pad, lubricate them and reinstall the rocker with the new lash pad. Repeat this exercise until rocker-arm geometry is right. Secure the jam nut so lash doesn't change.

While you have it nearby, check the wipe pattern on the original lash pad. If the cam-lobe contact patch was off center, so should be the rocker-arm wipe pattern

Lubricate rocker-arm pivots and cam lobes.

on the lash pad—and in the same direction. Centering the cam-lobe wipe pattern should also correct the wipe pattern on the lash pad.

Let's hope that the machinist who did the valve-and-seat work on your head *equalized* the stems—they should project from their guides an equal amount. If this is the case, the rest of the rocker-arm geometry-checking job should be relatively easy. If not, who knows?

The reason I say checking rocker geometry should be relatively easy with equalized valve stems is because all stem tips will have the same relationship to their cam lobes. Therefore, what you find to be correct for one rocker arm should hold true for all rockers. Consequently, the lash-cap thickness used for one rocker arm should work for all rocker arms.

This doesn't mean your geometry checking job is finished. On the contrary. It simply means that you shouldn't have to remove any rocker arms to refit different-thickness caps. All you should have to do is blue, lubricate and install caps and rocker arms, then make your confirmation checks. You should only have to install the remaining rocker arms once. However, if your valves weren't equalized, you're in for a long day.

After you've checked all rocker arms, install them, set valve lash and secure their pivot jam nuts. After you tighten each jam nut, recheck lash. It may have decreased because when the jam nut was tightened, it may have pulled the pivot up. So recheck and adjust as necessary. Now you're ready to complete cylinder-head assembly.

Lubricate rocker-arm tip and install rocker arm. Compress spring a slight amount and slip rocker onto pivot.

Rotate cam with wrench at square bosses.

Set valve lash as you go. Once desired clearance is set—0.20 in. (0.008mm) intakes; 0.24 in. (0.010mm) exhausts . . .

. . . . tighten pivot jam nut while holding pivot. Recheck lash and readjust if necessary.

To complete valve-train assembly, install lash spring. Hook under retaining spring, then lift into groove at pivot end of rocker arm.

Install Rocker-Arm Spring—Dig out the rocker-arm springs—the little mouse-trap-looking springs. Check that the spring retainers on the rocker-pivot bushings point toward the valve springs. To install the springs, hook the ends of each spring under the looped ends of the retainer. Then, force the spring up and over the pivot end of the rocker. Let the spring snap into the groove in the end of the rocker arm.

Time Camshaft—While you are working with the cylinder head, get it ready to install on the engine. This involves timing the camshaft, or setting number-1 cylinder on the power stroke.

Timing the cam is a relatively simple process. All you need to do is rotate the cam so the sprocket dowel aligns with the thrust-plate timing mark. The mark is below and slightly to the left of the top thrustplate bolt. If the sprocket is still on the cam, look through one of its lightening holes to find the timing mark. You can see the dowel through one of the three dowel holes in the sprocket.

Turn the cam with the sprocket bolt until the dowel aligns with—is below—the mark. The notch on the sprocket hub should align with the thrust-plate timing mark.

You're now finished with cylinder-head assembly. You'll next need the head when it's time to install it on the block. Slide it back into the plastic bag and store it under your workbench for now. Note that some valves will be open with their heads protruding below the head-gasket surface, so do *not* rest the head on the head-gasket surface.

CHAPTER EIGHT

Engine Assembly

Putting it back together is the rewarding part of engine rebuilding. All dirty and tedious jobs are over. To help ensure everything goes right, be organized and keep things clean.

To assemble your engine, you'll need an *overhaul* (complete) gasket set. This regrind gasket set must be combined with a conversion gasket set to make a complete overhaul set. You'll also need a set of 40mm core plugs.

This is *the* most pleasant part of engine building. Everything is clean, the parts are new or reconditioned and most of the hard work is behind you. The running around associated with getting parts and jobs done that you couldn't handle is just about over. It's time to assemble your engine.

Things You Need—Just like the jobs you've already done, there are additional items you'll need for assembling your engine. As you know, trash bags are useful for keeping parts clean. You'll need a big one for covering the block during assembly. You'll also need some assembly lubricant, a complete gasket set, gasket sealer, gasket or weather-strip adhesive and, maybe, a spray can of high-temperature aluminum paint or head-gasket sealer. Finally, you'll need a few special tools.

Gaskets—Rather than supplying complete gasket sets—*rebuild sets*—many gasket manufacturers supply a bottom-end—*lower* or *conversion*—set in combination with an upper—*valve-grind*—set. For example, Repco® sells a complete rebuild set; as pictured, Fel-Pro® does the same with two sets. The advantage of doing it by the two-set method is that users don't have to buy more gaskets than they need. Either way, it shouldn't make much difference to you.

Sealers—All sorts of sealers are available. I'll list a few that work particularly well in certain applications. First is room-temperature-vulcanizing (RTV) silicone sealer. It's great if used in the right place and in the right amount. Used incorrectly, it can break off and clog oil passages, leading to disaster. It's not a cure-all.

WARNING: The fumes (out-gassing) from incompletely cured silicone sealer in the intake or exhaust path can permanently damage O_2 sensors. So, if your car has an O_2 senser and you are working with silicone sealer in these areas, remove the O_2 sensor until the silicone has cured at least 24 hours.

You'll also want some non-hardening sealer such as Permatex® No. 2. Ford markets some fine sealers. Perfect Sealing Compound, B5A-19554-A, is a general-purpose sealer. Gasket and Seal Contact Adhesive, D7AZ- 19B508-A, is especially good for installing intake-manifold gaskets. Another good one for this purpose is OMC's (Outboard Marine Corporation) Adhesive Type M. You can also use weather-strip adhesive as a contact-type gasket adhesive. Just hope and pray you don't have to remove the gasket later.

Lubricants—Lubricants are a necessity when assembling an engine. How well an

Apply thin bead of silicone sealer to core-plug flange.

Install core plugs with hammer and punch, short section of pipe or socket about 1/16 in. smaller than inside of plug. Soft mallet will not damage socket.

Install core plugs with flange even with bottom edge of chamfer in block.

engine is lubricated during the first few minutes of running is critical to its durability. Remember this during the assembly process.

Lubricants you'll need include at least a quart of the oil you intend to use in your engine's crankcase—probably a multi-grade detergent type—a can of oil additive and some moly grease. As for the brand of oil to use, you decide. The brand isn't as important as the grade. So, regardless of the brand you use, grade SG is best.

In addition to crankcase oil, get a couple of cans of Ford's Oil Conditioner or GM's Engine Oil Supplement (EOS) for general engine assembly, initial bearing lubrication and to put in the first crankcase fill. Finally, fill a squirt can with motor oil.

Tools—You'll need some special tools other than those that normally reside in a toolbox. One of the most important is a torque wrench. *An engine cannot be assembled correctly without a torque wrench.* Even the most experienced mechanic doesn't rely on feel when tightening a critical nut or bolt. He uses a torque wrench. Put this tool at the top of your list.

Clean all of your sockets before you start assembly. Chances are they are full of crud from disassembly. Why put even a little of this back into your clean fresh engine?

Plastigage—I don't consider the next item to be necessary because bearings are made to such close tolerances. But it's a good idea to use *Plastigage®* as a check to

make sure you get the right bearings. It's not uncommon for the *wrong bearings* to be in the *right box.* Plastigage is a colored strip of wax used for checking assembled bearing-to-journal clearances. All you need to know about it at this point is that you'll need *green* Plastigage. It measures 0.001—0.003-in.   (0.0254—0.0762mm) clearances. Get one envelope or strip of *fresh* Plastigage—you won't need much. If it's not fresh, it won't be accurate.

ASSEMBLE BLOCK

Install Plugs—Two types of plugs install in the block: core plugs and oil-gallery plugs. There's also a block drain plug that you may have removed.

You'll need 40mm cup-type core plugs to seal the water-jacket core holes. These plugs go in the sides and ends of the block. As shown, core plugs are packaged for specific engines. If your engine machine shop doesn't have them, check with an auto-parts store.

Install Core Plugs—Although it's not essential to use sealer on core plugs, I do it just to be sure. Run a small bead of RTV sealer around the edge of the plug. With the flange pointing out, set the plug squarely over its hole—you should be looking *into* the concave side of the plug.

Use a mallet and large-diameter punch or socket to drive the plug into place. A punch about 1/16-in. smaller than the ID of the plug is ideal. Don't use a punch smaller than 1/2-in. diameter because it may distort the plug, causing it to leak. For the

Slug-type plugs install in block at ends of main oil gallery.

same reason, don't drive in a plug by hitting the edge of its flange.

Tap the plug into place. With a small punch, work around the inside edge of the plug, making sure it goes in squarely. When the outer edge of the plug is just past the inside edge of the hole chamfer—say 1/32 in.—the plug is in far enough.

Oil-Gallery Plugs—If you removed the main oil-gallery plugs—the ones that go in the front and rear faces of the block—install them now. You can either install the original 13mm (0.503-in.) slug-type plugs or pipe plugs. In either case, you should have the plugs on hand.

To install slug-type oil-gallery plugs, drive them into place with a hammer and punch. Sealer should not be necessary with these plugs. Drive in each plug so it's just behind the front surface of the block.

Note: Be careful that the front plug doesn't extend too far into the gallery. Otherwise, it will block off the oil gallery

Drive in plug—thread in if using pipe plug—until flush with front face of block. Plug at front must not cover oil gallery that branches off main gallery. Check its depth versus plug length before installing plug so this won't occur.

If you're using pipe plugs at ends of oil galleries, front plug must be flush or below front face of block and doesn't block oil gallery at other end. Photo by Frank Honsowetz.

Clean, then install crankcase-breather screen in block . . .

. . . and retain with baffle. Secure baffle with two Phillips-head screws and lock washers.

If chain oiler was removed—on engines so equipped—install it now. Position oiler so squirt hole aims at inside corner of left main-bearing parting line. Dot on oiler should point straight up.

that goes to the front of the cylinder head. Measure how deep the cylinder-head oil gallery hole is from the front face of the block, then shorten the plug if necessary.

If you are installing threaded pipe plugs, this is NOT the time to be tapping the holes. I explained how to do that back on page 52. If you decide at this time that you must have threaded pipe plugs then this block will have to be completely disassembled (again!) and recleaned. There are no shortcuts when it comes to getting the block oil passages totally clean. Fail in this and you can expect to buy a new crank and main and rod bearings.

Make sure you install them below the block surface. Don't use silicone sealer or Teflon tape on the plugs. A glob of sealer or a hunk of tape floating around in the lubrication system could ruin an otherwise

perfect rebuild if it restricts oil flow. Rather, seal the threads with a non-hardening sealer such as Permatex No. 2. Run the plugs in tight. If the front plug extends past the front face of the block, remove the plug and grind it down. Again, make sure it doesn't extend so far into the hole that it blocks off the cylinder-head oil gallery hole.

Drain Plug—If you removed the drain plug, seal its threads and run it in tight.

Replace Crankcase-Breather Baffle & Screen—Clean the breather baffle and screen if you haven't done so. The best way to do this is to soak the screen in carburetor cleaner. Just don't get the stuff on your skin. After soaking it for an hour or so, rinse off the carb cleaner with water.

Fit the screen into its pocket in the block. You'll have to roll the block over on its back to do this. Position the baffle over the screen and secure it with the two Phillips-head screws and lock washers.

Timing-Chain Oiler—If you removed the timing-chain oiler—on four-cylinder engines only—install it now. Position it in its hole in the front face of the block. The hole is immediately above and offset to the right of the front main-bearing bore as you look at the front of the block.

Position the oiler squirt hole, directing it at the chain-to-crankshaft sprocket crotch. This way the timing chain will receive maximum lubrication as it *engages* the crank sprocket. See the nearby photo. Note that the squirt hole is directed at the inside right corner—viewed from the front—of the number-1 main-bearing-cap parting line.

Once you have the oiler positioned, tap it into place with a punch and hammer. Don't use sealer. Drive it in until its shoulder bottoms.

Pressure-Relief Valve—The oil-filter pressure-relief valve is in the right side of the block, immediately rear of the oil-filter adapter. To check its spring, push in on the valve—the ball—with your thumb or a screwdriver. If there is noticeable resistance as it is pushed off its seat and the ball seats firmly after it's released, the spring is OK. If the valve doesn't have much resistance or doesn't reseat, the spring is probably broken.

To replace the spring, pry the relief-valve retaining washer out of the block with a screwdriver. Note the position of the retainer so you'll know how to reinstall

MAIN-BEARING IDENTIFICATION			
Engine	Journal Diameter (in./mm)	Journal Number	Bearing Length (in./mm)
L14, 16, 18	2.1631-2.1636/54.942-54.955	1, 5	1.027/26.00
		2, 4	0.949/24.00
		3*	1.258/32.00
L20B	2.3599-2.3604/59.942-59.955	1, 5	1.027/26.00
		2, 4	0.949/24.00
		3*	1.258/32.00
L20A, 24, 26, 28	2.1631-2.1636/54.942-54.955	1, 7	1.027/26.00
		2, 3, 5, 6	0.949/24.00
		4*	1.258/32.00

*Thrust bearing

STD—for standard—stamped on back side of bearing indicates bearing size. A **010** indicates 0.010-in. undersize—smaller ID—bearing.

it. This will free the relief-valve ball and spring. Be ready to catch the ball.

Pull the spring from its bore—both halves if it's broken. Get a new one at your Nissan dealer. Insert the new spring, compress it with the ball on top, and tap the retainer in place to secure the relief-valve assembly. Drive it in with a socket that just fits inside the valve bore and fully bears against the retainer.

CRANKSHAFT INSTALLATION

Turn your attention to the crankshaft, its bearings and rear-main oil seal. Choose the bearings according to the size of the main-bearing journals. You'll find the crankshaft seals in the rebuild or conversion gasket set.

Size Bearings—Refer to your crankshaft inspection records to determine which bearing size to use—standard, or 0.010 in. (0.25mm), 0.020 in. (0.50mm), 0.030in. (0.75mm), etc. undersize. Or get out your 2—3-in. mikes and recheck the journals. Except for the L20B, all L-series-engine main-bearing journals are the same size at 2.1631—2.1636 in. (54.942—54.955mm). The L20B standard main-bearing journals are 0.197 in. (5mm) bigger at 2.3599—2.3604 in. (59.942—59.955mm). Undersize bearings for the L20B come in the same increments.

While you're at it, also purchase the connecting-rod bearings. Except for the L24 Maxima, all L-series engines have the same size connecting-rod journals, or 1.9670—1.9675 in. (49.961—49.974mm). Maxima rod-journal diameter is 1.7701—

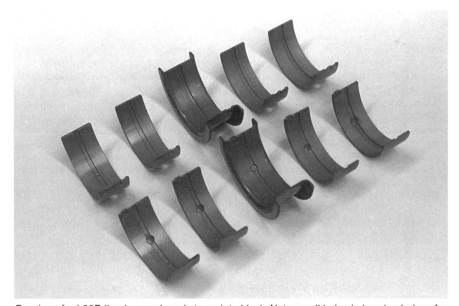

Bearings for L20B lined up and ready to go into block: Note small holes in bearing halves for number-1 journal. They also fit in rear bearing bore, so be careful. Hole is needed in insert at front that installs in block, not cap. It feeds chain oiler and tensioner. Note width difference between bearing inserts. Narrow inserts install in number-2 and -4 bearing bores in four-cylinder engines and number-2, -3, -5 and -6 bearing bores in sixes.

1.7706 in. (44.961—44.974mm). As with the mains, the rod bearings are available in undersizes of 0.010 in. (0.25mm), 0.020 in. (0.50mm), 0.030 in. (0.75mm), etc.

To determine which size bearings are needed, mike the journals. If the measurements fall within the standard range, get the standard bearings. However, if they mike some amount less, you'll need the same amount of bearing undersize as the difference from the standard nominal journal size, or average standard size.

For instance, if a bearing journal whose standard nominal size is 2.1634 in.

(54.948mm) measures at 2.1534 in. (54.722mm), use 0.010 in. (0.25mm) undersize bearings, or 2.1634 - 2.1534 = 0.010 in. (0.25mm). Just subtract the diameter of your bearing journals from the standard nominal bearing-journal diameter to determine undersize—if journal size does not fall in the standard-size range. Size is stamped on the backside of the bearing. It will say STD, 010, 020, etc. for standard, 0.010 in., 0.020 in., and so on.

Install Main-Bearing Inserts—With the engine block upside down, wipe the bearing bores clean so no dirt will get

CHECK BEARING OIL CLEARANCE

Cut strip of Plastigage to match journal length, then lay strip in place. Journals and bearing inserts should be free of oil. Install caps and torque to spec. Install the one you're checking last. Don't turn crank. Engine shown is not a Nissan/Datsun piece.

INSTALLATION METHOD

Oil clearance is the space between the bearing journal and bearing. More precisely, this is the difference between journal OD and bearing ID. Let's look at how to check main- and rod-bearing oil clearance.

Main Bearings—Install the crankshaft using the methods described in this chapter. With the crankshaft in place, the bearings and caps installed and bolts torqued to specification, rotate the crankshaft by hand. If it rotates freely, bearing clearances are sufficient. To check for excessive clearance, lift the crankshaft by its nose and try to wiggle it up and down. If you don't feel any movement, or play, clearance is not excessive and you can proceed with assembling your engine.

Connecting-Rod Bearings—Connecting-rod bearings should be checked with the crankshaft on the bench. This is because the piston cannot be assembled to its rod and in its bore for the check. Out of the bore, but in the block is too awkward.

With the crank on the bench, install the rod on its journal. Torque the rod-bolt nuts: 8mm nuts get 20—24 ft-lb (2.8—3.3 kg-m) and 9mm nuts get 33—40 ft-lb (4.4—5.4 kg-m). Rotate the rod on its journal. If it's free to rotate and there's no side-to-side wiggle, the bearings are OK.

PLASTIGAGE METHOD

Plastigage is a strip of wax that, when installed between a bearing and its journal, flattens or squeezes out to a width inversely proportional to the clearance between the journal and the bearing. Wider Plastigage means less oil clearance. The paper sleeve Plastigage comes in has a printed scale along one side for measuring Plastigage width. It reads out bearing-to-journal clearance directly in thousandths of an inch or millimeters. Green Plastigage measures a 0.001—0.003-in. clearance range.

To use Plastigage, cut a length about equal to the width of the bearing you're checking. Before you lay the Plastigage on the bearing or journal, make sure it's dry. Plastigage is oil-soluble, so oil will soften the wax and cause a false reading.

When checking the crankshaft, all other caps and bearings must be in place and torqued first. Do not oil any bearings or journals when checking the mains. Also, do not oil a rod journal or bearing when checking rod-bearing clearance.

Lay the Plastigage on top of the bearing journal or centered in the bearing. Carefully install the bearing cap. Do not rotate the crank or rod. It will smear the Plastigage. Torque the bolts or nuts to specification. Remember: Don't rotate the crankshaft or connecting rod. Otherwise, you'll have to remove the bearing cap and start over. After you've finished torquing the cap, carefully remove it and measure bearing clearance by comparing the squeezed wax width with the printed scale on the Plastigage sleeve.

It's not necessary to check all main or rod bearings unless you want to be absolutely certain. One thing for sure, you can't be faulted for checking.

trapped behind the bearing inserts. Use a clean paper towel and solvent, such as lacquer thinner, to wipe the bores in the block and caps. Wipe the back of the bearing inserts, too. The working surface of a bearing—the surface that goes against the bearing journal—is coated with a white residue as it comes from the box. Don't remove this residue; it's supposed to be there. Lightly wipe the working surface to ensure that it is clean.

At one end of each bearing-insert half is a tab. This tab—*locating lug or tang*—fits in a machined notch at the bearing-cap parting line to help position the insert in its bore. The bearing halves with the large oil holes go in the block. Those without holes go in the caps. The oil holes allow oil to pass to the main bearings. In addition,

some main bearings are fully grooved; some are not. If your bearings aren't fully grooved, the grooved halves go in the block and the plain halves go in the caps.

The front bearing-insert half that goes in the block has an additional hole. It supplies oil to the timing-chain tensioner and lubricator. Therefore, the main-bearing insert with two oil holes—one large and one small—must be installed in the block on the front journal, not the rear. I say rear because the front and rear main bearings are the same length—1.027 in. (26.00mm). You could mix them up if you don't pay attention.

Once you get the front and rear inserts installed, the others are relatively easy. For instance, the center bearing—number-3 or number-4, depending on whether it's a

four or six—is no problem because of its thrust flanges. Just make sure the half with the oil hole goes in the block. The remaining inserts can be installed in any bore because they are the same design and length—measuring 0.949 in. (24.00mm). They are a little more than 1/16 in. longer than the end bearings.

Install the bearings in the block by first putting the tab of each bearing in the notch at the edge of its bore. Hold the bearing flush with the cap's parting line with a finger or thumb, then force the bearing into place by pushing on the opposite end with the other thumb. All bearing halves will go in with little effort except for the center one. It requires more force because the thrust flanges fit tightly over the bearing web.

Remove cap with care and measure Plastigage width with scale at edge of sleeve to determine oil clearance. Plastigage may come off with bearing insert or stay on bearing journal.

Clean bearing bores before installing inserts. CAUTION: If half of bearing inserts are grooved, install grooved inserts in block; ungrooved inserts in caps.

Remove inserts from package and check size before installing. Don't trust what's printed on box. Instead, check backside of bearing for size.

After wiping off bearing insert, install in block. Note two oil holes in front bearing bore and matching holes in insert.

To knock off any imperfections on parting surface, lightly run file across caps.

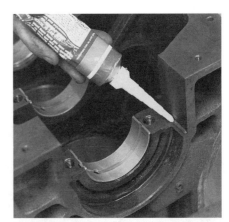

Before doing this, have crankshaft, bearing caps with inserts and cap bolts ready to install in block. Now, run a small bead of RTV sealer about halfway in corner of rear-main-cap register.

File Caps—Before installing the remaining halves in the caps, *lightly file* the cap-to-block mating surfaces. This will ensure that the caps will fit in their registers. To do this, you'll need a large flat, fine-tooth file. Lightly run the file back and forth on the cap-to-block parting line a few times. Even better, set the cap on the file and hold the cap square against the file. Run the cap back and forth on the file.

Be careful not to remove any material from the cap except for nicks or burrs—small projections raised above the normal parting surface. After doing this, wipe the caps clean. Install the inserts in the caps just as you installed their partners in the block.

Check Bearing-to-Journal Clearance—You have already determined the correct size bearings for your main bearings by measuring the main journals with a micrometer. Due to the relatively close

accuracy of mikes and the close tolerances that bearings are manufactured to, direct clearance checks are unnecessary, *assuming the right bearings got in the right box.* However, assuming can cause considerable trouble, and checking merely takes time. I once got a Buick V6 bearing in a box marked for a small-block Ford!

Install Rear-Main Seal—If you are going to check main-bearing clearance with Plastigage, wait until afterward to install the rear-main seal. Otherwise, install the seal now.

Nissan/Datsun manuals show the rear main seal being installed after the crankshaft is positioned in the block. If you do it "the factory way" you'll have to use a special driver to install the seal, Crankshaft Rear Oil Seal Drift KV10105500. To avoid this expense, simply install the oil seal on the crank *before* setting the crank into the block. This eliminates the need for the

special driver and reduces the chance of damaging the seal.

If you're doing a Plastigage check, installing the rear-main oil seal can wait until afterward. Here's how to install the rear-main oil seal.

Find the rear-main oil seal in your gasket set. You'll also need the crankshaft. Wipe its machined surfaces clean with a clean paper towel soaked in solvent.

To install the seal, smear moly grease or petroleum jelly on the crankshaft-seal surface and the seal lip. With the seal lip pointing toward the crank, work the lip over the flywheel flange. Once the seal lip is over the flange, push the seal forward so it's about 1/8 in. short of the front edge of the flywheel flange.

Seal Rear Main-Bearing Cap—The rear-main cap must be sealed to the block. If you're doing a Plastigage check, this

Squirt oil on bearings and spread with fingertip. Don't forget center-bearing thrust faces.

With a good grip on crank, hold it straight over block and lower it square onto bearings. If you installed rear seal first, check that it is installed square on crank and in block. Depth-gage end of vernier caliper works well for this.

Nissan recommends installing rear-main seal after crank is in block. I do it before, but take special care to ensure that seal is square to crank. Oil seal lip before installing seal.

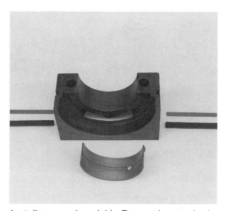

Install rear main quickly. Remember sealer in corners of rear-main register? Here's what you need: cap, bearing insert and side seals.

Run small bead of sealer in grooves at each side of cap.

sealing can wait until afterward. Here's how to seal the cap.

Find the two main-cap side seals and *nails* or *cores,* in your gasket set. The seals—flat metal strip with a beveled end—are slightly longer than the groove in each side of the cap. Each nail is approximately the same length as the grooves. Lay a side seal in one of the grooves and check how much of it should project when fully installed. Keep this amount in mind.

Start the sealing process by applying silicone sealer to the block. Using the tip that came with your tube of sealer, cut it off at the small end so it will lay a small bead. Seal the corners of the cap register in the block. As shown in the photo, page

117, start at the rear of the block and run a small 7/8-in.-long (22mm) bead of sealer in both corners. Keep the sealer handy. You'll need it soon.

Note: The crank and rear-main cap must be installed immediately after doing this, or the sealer will harden. Hardened sealer will prevent the cap from being pulled down square in its register. Get the crank in place without delay so you can finish sealing the main cap.

Install Crankshaft—Liberally oil the bearings in the caps and block. Also, oil the main-bearing journals. Worry less about making a mess and more about providing lubrication for the crank on initial startup.

With the block positioned upside

down, lift the crankshaft with two hands. Grab the crankshaft nose at one end and the center of the flywheel flange at the other. Lower the crank squarely into the block and onto its bearings. Reposition the rear main oil seal so it lines up with the rear face of the block. If there's a pronounced wear groove in the crankshaft seal surface, "cheat" the seal backward or forward about 1/8 in. so the new seal doesn't ride in the old groove. Give the bearing journals another shot of oil with your squirt can.

Install Rear-Main Cap—Turn your attention back to sealing the rear-main cap. Starting at the cap parting line, run a 1-in. (25mm)-long bead of sealer in each side-seal groove. Check that the bearing

With insert in place and journal oiled, tap bearing cap squarely into register. After oiling threads, install cap bolts and snug.

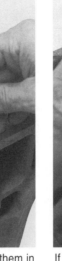

Slide side seals into grooves. Push them in as far as possible.

If metal side-seal expanders are used, check for angle-cut end. It's at right as shown.

insert is in place, then fit the cap to the block. Use the butt end of a hammer handle to tap the cap into its register until it's about 1/8 in. from fully seating.

Oil the side seals and insert them into their grooves with the lips pointing toward the block. Push in the seals until they bottom against the block. Finish tapping the cap into place. Check that the seals are fully installed by measuring how much they project from the block.

Oil two main-cap-bolt threads and thread them into the block. Snug them; they'll be torqued later.

Before installing the nails, check their points. The beveled points must go toward the cap, not the seals. This will keep the nails from digging into the seals. Insert the nail between the seal and cap, *pointing toward the cap*. As shown, I used a screwdriver to push in the nails. The nails should install flush or below the bottom of the block.

Finish the rear-main sealing job by trimming the ends of the seals so they project about 1/16 in. above the bottom of the block.

Install Remaining Main Caps—Install the remaining four or six main-bearing caps. Double-check that the bearing inserts are in place and you have eight or 12 bolts. Their threads should be clean and oiled.

Give the remaining bearing journals a shot of oil, then fit the caps to the block. Check their numbers and arrows to make sure they are positioned correctly. Arrows point to the front.

With expander positioned so angled end points away from seal—so it doesn't dig in—push expander into groove behind seal. It should install flush with block.

Double-check that arrows on main caps point to front of block. If all is OK, use soft mallet or butt end of hammer handle to tap caps into engagement with registers. Don't pull caps into place by tightening bolts. This may damage caps or registers.

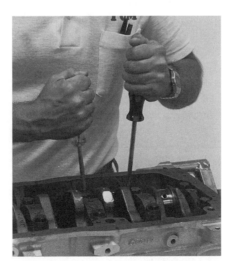

Align thrust-bearing faces by forcing crank back and forth with screwdrivers. Pry between main-bearing webs and crankshaft counterweights.

While forcing crankshaft forward, torque center main-bearing-cap bolts 33—40 ft-lb (4.4—5.5 kg-m). Finish torquing remaining main-cap bolts. Do so in sequence shown on page 120.

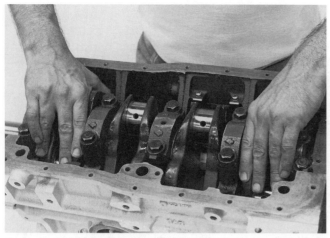

To confirm that all is OK, spin crank in block. If it binds, something is wrong. Don't go any further without finding and correcting problem.

To check crankshaft end play, force crank in one direction, zero gage, then force in opposite direction. Maximum reading is end play.

Set each cap on its journal and thread its bolts in a few turns to align the cap. Using a soft mallet or hammer handle, tap the cap into the register—don't tighten the bolts until the cap is hard against the block. Tightening the bolts to pull a cap into place could damage the cap or block. **Torque Main-Cap Bolts**—Tighten all main-cap bolts finger-tight. Align the center main-bearing thrust faces by forcing the crankshaft back and forth in the block. Use two big screwdrivers as levers to pry between other bearing caps and a crank-shaft throw or counterweight.

After doing this a few times, pry the crankshaft forward. Hold it in this position and torque the center main-cap bolts 33—40 ft-lb (4.4—5.5 kg-m). Follow the prop-er torque sequence shown nearby. Basically, start at the center cap and alter-nate back and forth to each cap. Work toward the ends until all cap bolts are torqued to specification.

After all bolts are torqued, spin the crank to make sure it turns freely. **Crankshaft End Play**—sometimes called *float*—is 0.002—0.007 in. (0.051—0.18mm) with a 0.012 in. (0.3mm) limit. End play is how much the crank moves longitudinally in the block. It's controlled by the crankshaft thrust bearing.

Two methods can be used to check crankshaft end play. One requires a dial indicator; the other, feeler gages. Although feeler gages are less accurate than a dial indicator, they are adequate.

To check end play with a dial indica-tor, secure the indicator base to the front of the block. If it has a magnetic base like

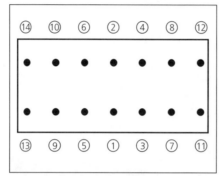

Torque main-bearing-cap bolts in sequence. Torque chart is for six-cylinder engine. If assembling a four, you'll have four fewer main bolts to torque. Drawing courtesy Nissan.

the one pictured above, this is easy. Otherwise, bolt it to the block. Position the indicator so its plunger bears against the nose of the crank and is parallel to the crank center line. Using a screwdriver between a main-bearing cap and the crank, pry the crankshaft forward. Hold it there and zero the indicator. To determine end play, pry the crank to the rear. End play is read directly.

If you don't have a dial indicator, feel-er gages will do. Pry the crankshaft in one direction or the other. With the crank held in that position, measure between the crank thrust face and bearing with a 0.007 in. (0.18mm) feeler gage. If the gage does not fit, end play is not excessive. Check with a 0.002 in. (0.05lmm) gage next. If it fits, end play is OK.

If, by rare chance, end play is under the 0.002 in. minimum, the thrust-bearing flanges will have to be thinned. This

If you don't have a dial indicator, use feeler gages to measure end play. Force crank in one direction, hold it there, then check clearance between thrust bearing and crank. Thrust clearance represents end play.

means you must remove the crank and the center bearing inserts.

To *increase* end play, thin the thrust bearing's front flange with 320-grit sand-paper on a *flat surface*. Before doing any sanding, use a micrometer to measure the width across the bearing flanges. Record this amount. How far end play is off gov-erns how much material should be removed from the thrust flange.

Hold the inserts end to end and *lap* away bearing material until end play is within tolerance. Holding the inserts this way squares them to the sandpaper and minimizes rocking motion. This ensures material removal is even around the thrust flange. Check flange width frequently so

When purchasing new pistons, rings may or may not accompany them, depending on the manufacturer. Here, piston and rings come separately.

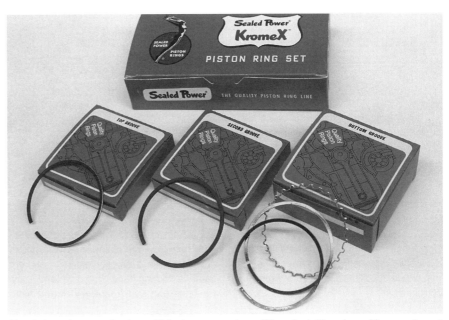

It's obvious from packaging which ring goes where. When installing rings, it's easy to get compression rings in wrong grooves and upside down. Study manufacturer's instructions before installing rings on pistons.

you don't remove too much material.

When flange width appears to be correct, clean the bearings and reinstall them and the crankshaft. Double-check end play to confirm that it is correct.

If end play exceeds 0.012 in. (0.3mm), remove the crank and trade it in on a crank kit. Let the reconditioner worry about the worn one. Too much end clearance is highly unlikely, considering you've inspected your crankshaft and declared it sound, or had it reconditioned or replaced.

Unlikely or not, end play is one of those items that must be checked regardless of the consequences. Like the man says, "Pay me now or pay me later." What you'll have to pay now will be a fraction of the cost later in both time and money.

GAPPING & INSTALLING PISTON RINGS

If you haven't assembled the pistons and connecting rods, refer back to page 80 for how it's done. However, if they are assembled, ready them for installation.

The equipment you'll need for gapping and installing rings includes a small flat file and a ring expander. It's possible to install rings without an expander, but it's easier and there's less chance of breaking a ring or scratching a piston if you use one.

Piston-Ring Gap—Piston rings are manufactured to close tolerances to fit specific bore sizes. Regardless, check their end gaps just the same. Just as with bearings, wrong rings can find their way into the right boxes. Once they're on the pistons and in their bores, you'll never know

Although ring end gaps should be OK as delivered, don't assume so. Fit ring into bore . . .

. . . and, using top of piston, square ring in bore.

until it's too late. Also, some rings designed for high-performance use must be gapped.

Top compression rings should be gapped to 0.014 in. (0.36mm), or about 0.004 in. (0.10mm) for each inch of bore diameter. For example, compression rings for a 3.5 in. (88.9mm) bore should be gapped at 0.004 X 3.5 = 0.014 in. (0.36mm). If ring gaps measure in the 0.012—0.017-in. (0.30—0.43mm) range, they should be OK.

Because they operate cooler, second compression rings should have a gap about 0.002 in. less than top compression rings. Gaps for oil rings depend on the

type. Regardless, oil-ring-gap ranges are wider at about 0.012—0.035 in. (0.30—0.89mm). The exact range depends on whether the oil ring is the single-piece or the three-piece rail type—a center expander/spacer and two rails.

Use the above figures only as a guide. Follow the recommendations accompanying your ring set. The ring manufacturer established specifications based on testing with his piston rings.

Check Ring Gap—To check piston-ring end gap, install the ring in a cylinder bore. Use cylinder-1 to start with. Pinch the ring ends together and carefully fit the ring in

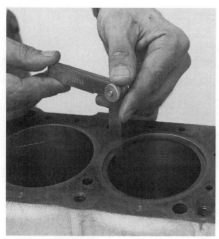

Check end gap with feeler gages. If gap is excessive, replace rings. If not enough, set ring gap to specifications listed or from your calculations.

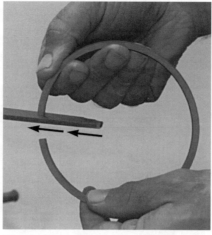

With fine-tooth file clamped in vise, move ring toward file in direction shown to prevent damage to ring face. File one end only. Recheck ring gap frequently during filing process.

Sealed Power's rotary ring filer makes ring-gapping job relatively easy. Because it removes material quickly, be sure to check ring gap frequently.

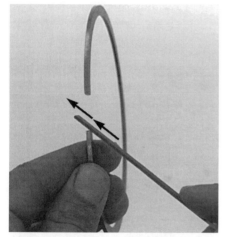

After correct gap is achieved, break sharp edges and remove burrs by lightly touching file to corners of filed end. Move file in direction shown.

the bore. Square the ring in the bore with the top of a piston.

There's no need to push the ring down the bore more than 1/2 in. (13mm) if the bores are fresh. But, if your block hasn't been rebored, push the ring about 3 in. down the bore. Taper in a worn bore causes a ring gap to close up at the bottom of the stroke. Therefore, end gap should be checked where it's least likely to prevent the ends of a ring from butting when the engine is at maximum operating temperature. If this occurs, the bore will be scored or the ring can seize or break, causing severe engine damage.

When you get the ring where you want it and it's square in the bore, measure end gap with feeler gages. Stack feeler gages

together until you get that all-important light drag. Add up the thickness of the gages to get end gap.

Set Ring End Gap—If any ring end gaps are excessive, return the complete set of rings and get a new set. Check the new ones, too. If a gap is too small, increase end gap by filing or grinding one end of the ring.

When filing or grinding a piston ring, the first rule is to file or grind the end of the ring *from its outside edge toward its inside edge*. This is particularly important with moly rings. The moly filling or coating on the outer edge will otherwise chip or peel off.

When filing, don't hold the ring *and* file in your hands. Rather, clamp the file in a vise or onto a bench with a C-clamp or Vise-Grip pliers. You can then move the ring against the file with much more control. For grinding a ring, use a thin grinding disc—one that will fit between the two ends. Just make certain that disc rotation grinds the end from the outside in. Hold the ring securely so you don't break it as you grind it. Frequently pinch the ends of the ring together to check that the end you're filing or grinding remains square.

Break the sharp edges at the end of the ring after you file or grind it. Use a *very fine-tooth* file or 400-grit sandpaper. The inside edge will have the biggest burr, the outside edge shouldn't have any and the sides will be somewhere in between. Just touch the edges with your file or sandpaper. Remove only enough material

so you can't feel any burrs.

When you finish gapping one complete ring set—two compression rings and one oil ring—put the rings back in the envelopes they came in. The ring manufacturer usually organizes the rings in sets and in order—top compression ring, second compression ring and oil-ring assembly. Be careful not to mix up the rings, particularly the compression rings. The differences between them are not readily apparent, so keep each ring set in order to avoid installing them incorrectly.

Also, store each piston-ring set with the piston-and-rod assembly that goes in the bore you used for checking and fitting that particular set. Move to the next bore and repeat this procedure until you've checked and fitted all rings.

Install Piston Rings—Once all of the rings are gapped, you're ready to install them on their pistons.

Piston rings can be installed without special tools, but I recommend using a *ring expander*. Like most engine-assembly tools, you don't have to lay out a lot of money to get a ring expander that will do an adequate job. There are different styles of expanders. The top-of-the-line type has a circular channel for the ring to lay in while it is expanded. Sealed Power's less exotic MT-2 expander, shown above, doesn't have this channel. Even if you buy the most expensive expander, it will be considerably cheaper than another set of rings. And, think back to when you removed the old rings from the pistons.

Make it easy on your thumbs and install compression rings using ring expander such as this one from Sealed Power. Although you can install rings with your thumbs, chances of breaking a ring are much higher.

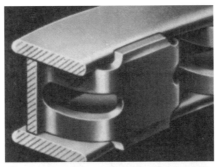

Three-piece oil-ring assembly consists of two side rails and one expander/spacer. Expander/spacer separates and forces rails against bore. Drawing courtesy Sealed Power Corporation.

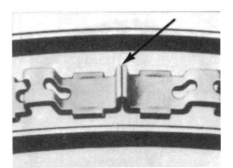

Expander/spacer ends must butt (arrow), not overlap. Triple-check during and after installing oil ring. Otherwise, serious engine damage can result. Photo courtesy Sealed Power Corporation.

With piston lightly clamped in vise or to workbench, start by installing oil ring. Expander/spacer goes on first.

Next on is oil-ring rail. Install on top of expander/spacer. Install bottom rail next.

Don't forget to check expander/spacer ends.

Your thumbs can be spared a lot of pain and suffering while installing the stiffer new rings.

Secure the piston-and-rod assembly so you don't have to horse around trying to hold it and the rod while installing rings. Lightly clamp the rod in a vise between two wood blocks. Be extremely careful here. Too much clamping force can bend a rod easier than you might imagine.

Position the piston so the bottom of its skirts rest against the vise jaws. This will keep the piston from rocking back and forth so your hands will be free to install the rings.

Don't clamp on the piston. If you don't have a vise, make yourself comfortable by sitting in a chair and clamp the rod and piston between your knees. Installing rings this way is about as easy as using a vise.

Oil Rings—When installing rings on a piston, start with the oil ring and work up.

You won't need the ring-expanding tool to install a three-piece oil ring. It has three components: an expander/spacer and two side rails. However, you can save yourself some time later on by installing the three oil-ring components so their end gaps are in the right relationship to one another rather than waiting until it's time to install the piston and rod in its bore. The idea is to *stagger* the gaps so the oil-ring assembly doesn't pass excessive amounts of oil.

Install the expander/spacer with its gap directly over one end of the piston pin and facing toward the front. The piston front is indicated by a notch or arrow stamped in its dome. The expander/spacer's job is to position the two rails in the oil-ring groove and to preload them against the cylinder wall. Be careful when installing the expander/spacer. Make sure its ends butt and don't overlap. You really have to work at keeping this from happening with some expander/spacer designs.

Now you're ready for the rails. Insert one end in the oil-ring groove *on top of the expander/spacer.* Hold the free end of it

with one hand and run the thumb of your other hand around on top of the rail to slip the rail into the groove. Don't let the free end of the ring dig into the piston as you bring it down over the piston. Install the other rail below the expander/spacer using the same method.

Position Oil-Ring Gaps—With the expander/spacer gap at the 12-o'clock position—at the front of the piston—position the top-rail gap at 10 o'clock, and the bottom rail at four o'clock as shown, page 125.

Double-check that the expander/spacer ends are not overlapping. If they are, remove and reinstall the rails.

Compression Rings—These rings—one-piece affairs—are more difficult to install because of their stiffness. Too, compression rings easily damaged and can damage the piston if installed incorrectly.

Keep your eyes open when installing these guys. Look for the *pip* mark—a little dot or indentation—that indicates the top side of a compression ring. The *pip* mark *must be up when the ring is installed.*

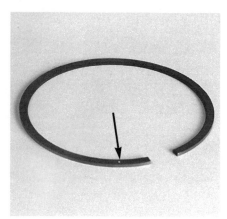

Some compression rings have a pip mark to indicate top side; some don't. Check instructions that came with ring set.

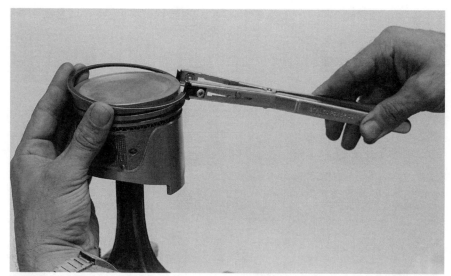

Next on is second compression ring. Make sure you know which is top side of ring. Expand ring only enough to get over piston. Guide open end of ring over piston and toward second groove, then rotate opposite side over piston. Release ring into second groove. Install top ring next.

Otherwise, the twist will be in the wrong direction, causing excessive blowby and ring and ring-groove side wear.

Twist describes how a ring bends, or the shape it takes when installed. Twist is used for oil control and for sealing combustion pressures. Compression rings with no twist have no pip marks. If you get a set like this, although unlikely, you can install them either way. But inspect the rings to be absolutely sure. Also, read the instructions that accompany the rings and follow them *exactly.*

The difficult thing about installing a compression ring is expanding it. Incorrectly done, you can twist or break the ring, or gouge or scratch the piston with the ring ends. This is why I recommend using a ring expander.

When using an expander, use one hand to expand the ring and your other hand to control it. Don't expand the ring more than necessary to get it over the piston and into its groove.

If you insist on installing the compression rings by hand, here's how to do it right. Wrap the ends of your thumbs with tape. The sharp ends really dig in when you're spreading the ring.

Position the second compression ring over the piston. Rotate the ring over the edge of the piston so its ends are lower on the piston than the rest of the ring. Expand the ring with your thumbs and control it with your fingers at the side. Rotate the ring down over the piston and position the ends over the groove. When the ring aligns with the groove all the way around,

Tools you'll need for installing pistons and connecting rods: oil squirt can, thread protectors, ring compressor, hammer or mallet, and large can with about 3 in. of oil—enough to cover piston pin.

release it.

When your thumbs recover, install the top ring using the same method. It will be easier because you won't have to bring it down over the piston as far.

Rotate the top compression ring so its gap is immediately above the top oil-ring rail gap, or 10 o'clock. Position the bottom compression-ring gap over the lower-rail gap so it's at the four-o'clock position.

Recheck end gaps *immediately before* installing the piston in its bore. Compression rings move when a piston-and-connecting rod assembly is handled.

PISTON & CONNECTING-ROD INSTALLATION

There are some tools you'll need to install the pistons and rods. You must have a ring compressor, two bearing-journal protec-

Install pulley bolt and washer in crank nose. Rotate crank throw to BC before installing piston and rod.

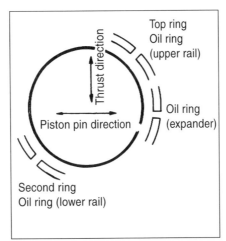

Before compressing rings, position them as shown. Oil-ring expander/spacer goes at back side of piston—opposite piston notch or arrow. Position top oil-ring rail under top compression ring and bottom rail under bottom compression ring. Drawing Courtesy Nissan.

Dunk piston in oil so it covers piston pin. Move rod back and forth to work oil into piston-pin bore. Lift piston out of oil and over can to let it drain so mess won't be excessive. Note sleeves on rod bolts and bearing insert in rod. Install them if you haven't yet. Install inserts in caps, too.

With rings compressed—make sure ring compressor is installed in right direction-wiggle piston back and forth in compressor. This will relax rings so they'll fully compress. Double-check rod number to bore. If all is OK, guide rod and piston into bore.

tors for the rod bolts, an oil can, something to push the piston into its bore—a hammer handle will do—and a large can with about 3 in. of motor oil in it. You don't absolutely need the last item, but it's the most convenient way I know to prelube rings and pistons.

Get Everything Ready—Just like other facets of engine building, you have to be organized when installing pistons and rods. All tools must be within reach, everything must be clean and the engine positioned so you'll be able to insert each piston and rod into its bore while guiding the rod onto the crank journal.

Before you start the actual installation, clean the cylinder bores. Use paper towels, not rags. Other than smears of rust-preventive oil, the towels must come out perfectly clean. Look over the pistons and rods, too. Regardless of how clean they appear, wipe out the bearing bores in the rods and caps. Give the bearings the same treatment you gave the main bearings. Make certain their backsides are perfectly clean.

If you are assembling your engine on a bench, roll the block over on its side with the deck surface toward the edge of the bench. This will give you clear access to both ends. You may have to block up the front of the engine to level it because the back of the block is propped up by the bell housing boss. If you are using an engine stand, rotate the block so the crankcase is down.

Organize the pistons and rods so they're close at hand and in order. This way, you won't have to hunt for each pis-

ton, even though it gets easier as you go along. With all the tools ready, you should be ready to slip the rods and pistons into their holes.

Crankshaft Throws at BC—Install the damper bolt with its washer in the crank nose. You'll then use it to turn the crank during rod-and-piston installation. When installing a piston and rod, its throw must be at BC so you'll have room to guide the rod onto its journal and install the bearing cap.

Position the crank, then remove the bearing cap from the rod you're going to install. Be careful not to knock the bearing inserts loose if you installed them earlier. Above all, don't mix them with other inserts. Avoid this by removing only one rod cap at a time. If you didn't install the bearing, do it now. Slip the protectors over the rod bolts. They'll protect the bores and bearing journals, plus they'll hold the bearings in place.

Liberally oil the piston rings, skirts and piston pin. Here's where the can of oil comes in handy. Immerse the piston so oil is over the piston pin. While immersed, spread oil over the piston skirt and bearing inserts with your fingertips. You're now ready to compress the rings.

Compress Rings—Ring compressors vary in design, so follow the directions that accompanied yours. If you don't have the directions, here's how to use one.

There are three basic styles of ring compressors. The most common and least

expensive operates with an Allen wrench or an over-center handle. Once compressed-rings are forced flush with the side of the piston—the compressor is held in position by a ratchet or the over-centering effect of the handle. The ratchet is released by a lever on the side of the compressor sleeve. The over-center handle is simply lifted.

The second type uses a pliers arrangement. A ratchet on the pliers handle holds the rings in the compressed position. This type is available from Sealed Power

Lightly tap piston into bore. If piston stops, don't force it. Remove and check compressor. Recompress rings and try again.

When compressor relaxes, rings are in bore. Set compressor aside and push piston down in bore and guide rod over crank journal with free hand. With insert installed and oiled, fit cap to rod and secure with nuts.

Double-check: Cap and rod numbers must match, agree with cylinder number, and be on side opposite oil filter . . .

. . . and piston notch or arrow must be to front of block.

Torque rod nuts to specification: 8mm bolt: 20—24 ft-lb (2.8—3.4 kg-m); 9mm bolt: 33—40 ft-lb (4.5—5.5 kg-m).

Corporation with sleeves or bands to accommodate 2-7/8—4-3/8-in. pistons.

A third type favored by high-performance engine builders is a sleeve with a tapered opening at the top and a bottom opening equal to the bore size. The lubricated piston assembly is slipped into the sleeve and the rings are compressed as they pass from the tapered opening into the bore-size diameter of the sleeve. As the sleeve is held against the block, the piston is pushed into the bore. The only problem with the sleeve type compressor is that you have to have one for each bore size you will be working with.

To use the pliers-type ring compressor, fit it loosely around the piston with the long side of the sleeve pointing up in relation to the piston. With the clamping portion of the compressor centered on the three rings, compress the rings. While you're tightening or clamping the compressor, wiggle it on the piston. This helps to compress the rings fully. The piston is ready for installation once the compressor band is tight against the piston.

Install Pistons & Rods—Use the notch or arrow on the piston dome, rod number and oil squirt hole in the rod as reference for positioning the piston and rod. The notch or arrow must point to the front of the block; number to the left and squirt hole to the right.

Insert the piston and rod in its bore. Guide the rod in, being careful not to let it bang against the cylinder wall. Insert the piston in the bore so the compressor is flush against the block deck. Holding the hammer at the head end, push or lightly tap the piston into the bore with the hammer handle.

If the piston hangs up before it's all the way in its bore, **STOP. Don't force the piston.** What has happened is a ring has popped out from under the compressor sleeve before entering the bore. Oil-ring rails are the worst. If you force the piston any farther, you'll probably break a ring and perhaps a ring land, resulting in a junked piston and ring(s). Release the compressor, remove the piston and start over. All you'll lose is a couple of minutes rather than a piston and ring.

When the last ring leaves the compressor and enters the bore, the compressor will relax. Remove it, set it aside and finish installing the piston and rod.

Use one hand to push on the piston and the other to guide the rod into engagement with the bearing journal. Guide the rod bolts so they straddle the journal, then tap lightly on the piston dome with the hammer handle to seat the rod bearing on the crankshaft.

Remove the sleeves from the rod bolts and install the bearing cap. Oil its bearing insert and the nut bearing surfaces. Make sure the cap number coincides with the one on the rod; the squirt hole goes to the opposite side. Install the rod-bolt nuts after oiling the bolt threads. Torque 8mm rod nuts 20—24 ft-lb (2.8—3.4 kg-m); 9mm nuts are torqued 33—40 ft-lb (4.5—5.5 kg-m).

With the first rod and piston installed, turn the crank so the next throw is at BC and install the next rod and piston. When you install the last rod and piston, step back and take a good look at your engine—it's beginning to look like one. While you're looking, double-check that

Preferred rod side clearance is 0.008—0.012 in. (0.2—0.3mm). Absolute maximum clearance is 0.024 in. (0.6mm). Using feeler gages, check between rod big end and crank-throw face.

While at TC, pointer is secured to front cover with 0 mark pointing directly at damper/pulley mark. Damper/pulley and front cover can now be removed.

If you removed cylinder-head dowels, install them now. Tap in until dowel bottoms.

the piston notches or arrows and rod number and squirt holes are all pointing in the same directions.

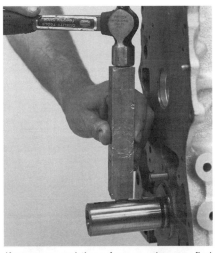

If you removed them from crank nose, find the three Woodruff keys. File smooth any burrs and install each key with hammer and soft punch. Drive in until key bottoms.

INSTALL CYLINDER HEAD

Before you think about setting the cylinder head on the block, you have to do two things: make sure the cylinder-head-locating dowels are installed, and set number-1 piston at TC.

Crank at TC—On page 111 of the cylinder-head chapter, I had you time the cam. Do the same with the crank. There's a very good reason for doing this. If the head was installed without regard to cam or crank position, valve damage would likely result. It doesn't take much imagination to understand this. Visualize a piston at TC and a fully opened valve in its combustion chamber on a collision course as the head is installed. Result—a bent valve.

Rotate the crank until piston number 1 is at TC—it's all the way to the top of its bore. You won't be able to get it right on, but getting the crank within a few degrees of TC is close enough.

If you are a fanatic—like I am—take this opportunity to get the crank right on TC. First, install the Woodruff keys in the crank nose, if they were removed. Check the keys and key slots for burrs. If you find any, use a file to remove them. With the key slots pointing up, position each key in its slot. Use a hammer and soft punch to drive the key into place. Temporarily install in the following order: crank sprocket, oil-pump/distributor-drive gear, front cover and crankshaft damper. Don't tighten the damper bolt. Only let the force of turning the crank tighten it; no more.

Although not necessary, I'm finding TC with dial indicator at top of number-1 piston. Front cover and pulley are temporarily installed so timing pointer can be checked for accuracy.

With a wrench on the damper bolt, turn the crank until the damper and timing pointer indicate TC—0 aligns with the damper mark. To double-check the accuracy of the pointer and damper marks, I use a dial indicator mounted on the block deck to find piston TC. When maximum indicator reading is found by rotating the crank to both sides of indicated TC—at the damper—you've also found actual TC. At actual TC, the timing pointer and damper/pulley marks should align. If they don't agree, you can make adjustments now or later.

Note where the damper/pulley mark and timing pointer align at actual TC. A piece of masking tape on the pointer with a felt-tip or ball-point pen mark aligned with the damper mark works well. Now that you've found actual TC, don't move the crank.

Remove the damper, sprocket and oil-pump/distributor gear from the crank. To prevent crank movement when loosening the damper bolt, put a wrench on the bolt and hit the end of its handle with a hammer. This will shock the bolt loose without—we hope—turning the crank. The same thing can be done with an impact wrench, providing you have one. If the crank turns, return it to TC, using your mark as reference.

Cylinder-Head Dowels—Two hollow dowels are used to position the cylinder head on the block. They install in two head-bolt counterbores. If you removed

Clean head-gasket surface with lacquer thinner and rag or paper towel prior to installing gasket.

. . . then install cylinder head. Lower head easily and shift around as necessary to engage dowels.

A 10mm, 1/2-in.-drive Allen wrench is used to torque head bolts.

Position head gasket to dowels on deck surface . . .

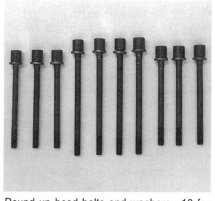

Round up head bolts and washers—10 for four-cylinder engines and 14 for sixes—and clean their threads. Long bolts also secure cam towers.

Oil threads and undersides of bolt heads, then thread-in bolts.

Install Cylinder Head—Prepare the cylinder-block deck surface by wiping it with a solvent-soaked paper towel. Give the cylinder head the same treatment. These surfaces must be absolutely clean; free of old gasket material, oil and grease.

Find the cylinder-head gasket in your gasket set. It may or may not need to be sealed. Read the instructions that came with the gaskets to determine this. If nothing is said about sealer, assume it's OK to use it as is.

To seal a head gasket, coat it with high-temperature aluminum paint, Copper Coat®, High Tack® or equivalent. Regardless of what you use, applying the sealer with a spray can works best. After you've sprayed the gasket on both sides and the sealer has dried, or tacked, you're ready to install the gasket and head.

these dowels, reinstall them. They are a must. To install a cylinder-head dowel, tap it until it bottoms in its counterbore.

Lay the gasket on the block and fit it to the dowels. Check that the gasket is right-side up; timing-chain offset to the left of the block and water-jacket holes and cylinder-head oil-feed hole lined up with those in the block.

Once you're satisfied that the gasket is positioned correctly and both the crank and cam are at TC, install the cylinder head. Grasp the head at both ends, center it over the block and lower it squarely onto the deck, engaging it with the dowels.

Find the 10 or 14 socket-head cylinder-head bolts and their hardened flat washers. The long bolts—four for four-cylinders and five for six-cylinders—install in the cam towers on the manifold side of the head. Make sure the bolt threads are clean, then oil them. Drop the bolts into the head and thread them into the block.

CYLINDER-HEAD BOLT TORQUE	
Engine	Final Torque ft-lb (kg-m)
L13, 16, 20A	40 (5.5)
L18, 20B, 24, 26, 28	61 (8.5)
L28 Turbo	65 (9.0)

Torque bolts in 20-ft-lb increments, then final-torque as specified.

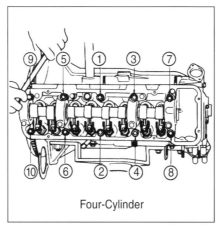

Four-Cylinder

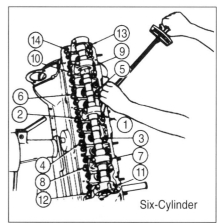

Six-Cylinder

After snugging head bolts in sequence, final-torque in two steps using same sequence. Note: Loosen head bolts in reverse sequence. Use L28 Turbo head bolts in all L28 engines.

New cam-drive components in relative installed positions: chain, crank and cam sprockets, tight- and slack-side chain guides and chain tensioner. Bright links on chain must align with sprocket timing marks. Note shorter distance between bright links on tight side of chain.

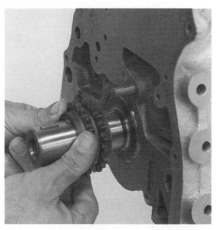

Begin chain installation by installing crankshaft sprocket with timing mark to front. Slide sprocket on to about position shown. It should go on with ease. Position crank so keys are straight up and cam so notch in hub aligns with groove in thrust plate. Cam dowel will be straight up.

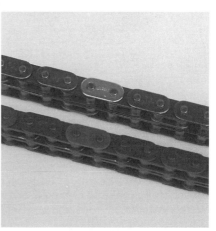

Old chain compared to new one: If original chain is used, bright links may not be . . . bright, that is.

To run the bolts down and torque them, you'll need a 10mm Allen wrench with a 1/2-in. socket drive. As I explained earlier, if you don't have a socket-drive Allen wrench, make one. Cut an Allen wrench 3-in. long, then insert it in a 10mm socket.

Run the bolts down and torque them in steps in the sequence shown in the chart. Work out from the center head bolts.

Torque them in pairs, alternating from end to end until you get to the end head bolts.

As a safety measure, install some old spark plugs loosely in the head to keep foreign material from entering the plug holes.

INSTALL TIMING CHAIN

Because of the critical nature of the L-series cam-drive system and the severe damage that can result if a failure occurs, I recommend that you replace all cam-drive components. These include: timing chain and sprockets, tight- and slack-side chain guides and chain-tensioner shoe. A possible exception is the tight-side chain guide—the straight one. If it doesn't have deep grooves from the chain, it should be

OK. Let's start by installing the crank sprocket.

Install Crank Sprocket—All three crank keys should be in the crank. There's a Woodruff key for the sprocket, one for the oil-pump/distributor gear and one for the damper. Slip the sprocket on the crank so the timing mark is forward and its bore chamfer is toward the number-1 main-bearing journal. Rotate the sprocket into engagement with the first key and slide it back against the front journal.

Install Chain—Lay the timing chain on your clean bench and look for the two bright links. As you can see from the photo, if you are reusing your chain, these links are hard to find. The used one only had 15,000 miles on it.

With chain draped over cam sprocket and bright link aligned with **1, 2** or **3**, lower chain through head and slip it under crank sprocket. Align bright link with crank-sprocket mark and pull chain up into engagement. Thread bolt with washer and fuel-pump eccentric—if used—into cam nose. Have wrench on cam to turn it and align dowel with matching hole in sprocket.

Remove the camshaft sprocket, but don't let the cam rotate while removing the sprocket bolt. Use an adjustable wrench on the cast-in knobs on the four-cylinder cam to hold it while you break the bolt loose. Vise-Grips can be used to hang on to the six-cylinder cam.

With the short distance between bright links to your right when you hold the chain up to the front of the engine, feed it down through the head. Slip the chain under the crank sprocket. Fit the chain to the crank sprocket so the bright link aligns with the crank-sprocket timing mark.

Pull up on the chain and slip the cam sprocket underneath. The bright link must align with the proper timing mark—there are three of them. If the number-1 dowel hole is used, use the number-1 timing mark. The same thing goes for the other two timing marks. If the number-2 dowel hole is used, align the bright link to the number-2 mark. Likewise for number-3. To repeat: *The bright chain link must align with the cam-sprocket timing mark that*

New chain is timed to 1 mark. At TC, sprocket-hub notch should align with thrust-plate groove.

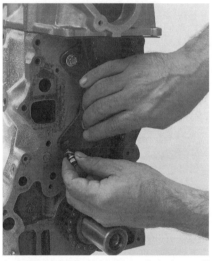

Install slack-side guide with top bolt, then pull guide against chain until bottom surface of guide is tangent—lines up—with curve at bottom of guide. Secure guide with bottom bolt.

agrees with the dowel hole engaging the cam-drive dowel.

Install the camshaft-sprocket bolt, fuel-pump eccentric or flat washer and lock washer. Don't tighten the bolt yet. Look through the sprocket—the top lightening hole—and check the sprocket notch or timing mark on the sprocket hub and thrust-plate timing mark. They should still be in line if you haven't turned the cam. Cam timing is covered on page 131 after the procedures for installing the chain guides and tensioner.

Install Slack-Side Chain Guide—The slack-side chain guide—the curved one—must be installed so its straight end is *tangent to*—aligned with—the chain. The end of the guide and the chain must touch and point in the same direction. To adjust for

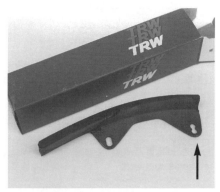

Don't even think about using old chain guides unless they are relatively new. Slack-side guide with siamesed guide bolt hole (arrow) is shown.

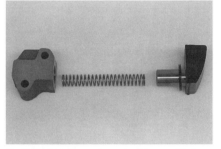

If chain tensioner is reusable—unlikely— clean with solvent. Slide bolts into tensioner body and install gasket over bolts.

this, the guide bolt holes are both slotted or slotted and siamesed—one hole runs into the other to form a figure 8. The second arrangement is shown above.

With the straight end up and the chain pushed toward the center of the engine, install the slack-side guide. Install the two guide bolts with their flat washers and lock washers. Start with the top bolt, then push the guide over to install the second. Check chain and guide alignment at the top through the cylinder-head inspection window.

Adjust the top of the guide as necessary to make it tangent to the chain; snug the bolt. If the chain is new, install the bottom bolt so the guide is away from the chain. Recheck top chain-to-guide alignment and readjust as necessary. Torque the guide bolts 4—7 ft-lb (0.6—1.0 kg-m).

Install Chain Tensioner—The chain tensioner consists of three major parts: shoe, spring and housing. There's also a plastic washer that fits over the shoe plunger. If you are using the old tensioner, clean and oil its separate parts, particularly the shoe plunger and its bore.

Compress spring in bore with shoe and force tensioner against chain. Align tensioner to bolt holes and start bolts.

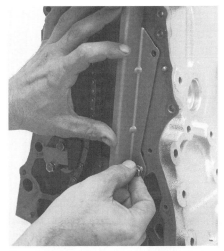

Secure tight-side chain tensioner with two bolts to complete timing-chain installation.

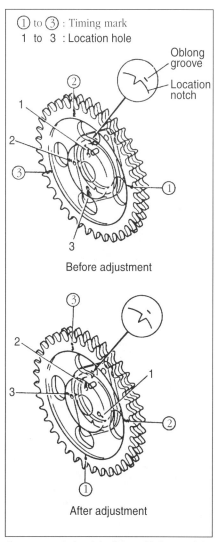

If cam-sprocket notch aligns with thrust-plate groove with crank set at TC, cam is timed. If notch is to left of groove (left), cam is retarded. Remove and reposition sprocket clockwise to next dowel hole and align 2 timing mark at teeth—if originally at 1—to bright link. Recheck notch alignment with groove. Move to 3 groove and mark if originally set at 2. Drawing courtesy Nissan.

To install the tensioner, first find the two tensioner mounting bolts and their lock washers. Slip the bolts through their holes in the tensioner housing. Don't forget the gasket that installs between the tensioner housing and the block. It's in the gasket set.

Return to the slack-side chain guide and adjust it so there is no clearance between the backside of the tensioner shoe and housing. Do this by loosening the bottom guide bolt and moving the guide so the tensioner shoe all but touches its housing. Secure the bolts.

With the spring in the housing, the gasket on the bolts and washer over the shoe plunger, compress the spring in the housing bore by forcing the shoe against the chain. Guide the plunger into its bore and hold it there. When the bolts align with the holes in the block, thread them in. Torque chain-tensioner bolts 4—7 ft-lb (0.6—1.0 kg-m).

Install Tight-Side Chain Guide— Install the tight-side chain guide with the long end up. No adjustments are necessary. Simply secure it with its two bolts and lock washers. Torque these bolts the same as above.

Time Camshaft—If you are *absolutely sure* that the crankshaft didn't move off TC, you won't have to fit the front cover to the engine. Otherwise, temporarily install the oil-pump/distributor gear, front cover and damper to recheck TC. Installing the cover will be a little different this time. It must fit under the head and onto the dowels. Otherwise, the process is the same.

Check the cam sprocket-to-thrust plate timing marks. If they align, cam timing is OK. However, if the sprocket mark *trails*—is to the left of the thrust-plate mark—the cam must be *advanced* to the next dowel hole in sequence to advance the cam. Each dowel hole advances the cam four *crankshaft degrees*—two camshaft degrees because the camshaft turns at half engine speed.

If, however, you installed the cam sprocket in the number-2 or -3 holes, you must *retard* the cam if it is to the right of the thrust-plate mark. It's highly unlikely that a cam would need retarding if it were in the number-1 hole unless something is wrong.

To change cam timing, remove the cam sprocket and reposition it. If you installed the damper, front cover and oil-pump/distributor gear to find TC, remove them. Drive a wooden wedge between the tight and slack sides of the chain at the guides. This will hold the chain in place while you change the cam sprocket.

After you have the wedge tightly in place, remove the cam sprocket. Reposition the next timing mark—advance or retard—to the bright chain link and engage the corresponding dowel hole to the dowel. To engage the sprocket to the dowel and cam nose, turn the cam with a wrench on the knobs. Recheck cam timing. If it's OK, secure the cam sprocket. If not, move to the last dowel hole—if there is another one. If not, and the cam is still retarded, you should have replaced the chain. You will have to now. Remove the cam sprocket, chain, guides and tension-

er, and start over with a new chain. Better recheck the guides and tensioner, too.

Once you're satisfied with cam timing, install the chain-sprocket bolt and washers or washer and fuel-pump eccentric. Torque the sprocket bolt 92—108 ft-lb (12.7—14.7 kg-m). Hold the cam with your wrench on the cam knobs or Vise-Grips on a six cylinder.

TIMING-CHAIN COVER & CRANKSHAFT DAMPER
You are probably familiar with installing the front cover if you've had it on and off

Torque cam-sprocket bolt 94—108 ft-lb (12.8—14.7 kg-m). Hold cam with wrench at square bosses to keep it from rotating.

Clean seal bore, then turn over cover and support on back side behind seal bore. With seal positioned squarely over bore—lip pointing down—tap around periphery with soft mallet. Gradually work seal into bore.

Check oil-pump-drive spindle in front-cover bore. If there's no "wiggle," spindle-to-bore clearance is OK.

Using telescoping gage, measure bore diameter. Compare to shaft diameter. Clearance should not exceed 0.006 in. (0.15mm). If clearance is excessive, replace front cover.

If you suspect spindle-bore wear to be excessive, check shaft-to-bore clearance by first measuring shaft diameter.

With front side of cover supported in immediate area of seal bore, drive out seal using punch and hammer. Gradually work around back side of seal until it pops out.

for timing the engine and camshaft. However, this time you must prepare it for permanent installation. Start by checking the oil-pump/distributor driveshaft—*spindle* in Nissan terminology—in the front cover.

Inspect Oil-Pump/Distributor-Drive Bore—Slip the shaft in the front cover and try wiggling it. There should be little movement. If you feel much movement, use a 0—1-in. mike and telescoping gage to measure the shaft OD and bearing bore in the cover. If the bore is more than 0.006 in. (0.l5mm) bigger than the shaft, replace the cover.

Install Crankshaft Seal—If you

haven't cleaned the front cover, do it now. Remove all dirt, grease and old gasket material. Use a punch and a hammer to remove the crankshaft oil seal. Don't try to knock it out with one whack or you may break the aluminum cover. Support the front of the cover close to the seal bore and carefully work around the seal until it falls out.

With the old seal out, clean the seal bore. You can now install a new front crankshaft seal from the gasket set. While you're looking, also find the two front-cover gaskets.

Lay the cover down with its gasket surface against a clean, smooth surface. Place a shop rag or piece of cardboard underneath if the surface is not smooth. Position the seal over the seal bore with the lip pointing down. Using a hammer—prefer-

ably a soft mallet—tap the seal into the bore until it bottoms.

Install Front Cover—Slip the oil-pump/distributor-drive gear over the crank nose and into engagement with its key and against the crank sprocket.

Here's where a common mistake is made. Don't you make it, too. *The large chamfer on the oil-pump/distributor-drive gear bore goes toward the engine*—against the crank sprocket. Install the oil slinger—flange forward—on the crank nose and against the gear. The engine is now ready for the front cover.

Go to your collection of bolts and dig out the ones for the front cover. I hope you stored these in one container. Nissan engineers must have stayed up late nights figuring out ways to come up with as many different-length bolts as possible for

Slide oil-pump/distributor-drive gear onto crank nose with large chamfered end first. Double-check that chamfer is against chain sprocket. This is critical.

Oil slinger goes on next.

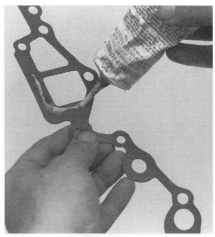

Prepare front-cover gasket by applying sealer around water-passage openings. Fit gaskets on dowels to front face of block.

Prelube front seal . . .

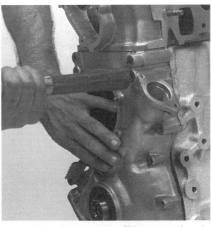

. . . and install front cover. Fit cover to dowels and tap into place with butt end of hammer. Fit is tight at cylinder head.

Before installing front-cover bolts, check lengths. It seems design objective was to make them all different. Check that there's sufficient thread engagement, but not so much that bolt bottoms in hole. Also, hold water pump up to cover to determine which bolts are not to be installed at this time. Some front-cover bolts double as water-pump bolts.

the front cover. Of the 13 bolts for the L20B, there are 87mm, 75mm, and 43mm long 8mm bolts, and 43mm and 16mm long 6mm bolts! The L20B has two extra bolts at the top of the cover.

When you think you have found all of the front-cover bolts, clean them. Soak them in solvent and wire-brush their threads. Carefully check sizes and lengths to the front cover to make sure you have all of the right bolts. If the water pump is not yet installed on the front cover, allow for the additional bolt length required to mount it.

Wipe the gasket surfaces clean and install the gaskets. Run a bead of sealer around the water passage on both sides of the right gasket. Place the gaskets against the front face of the block and over the dowels.

Lubricate the crankshaft oil-seal lip

with moly grease or petroleum jelly and fit the front cover to the block. Place the cover against the block, under the head and over the two dowels. Because the head is on, the fit will be tight, especially at the top. Tap against the top bolt bosses with the butt end of a hammer handle. Work from side to side until the cover is hard against the block.

Install all of the front-cover bolts that thread into the block and torque them: M6 (6mm) 2.9—7.2 ft-lb (0.4—1.0 kg-m); M8 (8mm) 7.2—12 ft-lb (1.0—1.6 kg-m). Now, install the two bolts that thread down into the cover at the front of the cylinder head. Torque them 2.9—7.2 ft-lb (0.4—1.0 kg-m).

Torquing the bolt under the timing-chain inspection window is virtually impossible because of tight access. So, tighten it with a box-end wrench using

your "calibrated" feel. Do not overtighten this bolt because it threads into aluminum. **Install Camshaft Cover**—Find the cam-cover bolts in your diminishing collection of parts and the gasket in the gasket set. No sealer is needed on the gasket. If you want to seal the cam-cover gasket, use silicone sealer on the cover only. Don't use sealer on the head side of the gasket. To hold the gasket in place—if you didn't use sealer—lay the gasket on the cam cover, then push the bolts through the gasket. The bolts will hold the gasket to the cover.

Set the cam cover on the head and thread in the bolts. As you snug the bolts,

Don't forget to install head-to-front cover bolts.

Close up top end of engine by installing chain-inspection cover and cam cover. Cam cover gasket may be pushed out of place as bolts are tightened, resulting in a massive oil leak if it isn't corrected. Use tab at center of gasket to align gasket. Install oil-filler cap.

Check damper/pulley nose for grooving. If OK, refinish seal surface with 400 grit emery cloth.

After oiling seal surface, fit damper/pulley to crank nose and rotate into engagement with keys.

Install pulley bolt and washer, and torque bolt 101—116 ft-lb (13.7—15.7 kg-m). Or, if engine is an L13, L16 or L20A, torque bolt 115—130 ft-lb (15.6—17.6 kg-m). Hold crank at flywheel flange with two bolts threaded in and a bar. Or use a wood block wedged between crank throw and bottom of block.

check that the gasket stays in place. Torque the cam-cover bolts 2.9—7.2 ft-lb (0.4—1.0 kg-m). Recheck the gasket and make sure the oil-filler cap is installed. The cam-cover gasket will relax, so retorque the cam-cover bolts.

Inspection & Fuel Pump or Pump Cover—To complete the "upstairs" sealing, install the timing-chain inspection cover and fuel-pump mounting cover. If a mechanical fuel pump is used, install it rather than the cover. Find the gaskets for these in the gasket set and install the covers. An insulating spacer installs between

the pump and head, requiring two gaskets for the pump. No sealer is required. Torque the bolts 2.9—7.2 ft-lb (0.4—1.0 kg-m).

If a mechanical fuel pump is used, lubricate the actuating-arm wear surface with moly grease. Place the gasket-insulator-gasket combo over the mounting studs and install the pump. If the eccentric is on its high spot, rotate the crank one revolution or force the pump against the head

and run in the mounting nuts. Torque the nuts 7.2—13 ft-lb (0.1—0.2 kg-m).

Prepare Crank Damper/Pulley—The L-series damper doubles as the accessory-drive pulley. Nissan-racing pulleys and dampers are separate—the pulley bolts to the damper. Standard four-cylinder L-series engines use solid dampers. If you haven't cleaned the damper, do so now.

If you have a six-cylinder engine, inspect the rubber bond between the outer ring and the damper center. Bonded six-cylinder dampers must be secure. Try forcing off the outer ring by placing the damper on the floor nose-down and standing on the ring. If the ring moves, the bond has failed; the damper should be replaced.

Check the crankshaft-seal surface; slight grooving is OK. Give it the same treatment you gave the crankshaft-bearing journals—but don't polish it. Similar to cylinder-bore crosshatching, some tooth is required to carry oil to lubricate the seal.

Install Damper/Pulley—Oil the damper-seal surface. Fit the damper to the crank nose and rotate it into engagement with its key. Push the damper all the way on and install the bolt and washer. Make sure the bolt threads are clean, then Loctite them.

Most L-series damper bolts are torqued 101—116 ft-lb (13.7—15.7 kg-m). The exceptions are the L13, 16 and 20A; torque their damper bolts 115—130 ft-lb (15.6—17.6 kg-m).

After installing oil-pump pickup with new gasket, bottom end can be sealed. Run bead of sealer across front-cover and rear-main-cap parting surfaces before installing pan gasket.

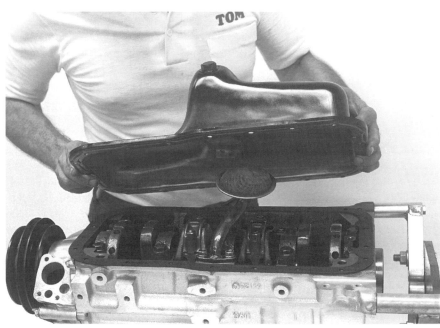

Set pan on block, being careful not to shift gasket out of position.

You'll find that you can't torque the damper bolt without turning the crankshaft. To hold the crank, install two bolts in the flywheel flange and bridge them with a large screwdriver or pry bar. This will give you a "handle" to prevent crankshaft rotation.

OIL-PUMP PICKUP & PAN
It's time to seal the bottom of your engine. Roll your engine over on its back—if it's on an engine stand. Otherwise, stand it on its rear face.

Install Oil-Pump Pickup—If you haven't cleaned the oil-pump pickup, do it now. Soak the pickup in solvent to loosen deposits. If they break off, the dirt particles go directly to the oil pump. Oil-pump damage is the likely result.

After soaking the pickup, blow out its screen with compressed air. If this doesn't get the screen clean, soak it again. Repeat this process until you get the pickup perfectly clean. Use carburetor cleaner if conventional solvent doesn't do the job.

Find the two pickup-mounting bolts and gasket. Do not use sealer on the gasket. Install the pump and torque the bolts 7 ft-lb (1.0 kg-m).
Install Oil Pan—With the pickup in place, take one last look at the bottom end. Take this opportunity to soak the tim-

ing chain with oil to give it some initial lubrication.

The oil pan must be clean. If it's not, clean it. While you're at it, check the mounting flange to make sure it's flat, particularly at the bolt holes. The flange must not be dimpled at the bolt holes.

To fix a bent or dimpled oil-pan flange, lay the pan upside down on a flat, sturdy surface. With a hammer and large punch, work around the reinforcing beads to straighten and flatten the flange. You may want to treat your pan to a fresh paint job.

Now you can install the oil pan. Gather all the parts you'll need: oil pan, pan gasket, bolts and silicone sealer.

Clean the gasket surfaces with lacquer thinner. Run small beads of sealer at the junctures of the bottom surface of the block and rear-main cap and front cover. No more sealer is required. Lay the pan gasket on the block. Without moving the gasket, fit the pan to the block. Run in all the pan bolts and gradually tighten them. Because the oil-pan gasket will relax as it's compressed, keep tightening the bolts until 4—7 ft-lb (0.6—1.0 kg-m) is maintained. Do not overtighten the bolts or you will dimple the pan flange.

Before shifting your attention from oil pan, make sure the drain plug is snug and its washer is in good condition—don't

put this off. Replace the plug if the washer is split or squeezed out. Replacing the plug-and-washer assembly is easier than replacing the washer on the plug. Correct torque for the oil-pan drain plug is 14—22 ft-lb (2.0—3.0 kg-m).

OIL PUMP
Before you install the oil pump, reset number-1 cylinder to TC if you moved the crank. To ensure that number-1 piston is at the top of its power stroke, look into cylinder-1 exhaust and intake ports. Both valves should be closed with the crank damper indicating 0 on the timing pointer.

To install the oil pump, you'll need the pump, gasket, oil-pump/distributor-drive shaft and four mounting bolts. Wipe off the gasket surfaces with lacquer thinner. Fit the gasket to the pump housing—no sealer required here.
Time Oil Pump—Apply moly grease to the oil-pump/distributor shaft on both sides of the gear and to the gear teeth.

To time the pump—actually it's the oil-pump/distributor shaft you are timing—insert the short end of the shaft in the pump. The shaft is fully engaged when the gear bottoms against the housing. Rotate the shaft so the timing mark on the gear hub aligns with the oil squirt hole. See photo, page 136. This is where the shaft must be when you install the pump. Insert one bolt with its flat washer and lock washer in the pump housing.

Without rotating the shaft, hold the pump up to the cover with the pressure-regulator-spring cap to the rear of the engine. Insert the shaft through its hole in the cover. Using the single pump mounting bolt as a guide, rotate the pump about 1/2-bolt hole to the right—clockwise. This compensates for the counterclockwise rotation of the shaft as the gear on the shaft engages its driving gear on the crank.

The object here is to end up with the tang on the distributor end of the shaft at 11:25 clock position as viewed through the distributor-mounting hole. Also, the tang offset should be to the front of the engine. As shown in the photo, page 137, the tang will align with the rear edge of the top distributor bolt hole at the 11:25 position. The tang will also line up with the front edge of the bottom hole.

If the tang doesn't line up as described, pull out the pump and shaft, rotate the shaft to compensate for how much it was off, then reinstall the shaft and pump. When the shaft aligns properly, line up the pump gasket, thread in the pump bolts and torque them 8—11 ft-lb (1.1—1.5 kg-m).

WATER PUMP

Before you install the water pump, turn the pump shaft and feel for roughness. If the bearings feel rough or there are signs of coolant leakage at the front of the water-pump housing, replace the pump.

Find the water-pump gasket. Most water pumps have two captive bolts; one short and one long. These bolts can't be removed with the pulley-and-viscous-drive assembly in place. The remaining bolts should be the only parts left in your loose front-cover-parts collection. Use silicone sealer on both sides of the gasket and fit it to the pump.

Fit pump to the front cover and thread in the bolts. Torque 6mm water-pump bolts 3—7 ft-lb (0.4—1.0 kg-m); torque 8mm bolts 8—12 ft-lb (1.2—1.6 kg-m).

Breather Tube—If you removed it, install the crankcase-breather tube. It installs in a hole in the left side of the block. Push it in as far as you can by hand, then tap the tube into place with a soft mallet. If the tube has a support bracket, such as the one shown, make sure it will line up with its mounting hole. This one bolts to a bracket on the exhaust manifold.

Run-in all pan bolts and torque 4—7 ft-lb (0.6—1.0 kg-m). Retorque several times to compensate for gasket relaxing.

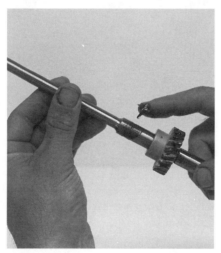

Prelube oil-pump-drive-spindle gear and bearing journals.

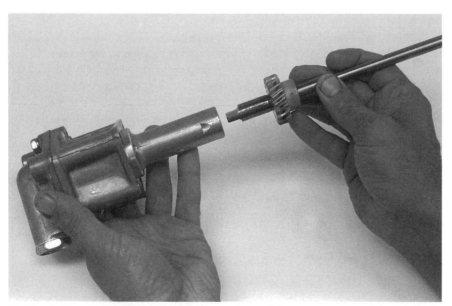

Position bottom end of spindle to oil pump as shown. Note mark on gear hub and notch in pump extension. Fit bolts, gasket and spindle to pump . . .

. . . and insert assembly into front cover. Engine should be at TC on firing stroke.

Shaft will rotate as spindle gear meshes with drive gear. Check drive tang at upper end of spindle when oil pump and gear are fully installed. Tang should be offset to front and pointing at back side of top distributor mounting hole.

COOLANT INLETS & OUTLETS

Thermostat Housing—The thermostat housing consists of upper and lower halves that bolt to the cylinder head. Bolt the bottom half to the head with its gasket and some sealer on both sides of the gasket. While you're looking for this gasket, find all coolant outlet and inlet gaskets.

Caution: You must use the correct length bolts in the thermostat housing, particularly the front one. A bolt that's too long in the front hole will shove the chain guide into the timing chain as it's tightened. This will wear out the guide in very short order. So, double-check the bolt before you install it.

Torque the thermostat-housing-to-head bolts 8—14 ft-lb (1.2—2.0 kg-m).

Test Thermostat—If your engine didn't experience overheating problems and it warmed up OK you may be able to reuse the original thermostat. Otherwise, install a new one. Don't do this before you test it.

Don't assume a new thermostat is OK just because it's new. More than one new thermostat has refused to open and caused the engine to overheat. You don't want this to happen to your newly rebuilt engine the first time it's run. To make sure you don't have this problem, heat the *new or old* thermostat in a pan of water. Use a kitchen thermometer in the water so you can observe its temperature.

Screwdriver is used to double-check tang position. Tang should align with rear edge of top distributor-adapter bolt hole.

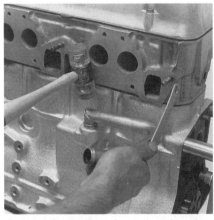

If removed, install crankcase-breather pipe. Using soft mallet, gradually tap into block. Support-bracket position is a guess. Reposition it after exhaust manifold is installed.

When the water reaches the temperature rating of the thermostat, it should begin to open. The thermostat should fully open when it's 5F above its rated temperature. If it doesn't, replace it. Check the replacement thermostat, too.

Install Thermostat—Set the thermostat in the recess in its housing with the spring down. The thermostat should have TOWARD ENGINE stamped on the underside of its flange. Apply sealer to both sides of the gasket and install it with the top half of the thermostat housing—coolant outlet. Bolt the housing halves together and torque the two bolts 7—12 ft-lb (1.0—1.6 kg-m). You may have to

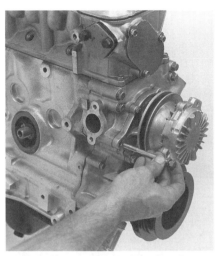

Apply sealer to front cover. Then install water pump and torque 6mm bolts 3—7 ft-lb (0.4—1.0 kg-m) and 8mm bolts 8—12 ft-lb (1.2—1.6 kg-m).

Next on is thermostat housing. You'll need upper and lower halves, mounting bolts, new gasket and thermostat. Make sure thermostat works, especially a new one, before installing. Immerse thermostat in boiling water and check to see if it opens. If it doesn't, replace thermostat and recheck.

remove the outboard bolt later to install a fuel-line or ignition-wire bracket.

Install Coolant-Inlet Neck—On the other side of the engine, install the coolant-inlet neck. With its gasket sealed and installed between the neck and front cover, install the bolts and torque them 7—12 ft-lb (1.0—1.6 kg-m).

Install Distributor Adapter—If you removed the distributor adapter on teardown, find the distributor-to-front cover adapter gasket. You probably ran across it in your search for the thermostat and coolant-inlet necks because it's easy to mistake it for one of these. Don't use sealer on this gasket. Install the adapter with

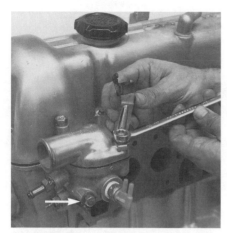

CAUTION: Do not install bolt that's too long in front thermostat-housing hole (arrow). This is a common cause of timing chains being destroyed. Thermostat spring installs down. Use RTV sealer on gaskets. Torque bolts 7—12 ft-lb (1.0—1.6 kg-m).

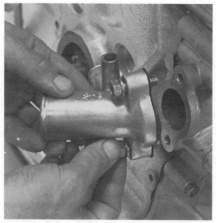

Go to other side of engine and install coolant inlet. Bolts get same torque as those for thermostat housing.

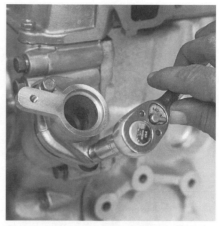

Back to other side, install distributor adapter. Adapter "ear" installs in 10:30 or 3:00 position, depending on engine. No sealer is needed on neck. Torque bolts 7—12 ft-lb (1.0—1.6 kg-m).

its "ear" in the 10:30 or 3:00 position—see the accompanying photo. Torque the bolts 7—12 ft-lb (1.0—1.6 kg-m).

MANIFOLDS

Install Gasket—Fit the one-piece intake/exhaust-manifold gasket over the exhaust-manifold studs and against the side of the head. If your manifolds are installed separately—unlike the bolt-together L20 manifolds shown—install the exhaust manifold first. Secure it with flat washers and finger-tight nuts.

WARNING: Be sure to use the correct manifold gasket for fuel-injected engines. It must have the small windows (rounded notches) that the injectors shoot through into the intake ports.

Some intake- and exhaust-manifold flanges are clamped at their edges with bolts and thick, flat washers that bridge their flanges; the bolts don't go through holes in the flanges. This makes it handy to install an intake manifold separately.

For those bolts with washers that straddle intake and exhaust flanges, loosely install them with their washers. The concave, or cupped, side of the washer goes against the manifold. You can now slip the intake manifold down between these washers and the head. This allows you to install the remaining bolts and washers without having to play gymnastics by holding the manifold and threading in a couple of bolts. A lifting lug installs with the rear exhaust-manifold stud. Don't forget it.

Fit manifold gasket to studs. No gasket sealer is required.

Install the remaining manifold bolts and washers. Access to these nuts and bolts is difficult. However, with the right combination of sockets, extensions and U-joints, you won't have any trouble. Once you have all the bolts, nuts and washers in place, torque them to the following values:

Thread Size	ft-lb	(N-m/kg-m)
8mm bolt	11—18	(15—25/1.5—2.5)
10mm bolt	25—33	(34—44/3.4—4.5)
8mm nut	9—12	(12—16/12—16)

Install Carburetor—If your engine is carbureted, install the carburetor(s) now rather than waiting after you've installed the engine. It is easier to do now. Set the carburetor(s) on the manifold with new gaskets and the carburetor insulator(s).

Install manifolds separately, unless bolted together such as this. Exhaust manifold goes on first if separate from intake manifold.

Thread on the nuts and torque them 3.6—7.2 ft-lb (0.5—1.0 kg-m).

Using your marked tags or masking-tape flags as reference, install as many lines, wires and hoses now as is practical. Again, it's much easier to do it now rather than after you've installed the engine.

Fuel Injection—If your engine is fuel-injected—unless it's turbocharged—you have no choice but to complete the induction-assembly installation after the engine is installed.

Turbocharger—If you have an L28ET (turbocharged L28), install the turbocharger. Start by installing the turbocharger oil line. It takes oil from the right side of the block at the oil-pressure sender and routes it over the back of the block to the turbocharger.

With the exhaust outlet bolted to the

Large washer bridges intake- and exhaust-manifold flanges, securing both to head. Concave side installs against manifolds. If manifolds are installed separately, start with exhaust. Loosely install these bolts and washers so you can slip intake manifold between washer and head.

Have a nut nearby when doing this. When manifold(s) is in place, install nut on stud to hold it (them) in place. After you have all nuts and bolts loosely installed, torque them according to specs.

turbo, fit a new gasket and the turbocharger to the exhaust manifold over the four mounting studs. Secure it with the mounting nuts and torque them 33—40 ft-lb 4.5—5.4 kg-m).

Don't forget the oil-drain pipe—it installs between the bottom of the turbocharger and the left side of the oil pan.

Connect the oil-feed line to the turbocharger.

DISTRIBUTOR

Now's a good time to install the distributor. First, mark the distributor housing to indicate the firing position of the number-1 cylinder. Do this by marking the

number-l distributor-cap terminal, page 140. Once you have the housing marked, remove the cap.

Insert the distributor into its adapter and align the adjustment tab on the distributor housing with the one on the adapter. Rotate the rotor shaft until it engages the drive-shaft tang. When the distributor shaft engages its drive shaft, the distributor can be inserted all the way into the adapter. Thread the bolt with its washer in the adjustment tab. Leave it loose.

To static-time the ignition, reposition the engine crank at 10° before top center (BTC). If the crank is on TC, simply rotate it backward, or counterclockwise, 10°. Rotate the distributor housing all the way to the left, or counterclockwise. If breaker points are used, check point gap. It should be 0.020 in. (0.50mm). Rotate the housing to the right—clockwise—until the points just begin to open. Secure the adjusting bolt.

If a solid-state ignition is used, rotate the distributor housing counterclockwise until the *reluctor* points—the pointed wheel on the distributor shaft—line up with the *stator* points—the ring with points

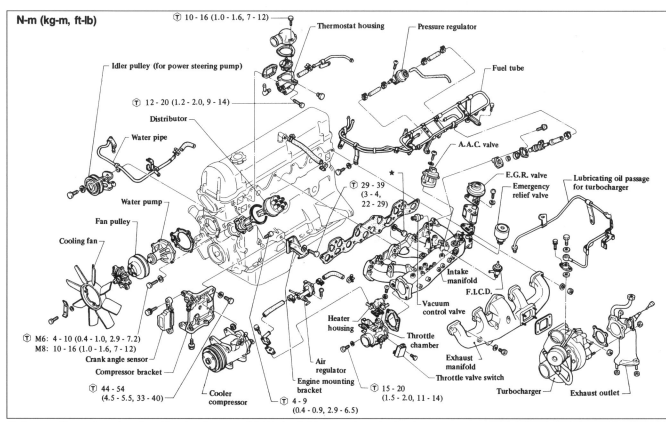

Reference illustration when installing hardware on L28 Turbo. With exception of turbocharger, torque values and many components are valid for other L-series engines. Drawing courtesy Nissan.

Using number-1 mark on cap as reference, transfer mark to distributor housing.

Loosen adjusting nut at base of distributor. Note timing marks (arrow).

With rotor pointing at reference mark on housing, install distributor. Turn rotor back and forth until shaft engages spindle tang and distributor drops into place. If it doesn't, remove distributor and check tang position. If you installed drive spindle correctly, return crank to TC and try again.

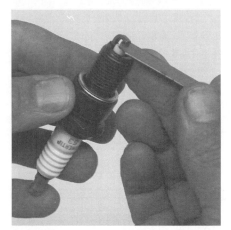

Don't assume spark plug gaps are OK just because plugs are new. Gap plugs for breaker-point ignition 0.032 in. (0.8mm) and 0.042 in. (1.1mm) for solid-state ignition. Install distributor cap and route wires to plugs. Firing orders are: 1-3-4-2 for four-cylinder engines; 1-5-3-6-2-4 for sixes.

surrounding the reluctor. Secure the adjusting bolt.

Install the distributor cap and route the wires to the spark plugs according to engine firing order. For fours, firing order is 1-3-4-2; firing order for sixes is 1-5-3-6-2-4. The distributor rotates in the counterclockwise direction. Starting at the number-1 distributor-cap terminal, follow the firing order to route each spark-plug wire separately.

Install Spark Plugs—Now is a good time to gap and install new spark plugs. Just because the plugs are new doesn't mean the gaps are right, even if they were OK when they left the factory. If a breaker-point ignition is used, set gap to 0.032 in. (0.8mm); 0.042-in. (1.1mm) gap for solid-state ignition.

Before you install the plugs, put some anti-seize compound on their threads—not the threads in the head. This will help

to ensure that the softer aluminum threads in the head will not gall. Do not get anti-seize compound on the two threads nearest the tip end of the plug. Anti-seize may end up on the plug tip, fouling it.

Install the plugs so they are against their gaskets—just finger-tight! To correctly tighten a plug with a new gasket, turn it 1/4 turn after the plug is *against its new gasket*. To eliminate guesswork, it's best to tighten the plugs with a torque wrench 11—15 ft-lb (1.5—2.0 kg-m).

Finish installing the plug wires by pushing them all the way on the plugs. Give them a tug to make sure they are fully seated.

SENDING UNITS

Oil-Pressure Sender—There are two types of oil-pressure senders: those for idiot lights and those for gauges. The idiot-light sender is much smaller than the large

canister-type gauge sender.

Regardless of the type of sender, they install in the same place—beside the oil filter. Put non-hardening sealer on the threads and screw-in the sending unit. Do not use Teflon tape. There are flats on a canister-type sender, allowing you to use an adjustable wrench for tightening it. Special sockets are available for installing an idiot-light sender, but an adjustable wrench will also work. Tighten both types 7—12 ft-lb (1.0—1.6 kg-m).

Coolant-Temperature Sender—The coolant temperature sender should already be installed. If it's not, install it now. It goes in the thermostat housing. Don't forget to seal its threads.

Oil Filter—You can either install the oil filter now or after the engine is installed. The advantage of doing it now is that the lubrication circuit will be completely sealed. The disadvantage is having the filter in the way while you're installing the engine. You be the judge.

Although there are other components that can go on the engine while it's on the stand or bench, let's move to the installation chapter. It makes more sense to install such items as the engine plate, clutch and flywheel, alternator, A/C-compressor bracket and engine mounts while the engine is "on the hook" and ready to install.

CHAPTER NINE

Engine Installation

Lift, such as cherry picker, and chain, cable or nylon strap are needed to install engine.

If automatic transmission is used, remove converter from transmission and drain fluid into container. Replace front transmission seal. It can be levered out, but take care not to damage stator support or input shaft. Install new seal, then converter.

It's time for the job you've been working toward—installing your newly rebuilt engine. Get those containers of fasteners and parts out from where they've been stored. You'll also need to round up the engine hoist, jack and jack stands again.

While you have the opportunity, clean the engine compartment, accessories, related brackets and hardware so everything under the hood will look as good as the engine. You'll need some degreaser, a stiff-bristle brush and a garden hose. Don't forget to protect the paint work on the fenders, cowl and other body surfaces. Degreaser is strong stuff. You can use the same materials to clean all bolt-on parts and accessories. Or, truck them to the local car wash and use their high-pressure washer. This will remove the resulting mess from your driveway. Once clean, some touch-up paint on key areas will enhance engine-compartment appearance once the new engine is back in place.

FRONT TRANSMISSION SEAL

Any leakage from the transmission into the clutch or bell housing should be corrected *now*. This is usually accomplished by replacing the transmission front seal.

Manual Transmission—Unless there are signs of gear lube in the bell housing or on the clutch, don't concern yourself with the front seal. Unlike an automatic-transmission front seal, this seal is not disturbed during engine removal and installation. Additionally, the liquid it seals is not pressurized, so its durability is much greater than an automatic-transmission front seal.

If there are signs of leakage from the input-shaft seal, replace it. To do this, remove the transmission front cover. Use a procedure similar to the one you used to remove and replace the crankshaft front seal. Pry it out with a screwdriver or a small pry bar.

After cleaning the seal bore with lac-

quer thinner, position the front cover on its nose. Run a thin film of silicone sealer around the periphery of the seal. Position the seal squarely over its bore with the seal lip pointing toward the transmission. Lightly tap the seal into place with a soft mallet. If the old seal isn't badly distorted, place it against the new seal to protect it during installation. Then, install the front cover with a new gasket.

Automatic Transmission—If you have an automatic transmission, replace the front-pump seal whether it shows signs of leaking or not. If it's bad, chances are it will start leaking soon after you get out of the driveway.

Before you can replace the front-pump seal, you'll have to remove the converter. Drain the converter after it's removed. This will make it much lighter and will prevent spilling fluid while reinstalling it. Also, if you haven't done so already, it's a good idea to get rid of old transmission fluid. So drain it now and fill the transmission with fresh ATF after you get everything back together.

Before pulling off the converter, measure the perpendicular distance from the nose of the converter to the front face of the bell housing. Rotate the converter and push it toward the transmission to make sure it is fully engaged. Lay a straightedge across the front of the bell housing and measure the distance to the converter nose. Record the distance. You'll need this dimension for checking converter installation later.

Have a bucket or drain pan close by. Be ready to handle some weight as you slide the converter forward and clear of the input shaft. Tilt the converter front-down so the fluid won't pour out before you can drain it into a bucket or pan.

Removing the converter exposes the front-pump seal. Put a screwdriver behind the seal lip and pry it out. Go around the seal, prying a little at a time and the seal will eventually pop out. If it's stubborn, the seal can be removed with a chisel and hammer, driving carefully against the little bit that extends beyond the front-pump bore. I don't recommend using the chisel-and-hammer method first because of the risk of damaging the *stator support* or the seal bore. So, attempt prying it out first.

Before installing the new seal, clean the front-pump bore by wiping it clean of any oil with a paper towel and lacquer thinner. Prelube the seal lip with some clean ATF. Place the seal squarely in the front-pump bore with the seal lip pointing toward the transmission. Tap lightly around the seal with a hammer, being careful it doesn't cock in the bore. Keep doing this until you feel the seal bottom firmly all the way around. Wipe any excess sealer off and you're ready for the converter.

While you're still in the engine compartment, clean the inside of the bell housing. Make sure the front face of the housing—the surface that mates with the engine—is clean and free of burrs and nicks. Smooth any imperfections with a flat file. This will ensure good engine and transmission alignment.

Before installing the converter, check the outer surface of the converter neck—the surface that runs against the seal. Be particularly attentive if the seal you replaced leaked. If it has any nicks or burrs or is at all rough, polish it with 400-grit paper. If the seal surface is deeply grooved, you'll have to replace the converter. Sorry! Otherwise, fluid will leak past the new seal.

If the converter's seal surface is OK, clean it with lacquer thinner on a rag or

Depth of rivets below friction surface is accurate indicator of clutch-disc wear. If less than 0.012 in. (0.3mm), replace disc.

If equipped with manual transmission, check pressure plate friction surface for warpage using straightedge. Check also for hot spots and heat checks—small cracks. Check spring for bent, cracked or broken fingers. If any problems are found, replace pressure plate. If OK, clean friction surface with lacquer thinner and give it a good sanding. Give flywheel same treatment.

paper towel. Then, give it the same treatment that you gave the crankshaft-seal surfaces. Use a strip of 400-grit emery cloth to put a new "tooth" on the converter's seal surface.

Now you're ready to install the converter. Lightly oil the surface you just cleaned. It's added insurance for the seal, even though you already lubricated the seal.

Start the converter on the transmission input shaft. Rotate the converter back and forth while pushing on it until you feel there is *full* engagement with the transmission. Be careful here because the converter must engage the transmission input shaft, stator support and front pump. You should feel at least two engagements, and probably all three.

When you think the converter is fully installed, remeasure the converter-to-bell housing distance. The distance from the front face of the bell housing and the front of any of the converter drive lugs should measure about 27/32 in. (0.84 in. or 21.5mm). Measure to a drive lug from the backside of a straightedge laid across the front of the converter.

If this measurement is less, the converter is not fully engaged. Stop and spin and push on it some more until it is engaged. Don't trash a converter and transmission by thinking you can pull it on the rest of the way with the bell hous-

ing-to-engine bolts. This will probably damage the transmission, sending metal chips through the transmission lube system. Say good-bye to any savings from doing your own engine rebuild.

Clutch & Flywheel—Now's the time to replace or recondition the clutch or flywheel, if necessary. Check these components for sure. Checking is purely academic if the clutch slipped before the rebuild. You'll already know something has to be replaced; the disc for sure, probably the pressure plate and maybe the flywheel. If the clutch didn't slip, inspect these items anyway.

Measure Clutch Disc—Inspect a clutch disc by simply measuring the depth of the friction-material rivets. This is best done using the depth-gauge end of vernier calipers. Nissan recommends a minimum depth of 0.012 in. (0.3mm).

If you're thinking of skimping here, don't. Clutch discs are relatively inexpensive. And one thing you know for sure—clutch-disc wear will continue. Why risk ruining the pressure plate and flywheel? Also, it's considerably easier to replace clutch components now than after the engine is back in place.

Pressure-Plate Inspection—The general rule is, if the clutch disc wore out in a short time, the pressure plate needs to be replaced as well. This is particularly true if more than two discs have been used with

Don't install old clutch-release bearing without checking. Rotate while pushing on bearing. If you feel any roughness, replace it.

this pressure plate. But if the clutch looks good and gave many miles of trouble-free service, chances are it's all right.

The first thing to do when inspecting a pressure plate is to look at its friction surface—the surface that is in direct contact with the disc. If this surface is bright and shiny, and free of deep grooves, the pressure plate is probably OK. However, dark spots (hot spots) or heat checks (small cracks) indicate excessive slippage and irreparable pressure-plate damage.

In any case, check the pressure-plate friction surface by laying a straightedge across it. If it is warped in the typical concave shape, there will be a widening gap between it and the straightedge, starting from zero at the outside edge and increasing toward the inside edge.

If the hot spots, heat checks or warpage don't look too bad and you're on a tight budget, compare the price of resurfacing the pressure plate versus the price of a new or rebuilt one. Otherwise, don't waste time—replace it.

Regardless, if the pressure plate has survived more than two discs, it should be replaced no matter how good the friction surface looks. The diaphragm spring and related components are probably weak from fatigue, resulting in reduced clutch capacity. You may have gotten away with it with a tired engine, but now your engine will be making more torque, thus the chance of a slipping clutch is increased.

Flywheel—Because the flywheel *sees* the same slippage as the pressure plate, it will suffer from similar ills. If the original pressure plate has problems, take a really good look at the flywheel. Chances are it will be

in better condition because it has more mass than the pressure-plate pressure ring to absorb heat. For instance, you probably won't see a warped flywheel. The heat required to warp a flywheel would destroy the friction facing first.

On the other hand, it's common for a flywheel *surface* to get hot enough to *heat-check*. Also, a flywheel is not immune to damage from contact with the friction-disc rivets. It can be grooved as easily as a pressure plate. So, if the pressure plate is grooved, the flywheel may be also.

If the flywheel is heat-checked or badly grooved, it should be resurfaced. In fact, some clutch suppliers won't warrant their clutches unless the flywheel it is installed against is new or resurfaced. It's possible that resurfacing won't correct serious heat-checking. Only so much material can be removed from a flywheel before it becomes dangerously thin. And reusing a heat-checked flywheel is dangerous, too.

Heat checks can develop into long, deep radial cracks (like the spokes of a wheel) toward the center of the flywheel. A cracked flywheel can easily come apart or "explode" at high engine rpm with the force of a hand grenade.

If resurfacing is necessary, take the flywheel to an engine machine shop. Make sure the resurfacing is done on a grinder rather than a lathe, particularly if the flywheel is hot-spotted. Hot spots are harder than the *parent* (surrounding) metal. Consequently, if the flywheel is resurfaced by conventional machining, the cutting tool will *jump* over the hard spots. This creates little bumps on the friction surface. A grinding stone cuts right through the hard spots.

How about a flywheel that appears to be in good condition? It should still be cleaned. The resins in the clutch will be deposited on the flywheel friction surface. To give the clutch disc a fresh start, clean the flywheel friction surface with fine-grit sandpaper. After sanding, wash it with a *non-petroleum* solvent such as alcohol or lacquer thinner. This will remove any oil deposits. Give the same treatment to the pressure plate.

Finally, clean the counterbore on the side opposite the flywheel friction surface. It pilots tightly over the crankshaft mounting flange. If this counterbore is not clean and free of rust, flywheel installation will be dif-

ficult. You can use coarse sandpaper here.

Clutch-Release Bearing—I recommend replacing the release, or throwout, bearing regardless of its condition. The relative cost of a new bearing and the effort required to replace it once the engine is back in makes this a good insurance policy.

To replace the release bearing, slide it forward off the transmission input shaft and unclip it from the release lever. The old bearing will have to be pressed off its hub and the new one pressed on. To remove the old bearing, you'll need a pipe, hole in a wooden or steel block, or something of the kind that will clear the bearing hub, but still support the backside of the bearing. Next, you'll need something to act as a large punch that will seat against the front of the bearing hub, but will clear the bearing inner race as the hub is driven out.

Ready the hub for the new bearing by cleaning it and checking the surface that slides on the transmission-bearing retainer. Any burrs can be smoothed with a half-round or round file, preferably having a *mill cut*—the file teeth are in a X-pattern.

Although not a concern when removing the old bearing, the problem now is how to put the new bearing on the hub without damaging it providing it doesn't come preassembled to a hub. If this isn't done right, chances are the release-bearing races will be damaged.

To do this right, you'll need a *mandrel* that fits firmly against the front edge of the inner bearing race—it must not bear against the outer race. This mandrel can be a short section of pipe or tubing, or a large socket. Some experts even use the old bearing to push on the new one during installation. Works great!

To install the bearing, stand the bearing hub upright on a solid surface or centered under a hydraulic press ram. Place the new bearing squarely over the end of the hub with its front face up. The seal will be down or facing the hub. Position the mandrel against the inner bearing race and push or drive the bearing onto the hub with the press or a hammer. Make sure the bearing starts straight. The bearing will be fully installed when it seats against the shoulder on the hub.

Fill the groove in the hub ID with moly grease. Don't overdo it. There's always the chance that excess grease in the bell

After placing engine plate onto dowels at rear face of block, fit flywheel or flexplate to crankshaft. Align holes to those in crank. Thread in bolt to keep flywheel or flexplate from falling.

Apply drop of locking fluid to bolt threads . . .

. . . and install in crankshaft. Torque bolts 101—108 ft-lb (14—15 kg-m) for all but L13 and L16 engines. Torque them 69—76 ft-lb (94—103 kg-m). Note flywheel lock at starter ring gear. This one is from Mr. Gasket.

housing will end up on the clutch. That would mean pulling the engine or transmission to clean the grease off of the disc, pressure plate and flywheel—a lot of work that you won't want to do.

Apply a thin film of grease to the release lever-to-bearing hub contact points. Reinstall the release-bearing assembly on the release lever and retain it with its clip. Apply a thin film of grease to the lever pivot and reinstall the lever and bearing.

EXTERIOR ENGINE HARDWARE
Before the engine can be installed, some exterior components must go on first. Make this job easier by lifting and supporting the engine with the same lifting device used to install the engine. Observe caution with the cherry picker, hoist or whatever, as discussed on page 27.

Hook a chain, cable or lifting strap between the two lifting eyes at opposite ends of the cylinder head. Then, hook the cherry picker or chain hoist to it and lift the engine. Adjust the position of the hook so the engine is slightly lower at the rear—about a 5° slant on the engine.

Manual-Transmission Pilot Bushing—
Engines that will be fitted to a manual transmission must have a pilot bushing installed in the counterbore at the crankshaft flywheel flange. This bushing supports the end of the transmission input shaft. If the engine you are installing with a manual transmission was previously used

behind an automatic transmission, you'll have to install a pilot bearing because automatic transmissions don't use one.

Check the existing pilot-bushing ID if you haven't removed the bushing already. Pilot-bushing ID should be no less than 0.635 in. (16.13mm). Measure bushing ID with a telescoping gauge and micrometers or a vernier caliper.

If bushing ID exceeds the maximum bore-diameter limit of 0.635 in., remove it with a *slide hammer* or a hammer and a thin chisel. A slide hammer has a heavy weight that slides on a rod. The rod has a handle at one end and several end attachments, one of which will fit through the bushing bore and hook to the back side of the bushing. The bushing is pulled out by banging the weight against the handle, gradually knocking it out of its bore.

To use the hammer and chisel, simply split the bushing. Do this with care to avoid damage to the crankshaft counterbore.

Regardless of the method used to remove the pilot bushing, measure its depth with a straightedge laid across the flywheel flange to the back side of the bushing. It should measure approximately 0.177 in. (4.5mm) when the new bushing is installed.

Although it's not necessary to lubricate an Oilite pilot bushing because of its self-lubricating qualities, I soak the bushing in oil for about 15 minutes before installa-

tion. Afterward, I wipe the excess oil off of the bushing. Other than this, don't lubricate a pilot bushing. The oil or grease will also lubricate the clutch.

Position the new pilot bushing squarely over its bore. Carefully drive it into place using a socket that matches its OD and a hammer. Use a brass hammer if you don't want to mar the socket or ruin its plating. If the bushing cocks, remove it and start over. When you think the bushing is approaching its specified depth, check it. It should be in 0.157—0.197 in. (4.0—5.0mm).

Engine Plate—Make sure the two transmission-alignment dowels are in the rear face of the engine block. A solid dowel is fitted to the block above and slightly to the right of the rear core plug. A hollow dowel is concentric with the lower-left bell housing-bolt hole. If you removed this dowel to mount the engine to a stand, you must replace it. Make sure both dowels are in place before proceeding with engine installation.

After cleaning and applying a fresh coat of paint to the engine plate, apply a thin bead of weather-strip adhesive to the block's rear face to keep the plate from falling off the dowels and sliding down between the block and flywheel/flexplate while you're concentrating on aligning the engine and transmission.

Fit the engine plate over the dowels and against the engine block. Take the

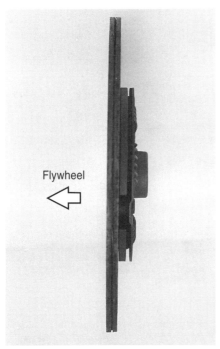

Clutch disc must install against flywheel as shown.

Center clutch disc to crankshaft input shaft with alignment tool. Tool will support disc while pressure date is installed.

plate on and off until the sealer tacks—gets sticky. Then, put it on for good.

Flywheel/Flexplate—Gather up all six flywheel bolts, clean them—especially the threads—and apply Lock N' Seal® Loctite® or equivalent to their threads. With one bolt handy, position the flywheel/flexplate on the crankshaft and rotate it so its holes line up with those in the crankshaft. Thread in one bolt to hold the flywheel/flexplate in place, then reinstall the remaining bolts. Gradually tighten the bolts and torque all but L13 and L16 engine bolts 101—108 ft-lb (13.7—14.6 kg-m). Torque L13 and L16 bolts 69—76 ft-lb (9.4—10.3 kg-m).

Use the handy device shown on page 144 to lock the flywheel while the bolts are being torqued. Or, use a strap bar bridging a couple of pressure-plate bolts threaded into the flywheel as shown on page 37.

Install Clutch—You can't just bolt the disc and pressure plate to the flywheel. The disc must be centered to the crankshaft, or you'll never get the engine and transmission bolted together.

To center the clutch disc to the crankshaft, you'll need a dummy transmission input shaft. K-D's universal clutch-alignment tool is shown here. Consider this the

"high-price spread." A spare input shaft works even better. Maybe you're lucky enough to have one. If not, a one-time job doesn't warrant buying an expensive tool. Many auto-parts stores sell less-expensive wooden alignment tools that work fine.

Install the clutch by first inserting the dummy shaft through the *back* of the disc splines. The portion of the clutch-disc hub with springs is on the back side. Hold the disc against the flywheel and insert the dummy shaft into the pilot bushing. The disc will stay there while you get the pressure plate into place.

Although it will fit and operate in any one of three positions on the flywheel, match the prick-punch marks on the flywheel and the old pressure plate—if you put them there at disassembly. I do this just as a precaution.

Although it's theoretically unnecessary, I know a part will fit in its original position with the least trouble. Of course, if you're installing a new pressure plate, install it in any position. The pressure plate may fit a little tightly. Carefully tap the pressure plate onto the dowels. Thread the six pressure-plate mounting bolts into the flywheel, then gradually tighten them. Stop tightening the pressure-plate bolts just before the disc is clamped to the flywheel.

Move the centering tool up and down to its limits until you find the center of movement, then hold the tool on this center. Continue tightening the bolts. When the pressure plate clamps the disc, check that the disc is centered. Pull the centering tool out. If it comes out and can be reinserted without difficulty, the disc is centered and the centering tool can be set aside. Finish tightening the pressure-plate bolts 12—15 ft-lb (1.6—2.1 kg-m).

Alternator—Hold the alternator bracket to the block and thread in the two bracket-to-block mounting bolts. Install the nut and washer before you run in the bolts too far. If the bracket you're installing uses a stud and nut in addition to the bolts, there's no room to get the washer and nut on the stud if you run the bolts in all the way. Tighten the bolts and nut 29—43 ft-lb (3.9—5.9 kg-m).

Fit the alternator to its bracket using the two lock washers and pivot bolts—one in front and one in back. Thread them in finger tight. Swing the alternator up into position and install the adjusting bracket. This sheet-metal bracket goes under the upper-right front-cover bolt. Install and lightly tighten the alternator bracket-to-alternator bolt to hold the alternator up.

Although I prefer waiting until the engine is installed, the alternator/water pump belt can be installed now. To do this, you'll have to loosely install the water-pump pulley without the fan. This will prevent fan damage.

A/C-Compressor Bracket—The factory A/C compressor uses a bracket similar to the alternator, though it's much larger. Additionally, it mounts the compressor idler pulley.

Four bolts with lock washers secure the A/C-compressor bracket to the block—the two long ones install at the top. Install the bracket and tighten the bolts 29—43 ft-lb (3.9—5.9 kg-m). Install the A/C compressor after the engine is installed.

Engine Mounts—Using two bolts with lock washers, install each mount with the ears at the outboard end facing down. The mount with the long bracket goes on the left side of the engine. Don't tighten the bolts for now. Leave them loose.

Oil Filter & Oil-Pressure Sender—Spread a film of oil on the new filter's seal, thread it onto its adapter and hand tighten

Position pressure plate to flywheel using match marks as reference. Install pressure-plate cover to dowels and secure with bolts. Gradually tighten bolts in rotation to pull down pressure plate evenly. Check alignment tool as you go and recenter disc as needed. When disc is clamped against flywheel and tool slips in and out freely, it can be removed. Torque bolts 12—15 ft-lb (1.6—2.1 kg-m).

Install some accessories now rather than after engine is installed. Access is much easier. Alternator and bottom bracket go on first. Then, swing alternator up and loosely install adjuster bracket.

Install A/C compressor bracket with idler pulley.

Install engine-mount brackets to block.

Prepare mounts to accept engine. Metal stopper is installed over rubber mount. It prevents engine from lifting while vehicle is under power if rubber mount fails.

it. If you use a wrench, don't tighten it more than 3/4 turn *after* its seal contacts the block.

Heater Hose—Install the heater outlet hose to the block; it's the long one. You'll need a hose clamp at the straight end and two mounting clips. The mounting clips should already be on the hose unless you're installing a new hose.

Position the hose along the right side of the block with its formed end to the rear and up. Push the straight end of the hose over the engine coolant inlet and secure it with the clamp. Slide the mounting clips along the hose to align them with their mounting bosses.

Find the two bolts, their lock washers, and two plastic-coated wiring-harness clips. These clips install between the engine block and the heater-hose clips.

INSTALL ENGINE

There's not much more you can install on the engine, so the big moment has come. If you wired the transmission up, place a jack under the transmission or bell housing. Raise the transmission enough to relieve the tension on the wires and remove them. Let the exhaust down, too, if it's wired up.

Lift Engine—With your engine hanging at the end of the cable, chain or strap, recheck its attitude. Its angle will have

changed after bolting on the extra hardware. The engine should be slightly lower at the rear, or at about a 5° slant. This is especially important with a manual transmission because of its long input shaft.

Raise the engine so it will clear the front of the car. Also, recheck that your lifting device will lower the engine all the way onto the engine mounts. Do this by measuring up from the ground to the engine—mount brackets on the engine when the engine is lowered all the way. Compare this height to the distance the engine mounts are from the ground. Remember that the car will settle a couple of inches when it supports the additional weight of the engine—if the car is sitting on its front suspension.

So, adjust the hookup to the engine now. Otherwise, you may have it down in

the engine compartment with two bolts in the bell housing and find it needs to be lowered a couple of inches but the lift is out of travel.

Many L-series engines have separate pieces, such as a baffle or *stopper,* that install between the rubber mount and engine-to-mount bracket. Baffles are used for shielding mounts from exhaust heat or other damaging elements. Stoppers limit fore-and-aft engine movement on the mounts. Position these necessary pieces on the mounts now. Don't leave them out.

If your vehicle has manual transmission, put it in gear. This will lock the input shaft so it will engage the clutch-disc splines. Equally important with an automatic transmission is to position one converter bolt hole directly at the bottom of the housing. If you are using the original

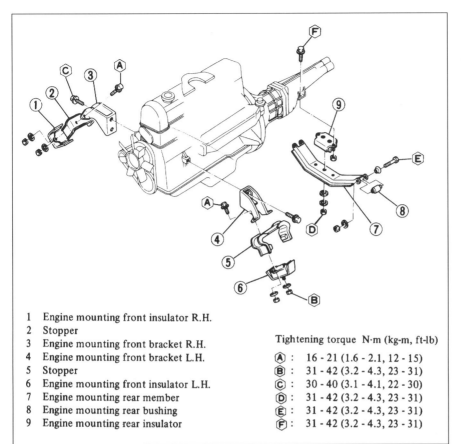

		Tightening torque N·m (kg-m, ft-lb)
1	Engine mounting front insulator R.H.	
2	Stopper	
3	Engine mounting front bracket R.H.	Ⓐ : 16 - 21 (1.6 - 2.1, 12 - 15)
4	Engine mounting front bracket L.H.	Ⓑ : 31 - 42 (3.2 - 4.3, 23 - 31)
5	Stopper	Ⓒ : 30 - 40 (3.1 - 4.1, 22 - 30)
6	Engine mounting front insulator L.H.	Ⓓ : 31 - 42 (3.2 - 4.3, 23 - 31)
7	Engine mounting rear member	Ⓔ : 31 - 42 (3.2 - 4.3, 23 - 31)
8	Engine mounting rear bushing	Ⓕ : 31 - 42 (3.2 - 4.3, 23 - 31)
9	Engine mounting rear insulator	

L28 engine and transmission mounts and fastener torques. Drawing courtesy Nissan.

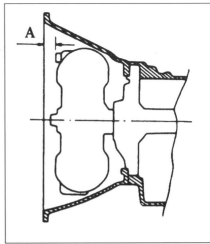

Rotate automatic-transmission converter into engagement with stator and input shafts, and front pump. Check for full engagement by measuring distance between converter-drive lug and straightedge placed across front face of bell housing. Distance A must be more than 0.846 in. (21.5mm). Drawing courtesy Nissan.

converter, it should be the marked one. Also, check that the matching flexplate hole is at the bottom.

Lower the engine into its compartment, being careful not to bump it into anything. There are several fragile and expensive components that will break if bumped. A helping hand from a friend would be in order for this reason.

Manual Transmission—Center the engine on the transmission. Be ready to raise or lower the transmission to get the two lined up.

Carefully move the engine back so the input-shaft pilot centers into the clutch disc. Adjust the jack and/or lift so the engine and transmission mating faces are parallel. Push the engine back and rock it from side to side. The clutch and input shaft should engage. If they don't, turn the crank with the crankshaft pulley bolt or move the car slightly while in gear. This will turn the input shaft slightly. Try engaging the engine to the transmission again. *Don't force anything!* It's like flipping a coin. Heads will come up sooner or later. Be calm and repeat this procedure until

the two sets of splines line up and engage.

Once engaged, put the transmission in neutral. Check that the engine and transmission mating faces are still parallel. When they are, rotate the engine to one side or the other to engage the alignment dowels with the bell housing. Have a bell housing-to-engine bolt and washer in hand. Once the engine "clicks" into engagement, keep it there. Thread-in the bolt finger-tight, then install another the same way. Torque these bolts 32—43 ft-lb (4.3—5.8 kg-m). You'll have to finish installing and torquing the engine-to-bell housing bolts from underneath. Remove the jack.

Automatic Transmission—Make one last check that the converter is on all the way and positioned with the marked drive lug at the bottom. Move the engine close to the converter housing, lining it up on center and with its rear face parallel to the transmission's front face. You may have to adjust the position of the transmission with the jack. Move the engine from side to side—rotate it—so the alignment dowels engage the bell housing.

Have a bell housing-to-engine bolt and washer in hand. Once the engine "clicks" into place, keep it there by threading in the bolt finger-tight. Install another bolt the same way. Torque these bolts 29—36 ft-lb (3.9—4.9 kg-m). You'll have to finish installing and torquing the engine-to-bell housing bolts from underneath. Remove the jack.

The next major step in the engine-to-transmission procedure is to bolt the converter to the flexplate. This can wait until you have the car up in the air to do the other "bottom-side" jobs.

Engine Mounts—Double-check the engine mounts. The baffle or stoppers should be in place and lined up.

Lower the engine *just short* of resting on its mounts. This can be a frustrating job if you don't keep calm. Getting the bolts started in 280Z-type mounts can be a pain because the mounts are at an angle. Mounts using studs, such as the L20 in the 200SX, are much simpler to get started. The main thing to watch for in this case is not to damage the stud threads.

If the mounts use bolts, use a punch or Phillips screwdriver to align the engine-mount bolt holes. Insert it through the front or rear mating holes. After one bolt is partially threaded in, remove the punch or screwdriver and thread-in the other one.

Go to the mount on the opposite side

When engine is engaged with transmission input shaft or converter nose and square against bell housing, install top bolt to keep engine and transmission together.

Once engine and transmission are together align mount bracket with mount by moving engine around. Don't tighten either mount until bolts for both sides are in.

Ground wire installs under top starter-mounting bolt. Using labels as guide, install remaining starter leads.

Reconnect heater hoses. If old or in bad condition, replace hoses.

Raise vehicle and support with jack stands. Make sure it's firmly supported before going underneath.

If old exhaust pipe-to-manifold gasket is OK, reuse it. Otherwise, install new one. This is easier to do from top on 280ZX.

and do the same thing. This is usually easier said than done. You should know by now why I suggested leaving the mounts loose. Adjust the engine up and down with the hoist to get things lined up. Once you've managed to get all the bolts started by juggling, prying and grumbling, snug the bolts and set the engine down on its rubber mounts.

As with many other fasteners, the right front engine-mount-to-insulator bolt may also secure a wiring-harness connector. Tighten the mount-to-insulator bracket bolt 12—15 ft-lb (1.6—2.1 kg-m). Torque engine-mount bolts that thread into the block 22—30 ft-lb (3.0—4.0 kg-m).

Route the wiring harness to the transmission through clips on the block under the heater hose.

Starter Motor—Install the starter motor. The engine ground-cable connector goes under the top mounting bolt, so have it in place before you wrestle the starter motor into place. After you have the top bolt started, thread-in the bottom bolt. You'll be able to reach it from above. Tighten bolts.

You'll now begin to appreciate those little identifying flags I had you install when you were disconnecting wires and hoses. Hook up the starter-motor leads. The battery hot-wire and ignition-lead connectors fit to a common post on the starter solenoid in this installation. The starter-switch wire uses a spade-type connector—push it on until it clicks in place.

Heater Hoses—Complete the heater-hose installation. Fit the short heater hose to the cylinder-head outlet and the heater-core inlet—it's the top tube. Connect the heater-outlet hose to the bottom heater-core tube. Tighten the clamps.

Oil-Pressure-Sender & Alternator Leads—Connect them. I hope you had

the leads tagged. You'll have three or four connections to make here: two loop-type connectors and two spade-type connectors. The spade, or bayonet, connectors may be in one terminal. I like these terminals because they can only be installed one way.

CHARGE BATTERY

Soon, you'll be ready for an initial engine startup. Your battery will have to be capable of cranking the engine for an extended time, so plan ahead. When you think you're about a day away from startup, have the battery charged.

BACK UNDERNEATH

It's now time to get your car back up in the air so the underside work can be completed. Don't forget the precautions: a

Push pipe up into engagement with manifold studs and start nuts. Using long extension from below, tighten nuts.

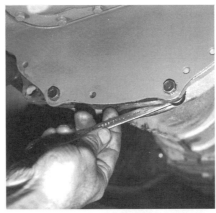

Install bottom engine-plate bolts. If automatic transmission is used, install flexplate-to-converter bolts. Use breaker bar at crank-pulley bolt to rotate crankshaft. Torque converter-drive bolts 29—36 ft-lb (4—5 kg-m). Install converter cover.

If so equipped, connect brake-booster vacuum hose. Using labels as guide, connect remaining vacuum hoses.

good jack, jack stands, blocked wheels, and jostle the car to make sure it's secure.

Exhaust System—After the car is firmly supported on jack stands, start by hooking up the exhaust system. Check the condition of the exhaust-manifold-to-pipe gasket. Replace it if it's not in good condition. Remember that this gasket is not included in most gasket sets.

As you may recall, it was necessary to loosen the 280Z's exhaust pipe at its mounting brackets in order to pull the exhaust off the manifold studs. This is because the studs don't point straight down; they angle down and back. If you have a similar situation, it'll be very difficult to lift the front section of the exhaust system into engagement with the manifold.

This is easily solved by placing a floor jack under the exhaust—near the transmission mount. Raise the pipe up so its mounting flange comes in light contact with the manifold studs. To install the gasket so it'll stay in place, push down on the pipe and slip the gasket between the studs and mounting flange. With a nut within reach, work the exhaust-pipe flange over the manifold studs, being careful not to damage the gasket. Thread the nut on a stud to keep the pipe in place, then install the other nut(s). Tighten the nuts 33—44 ft-lb (4.5—6.0 kg-m).

Don't forget the exhaust-pipe mount at the transmission. Get the complete exhaust system bolted back up in place.

Fuel Pump—Likewise, don't forget the fuel pump if you removed and stored it as suggested in the engine-removal chapter. Reinstall it so your engine will have fuel when it comes time for startup.

Torque Converter—If your vehicle is

equipped with an automatic transmission, bolt the flexplate to the torque converter. If you did all the preliminary work by placing the flexplate and torque-converter marks at the bottom, the flexplate and converter should be close to lining up. A Phillips screwdriver or punch inserted through a flexplate hole into the converter drive-lug hole should bring the two components into alignment.

Thread in a flexplate-to-converter bolt and torque it 29—36 ft-lb (4.0—5.0 kg-m). Now that one bolt is in, you'll have to rotate the crankshaft to gain access for installing the remaining three bolts. This can be done with the starter motor after you've installed the battery. I prefer turning the crank with a socket wrench on the crankshaft-pulley bolt. This beats inching the crank around using a large screwdriver to pry against the ring-gear teeth.

After rotating the crank 90° three times and installing the remaining bolts, install the bell housing cover plate. Tighten the bell housing cover-plate bolts 4—5 ft-lb (0.6—0.8 kg-m). Finish installing the bell housing-to-engine bolts. Torque the bolts 29—36 ft-lb (3.9—4.9 kg-m).

Engine Plate—For manual transmissions, install the engine-plate-to-bell housing bolts. Tighten them 6.5—8.7 ft-lb (0.9—1.2 kg-m). Finish installing the bell housing-to-engine bolts and torque them 32—43 ft-lb (4.3—5.8 kg-m).

Transmission Connectors—Depending on your vehicle, you'll have one or more electrical connections to make at the transmission. Do it now while the vehicle

is in the air and you are in the transmission area.

Splash Shield—Although your car may be equipped with a splash shield, don't install it now. It interferes with installing other components, and any tools or fasteners you drop may end up on the splash shield. It's much easier to pick things up off the floor or ground. So go back up top and set your vehicle back down.

TOPSIDE CONNECTIONS

Vacuum Hoses—Using your ID tags on the vacuum hoses as reference, hook them up. I hope you tagged them if you're working with an "emissions" engine. It will be overburdened with hoses.

Throttle Linkage—Install the firewall-to-engine throttle rod. First, remove the cotter pin, washer and spring from the rod. Slide the throttle rod into its companion linkage at the fire wall, fitting it into the rubber boot. The hooked forward end of the rod should be pointing down, not up.

Slip the spring into the throttle-shaft U-joint with the washer underneath the spring. Have the cotter pin handy. While you're holding the spring and washer in position with one hand, fit the hook end of the throttle rod into the two slots in the U-joint. Compress the spring with the washer and install the cotter pin. Check throttle operation.

For models using cable-type throttle linkage, route the cable around the carburetor. Hook the cable end to the carburetor throttle lever and end of the cable housing to its bracket. Check for proper

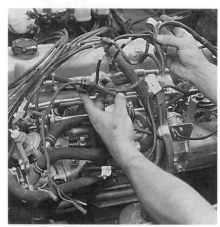

Without labels, this is just so much "spaghetti." Lay wires over engine so connectors are close to where they should go. After all are in place . . .

. . . reconnect loose ends. Three connections are made at thermostat on this 280ZX!

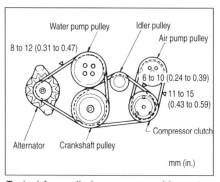

Typical four-cylinder accessory-drive setup is for 200SX: Use as reference when installing accessories and drive belts. Drawing courtesy Nissan.

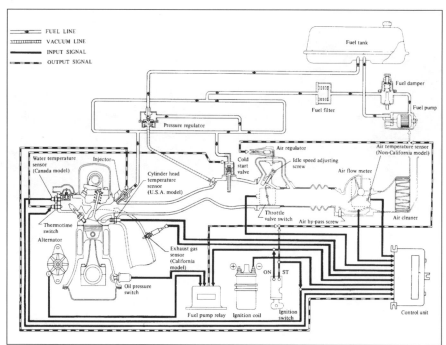

If you neglected to label electrical, fuel and vacuum connections on a fuel-injected 280ZX, you now know you blew it. However, all is not lost. Use diagram to trace and make connections correctly. Drawing courtesy Nissan.

Push on fuel-injection connectors and retain with wire clips. Finish job by securing wiring harness with clamps and tie wraps.

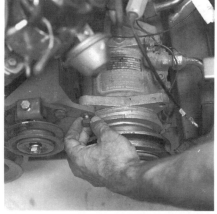

Unwire A/C compressor from body and install on bracket. If either hose was disconnected you must recharge system before A/C will operate.

throttle operation.

Wiring Hookups—If your engine is a fuel-injected L28 like the one pictured, I hope you tagged all the connectors. A few pictures will be of great help.

Start the wiring-harness installation by laying the harness on the engine and rout-

ing the individual leads to where they will be connected—*don't hook up anything yet.* Route the wires in, under and around the hoses and various components sitting atop the intake manifold.

After everything fits according to the identification tags and your satisfaction, make the final connections. Be very careful with installing connectors. If something doesn't fit, double-check its location. Don't force them.

After making all the connections, secure the wires and hoses with the tie-

wraps you saved. If you didn't save them, new ones can be purchased at most auto-supply stores. Regardless, make sure the wires and hoses are well secured. Floppy wires and hoses are likely to fail at their connections, chafe or get pulled loose.

A/C Compressor—Back to the heavy hardware: Unwire the A/C compressor from the inner fender and carefully lower it into position. Remember: Be careful not to bend the A/C lines. You don't want to crack one at this stage of the game and lose the refrigerant. You'll end up having

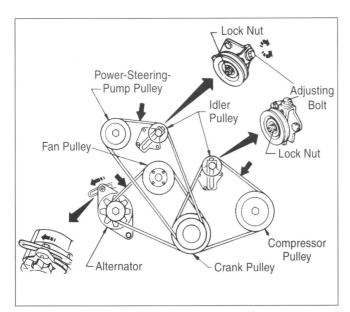

Accessory drive for 280ZX includes alternator, A/C compressor and power-steering pump. Drawing courtesy Nissan.

Fit belts to drive pulleys. When adjusted, belts should deflect approximately 1/2 in. when pushed on with thumb midway between pulleys. A/C-idler adjustment is secured with nut at center of pulley. Loosely install water-pump pulley.

to replace the hose and do what you were trying to avoid—the time and expense of recharging the A/C system.

Loosely mount the compressor to its bracket. There are two top bolts; one installs from the front and one from the back; two bolts install from the bottom. After you've gotten them all threaded in, snug them down and torque them 33—40 ft-lb (4.5—5.5 kg-m). These bolts thread into aluminum, so don't overtighten them.

Don't forget the compressor-clutch lead. Miss this connection and you'll wonder why you don't get cold air out of the A/C registers.

Belts—If you haven't checked the alternator/water-pump, power-steering pump, and A/C-compressor belts, do it now. If they are brittle and cracked, replace them. Regardless of their condition, it's good insurance to replace a belt if it's two years old or more.

Loosely install each belt in order, from back to front: alternator/water pump, A/C compressor and power-steering pump. Route the A/C-compressor and power-steering-pump belts over their idler pulleys. You can tighten them, but the alternator/water-pump belt will have to wait until after the water-pump pulley and fan are secured. Loosely fit the water-pump pulley to the water pump and route the belt over the pulley.

Tighten the pump and compressor belts by forcing the adjuster/idler pulleys

On fuel-injected models, install airflow meter. Connect hose, then secure to bracket.

Electronic-ignition leads are idiot-proofed. Each has different-size connector, stud and attaching nut and washer.

tight against the drive belts. Thread in the idler-pulley adjusting bolt to hold each pulley tight against its belt.

An improperly adjusted belt will either slip or overload the bearings of the accessory it's driving. Check belt tension by pushing against the belt with your thumb midway between two pulleys using about 20 pounds of force. A properly tensioned V-belt will deflect approximately 1/2 in. at the center of a 14—18-in. unsupported length. More or less belt length will result in proportionally more or less deflection. To accurately measure belt tension with long or short span belts, you'll need a belt-tension gauge.

A new belt should be rechecked after initial engine run-in. Ten minutes of running time is all that's necessary for a new belt to stretch and pull down into its pulley grooves.

Airflow Meter—Before bolting the airflow meter to its bracket, route its lead up through the hole in the center of the bracket. If you forget to do this, you'll have to remove the meter to route the lead.

Another job to do before securing the airflow meter: Connect the airflow-meter-manifold hose. This can be a tough job. Make sure the hose clamp is loose, and apply some soapy water to the inside of the hose. This will let the hose slip on the

With bottom hose and lower half of shroud installed, carefully lower radiator into position. Consider getting your radiator reconditioned before installing it.

Slip pump-mounting bolts into mounting flange, then lower fan into position over nose of water-pump shaft. Get all bolts started into pump flange and, for now, finger-tighten.

Use bar to tension alternator belt. Tighten adjusting bolt . . .

. . . and check belt tension. Readjust as necessary. It should deflect about 1/2 in.

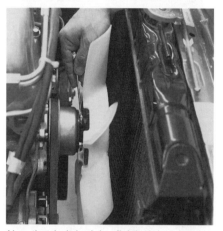

Now that belt is tight, finish tightening fan bolts.

airflow meter much easier—don't use oil to lubricate the hose.

Attach the airflow meter to its bracket using its mounting screws and washers. Then tighten the hose clamp.

Distributor Connections—My California calibrated, fuel-injected 280Z has three leads that connect to a junction block on the inner fender. The connectors are sized to the three different-size mounting studs, washers and nuts, making it *nearly* impossible to go wrong here. Hook them up at the left-front inner fender. Install the junction-block cover. Its two screws thread into plastic, so don't overtighten them.

Install Radiator—If your vehicle has a fan shroud, attach only the bottom half of the shroud to the radiator. Install the bottom radiator hose to the radiator now

rather than after the radiator is in place. To make radiator-hose installation easier, apply soapy water to the radiator nipple or hose ID.

Carefully lower the radiator into place. With the radiator properly located to the radiator support, secure the radiator with four bolts. These bolts install from the front through the radiator support and thread into weldnuts on the radiator flange.

Cooling Fan—With the radiator in place, you can now install the fan and belt. You'll be working with one of two basic types of fans: a plain fan, or a fan with an integral drive unit, or coupler. The plain fan bolts to a viscous-drive coupler that is integral with the water pump. You'll either be working between the fan and the radiator, or the fan and the water pump. Either way, installing the fan takes some finesse,

finger contortions and some dropped bolts or nuts. Now you'll find out why I suggested not installing the splash shield.

After all nuts or bolts are threaded into place and snugged down, how you proceed from here depends on which type of fan you're working with. If the fan bolts to the coupler, simply hold a fan blade while tightening each bolt. On the other hand, you won't be able to tighten the bolts or nuts to a viscous-drive fan because the water-pump shaft and pulley will turn. Holding a fan blade won't do any good because the coupler will let the whole works turn. Solve this little dilemma by doing a job you will be doing anyway.

Tighten the water-pump/alternator belt by levering the alternator away from the water pump as shown. Hold it in place while you tighten the adjusting bolt and pivot bolt. Check belt tension and finish tightening the fan nuts or bolts. Also, finish installing the top radiator hose.

Fan Shroud & Radiator Hoses—Complete the bottom radiator-hose hookup by connecting the hose to the water-pump inlet. Install the top half of the fan shroud. Its bolts will thread forward into the radiator or down into the bottom half of the shroud. Installing the left-side bolts is difficult on an injected Z—very tight quarters.

The engine-cooling circuit will be completed by installing the top radiator hose. I'll say it again: If these hoses are the least bit suspect, replace them.

Coolant Recovery—If your vehicle is equipped with a coolant-recovery system,

Set top half of fan shroud into place and secure to radiator and bottom half.

Install radiator hoses. Install engine-inlet hose to engine and radiator, and connect outlet hose to engine. Tighten clamps.

Coolant-recovery bottle installs to right of radiator—left side as viewed. Route hose to radiator neck and slip bottle over bracket.

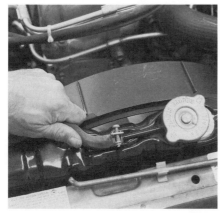

Connect coolant-recovery hose to radiator neck.

Secure charcoal-canister bracket to inside of right fender apron.

Slip canister into bracket, secure with clamp, and connect hoses using reference flags as guide.

complete its installation. The recovery bottle for the Datsun Z-car is located on a bayonet-type bracket at the right front of the radiator support. After routing its hose through the radiator support, simply slide the bottle down onto the bracket. Fit the recovery-bottle hose to the nipple that extends out from the radiator-filler neck and secure it with its clamp.

Charcoal Canister—If you had to remove the charcoal canister, install it now. Start with its bracket. It bolts to a companion bracket at the front of the inner fender. Slide the canister into place and secure it with the over-center clamp. Using your labels, fit the three hoses to their nipples on the canister. Soapy water will help here. Slide the hose clamps forward on the hoses and over the nipples. To open up the clamps so you can slide them, squeeze their ears with pliers.

One hose from the fuel tank supplies fuel vapor to the canister, and two hoses connect to the intake manifold. In case

On 280Z, hold air-cleaner assembly in position forward of left side of radiator . . .

. . . and guide connecting hose onto airflow meter. Soapy water on inside of hose makes this operation easier.

you didn't label these hoses, the nipple for the fuel-tank hose is labeled FUEL TANK. One of the two manifold hoses *purges* (removes) fuel vapor collected in the canister when a valve in the canister opens. This nipple is labeled PURGE on

the canister. Vapor in the canister is drawn into the engine where it is burned. The second hose supplies vacuum to the canister valve, opening it when a predetermined vacuum is reached. This nipple is labeled DIST VC.

Fit air-cleaner snorkel to open end of air cleaner.

Back underneath, install splash shield. You don't need to jack up front end to do this.

If fully charged, install battery. Starter will need all the cranking power it can get.

Air Cleaner—Start fuel-injected Z-car air-cleaner installation by routing the hose from the air cleaner to the airflow meter. This is not an easy job. Make sure the hose clamp is on the hose, but very loose. The hose is difficult to get on the EFI airflow meter, so consider using soapy water like you did on the radiator hoses. *Don't get any water in the meter.*

With the hose connected and clamped tightly to the airflow meter, bolt the air cleaner to the radiator support. Two bolts thread down into weldnuts. Install the air-cleaner snorkel. The snorkel routes back into the engine compartment and clamps to the end of the air-cleaner housing. Check the air filter. If it's dirty, replace it.

Splash Shield—Now you can install the splash shield. Do this without jacking up the front of the car by using a "very-low-profile" creeper—cardboard. Four bolts will do the job.

Install Battery—You're getting close to startup now. I hope you won't be disappointed by a dead battery. Install the battery and clamp it securely in its tray. Check the cable terminals and the battery posts. Clean them if they're corroded. Then, install the cables.

Engine Run-In Preparation—What you do prior to starting and running your newly rebuilt engine can dramatically affect its service life. The first 30 minutes of running are the most critical for a new engine.

Before Startup—Before starting your engine, make sure it has oil pressure. First, disable the ignition system by grounding the secondary lead coming from the coil. Crank the engine with the starter until oil pressure is indicated by the gauge or idiot light. Within 15 seconds, the gauge should indicate 35—40-psi oil pressure. If you have an idiot light, all you'll know by the

light going out is that the engine has minimum oil pressure. Cranking the engine will also help fill the float bowl of a carburetor, that being the case.

Reconnect the ignition. With your timing light ready to go, loosen the distributor-adjustment bolt so you can adjust timing. Disconnect and plug the vacuum-advance hose. Before firing your engine, have two items on hand. If you have an automatic transmission and have drained its torque converter, you'll need four quarts of ATF (automatic-transmission fluid). Also, have your timing light hooked up so you can set engine timing immediately after it fires. Adding ATF is important because the front pump will fill the torque converter once the engine starts turning. As a result, the rest of the transmission will be low on fluid. So the first thing you should do with an automatic is to add two quarts of ATF or the pump will suck air and aerate the fluid.

To ensure that your engine stays cool during run-in, put a garden hose into service. Fill the radiator with water, then open the drain and adjust water flow from the hose to the radiator to compensate for what is coming out the drain. This provides a source of cool water for your engine.

Startup—Start the engine, staying well clear of the axis of the fan while the engine is running. Don't be alarmed by the puff of blue smoke out the exhaust. It should disappear after a few minutes once the assembly oil is burned from the combustion chamber. Adjust idle speed if it's not right and keep your eye on the radiator. Set the timing. Turn the distributor *clockwise to advance timing* and *counterclockwise to retard timing.*

The rules: Once the engine is fired, it must be kept running at *no less than 1500 rpm* and it must be well lubricated and

cooled. Lubrication is particularly important to the camshaft and rocker arms. This is why the engine **should not be slow-idled** under any circumstances during initial run-in. If the engine won't maintain 1500 rpm, shut it off!

If the cam lobes aren't drenched in oil during run-in, it's quite possible that some will be damaged. This means a major repair job.

As for cooling, your car is stationary and, consequently, not getting full airflow through the radiator. This is aggravated by the fact that a new engine generates more heat than one that's broken in because of internal friction caused by tighter clearances. During run-in, you will notice engine rpm increasing gradually as the engine runs, indicating that the engine is *loosening up.*

When the thermostat opens, the water level will drop as water is drawn into the engine. Once you get the water level back up, readjust water flow from the hose to maintain that level. Keep the engine running. *Remember, don't let it idle below 1500 rpm. Shut off the engine first, if necessary.*

When you have the timing set, tighten the lock bolt and recheck timing. Wait until after you shut the engine down to reconnect the vacuum hose. It's too dangerous to be fiddling around the front of the engine when it's running. Not only is there danger from a fan blade coming off—extremely remote, but it has happened—the fan and accessory-drive belts and pulleys are just waiting to grab you. **Stay out of line with the fan.**

Post Run-In Checks—After you've run your engine for 20 minutes or so, shut it off. Let the engine sit 10—15 minutes. Then, shut off the hose and let the water drain out of the radiator. When it has drained, shut the drain cock so the engine

Fill radiator with water for initial run-in. With hose in radiator neck and drain cock open, compensate for radiator flow out of radiator by adjusting water flow from hose. Before starting engine, make sure it has oil pressure. Once started, let engine run for no less than 20 minutes at fast idle at not less than 1500 rpm.

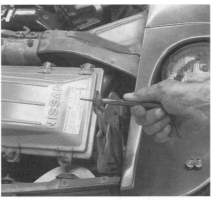

Punch is inserted into hood hinge to assist with installing and aligning hood. Although I did it "solo," I don't recommend installing hood by yourself.

Once bolts are installed, adjust hood to trace mark and tighten bolts. Carefully shut hood to check fit. It should be perfect or as good as original. Readjust as necessary.

and radiator can be filled with permanent coolant. Check the engine from top to bottom for fluid leaks: gas, oil and water. If you spot any, remedy them now.

Because gaskets, belts and hoses relax when they are loaded and heated, go over the entire engine and retighten a few things. High on the list are the manifold bolts, accessory-drive belts and hose clamps.

Engine Coolant—Even though your car may be operated in a warm climate where the temperature may never dip below freezing, water should not be used as the sole coolant. But, if water is all that's available, be sure to add rust inhibitor. This will prevent corrosion damage to the cooling system and will lubricate the water-pump seal. I believe the best practice is to use antifreeze so the coolant will have at least 0F capability. This not only provides corrosion protection, but it raises the temperature at which the coolant can operate before boiling—a real plus in hot climates.

Fill the radiator until it won't accept any more, then start the engine and wait for the thermostat to open. Have some antifreeze handy. The engine will begin to purge itself of air, so keep an eye on the coolant level. Don't forget the heater on vehicles so equipped. To fill it, put the heater control on HEAT so the water valve will open. Coolant will then flow through the heater core and hoses. When coolant level ceases to drop and is free of bubbles, bring it to about 1 in. (2.5cm) below the bottom of the radiator-filler neck. Cap the radiator. In the case of a coolant-recovery system, fill the recovery bottle to the MAX mark.

Install Hood—Time to rustle up some help. You'll need it to install the hood. Have the hood bolts and the proper wrenches handy. With the hood in place, run the bolts in just short of snug and adjust the hood to the reference marks. Or, with the ice pick or punch in the holes you drilled, tighten the bolts. Close the hood carefully to check its fit. It should be the same as before you removed it.

Trial Run—Now, with the satisfaction of having rebuilt your own engine, it's time to take it on its maiden voyage. Before charging out of the driveway, make sure you've collected all of your tools from the engine compartment. Your wrenches aren't going to do you any good scattered along the roadside. Take an inspection trip around your vehicle to make sure you don't end up flattening a creeper, a drain pan or anything that may have been left underneath in your haste to "see how she's gonna run."

It's not going to hurt your engine to operate it at highway speed on its first trip; just avoid accelerating hard. Also, vary the speed. Drive just long enough to get engine temperature stabilized. Keep alert for any ominous underhood sounds or warnings from the instrument panel. If something doesn't sound or look right, get off the road immediately and investigate.

After arriving back home, check fluid levels and look for any leaks that may have developed. Scan the engine com-partment with a critical eye. After everything appears to be OK, retorque the manifold bolts and check accessory drive-belt tension. You can now take a minute and admire your engine before you perform one more operation.

Hot-Lash Adjustment—Before your engine cools, remove the cam cover in preparation of checking hot valve clearance. If it has cooled, warm it up, then remove the cam cover. Don't run the engine with the cam cover off, particularly if top oiling is done through the cam lobes. You'll think your engine is lubricating the world.

Check valve clearance as detailed on page 14 in the troubleshooting chapter. Clearances are as follows: intake, 0.010 in. (0.25mm); exhaust, 0.012 in. (0.30mm). Torque the rocker-arm-pivot locknut 36—43 ft-lb (5.0—6.0 kg-m).

While putting the first 200 miles on your engine, constantly check fluid levels and be on guard for leaks. Keep checking things in the engine compartment. Correct any problems that might arise.

Don't get excited if your engine uses a little oil at first. If you installed chrome rings, expect it to use oil for a while until the rings bed in. Just keep the oil level between the dipstick marks and change the oil and filter after the first 500 miles. Avoid operating your vehicle at sustained or steady speeds. Vary speed as you drive. Avoid accelerating hard. Follow these rules and it will pay off in a longer lasting engine.

Retorque Head Bolts—As added insurance, retorque the head bolts *when the engine is cold*. Use sequence and torque values shown on page 129.

CHAPTER TEN

Tuneup

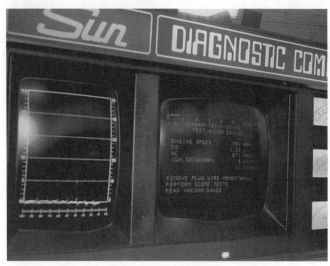

While on chassis dyno, engine can be tuned for emissions while idled or under power at various speeds and throttle settings.

Chassis dyno allows engine functions to be monitored while under simulated road load. No, this is not a Nissan or Datsun automobile.

After the initial break-in, have your rebuilt engine tuned for maximum performance. Performance includes three facets: power, economy and emissions.

If your engine is not experiencing any serious problems, such as detonation or overheating, put a few hundred miles on it before doing a final tuneup. Most engines will need repeated idle adjustments in the first 200—300 miles as the engine loosens up.

As the rings seat, they create less friction and seal better. As a result, engine power and economy increase. It will take about 1000 miles before you will have an accurate idea of the power and fuel economy the engine is capable of. The improvement will be dramatic for the first 200 miles, tapering off as miles accumulate. Most engines will deliver maximum performance after they have a few-thousand miles on them.

PERFORMANCE & EMISSION TUNING

The performance of your newly rebuilt engine should increase dramatically. Still, don't be satisfied with its performance until the engine has been thoroughly tuned. Just because it's better doesn't mean it's the best it can be.

You may be surprised at the unrealized power or economy in an engine. A computer-controlled, fuel-injected engine is calibrated to perform near maximum efficiency at the factory, but that of a conventional carbureted can usually be improved.

Depending on how much money you can spend, there are several ways to tune your engine. The first method is the most common—doing it yourself with a timing light and dwell/tachometer. With this method, you check initial timing, vacuum and mechanical advance, idle settings and point dwell. This works fine if you left the engine stock, but it's still not the best way.

An engine analyzer with an oscilloscope and four-gas analyzer is the next step up. With this setup, you can check air/fuel ratio, point dwell at various rpm levels, power balance, engine emissions and the primary and secondary circuits of the ignition system. Again, with a stock engine, this is a good way to tune the engine, and far better than the home tuneup.

The final method is to have your vehicle tuned and monitored on a *chassis dynamometer*. The chassis dyno measures drive-wheel power through a large set of rollers in the floor. Different loads are dialed into the roller to simulate changing road conditions. The engine is also connected to an electronic engine analyzer which monitors engine performance under road-load conditions.

A chassis-dynamometer tuneup costs a bit more than the others, but it is worth it to check out and improve engine performance. This tool can help to adjust the engine for performance under varying road conditions.

If the engine is tuned for power, good fuel economy and low emissions usually follow. It pays to have the engine tuned correctly.

METRIC CUSTOMARY-UNIT EQUIVALENTS

Multiply:		by:		to get:		Multiply:		by:		to get:
LINEAR										
inches	X	25.4	=	millimeters(mm)			X	0.03937	=	inches
miles	X	1.6093	=	kilometers (km)			X	0.6214	=	miles
inches	X	2.54	=	centimeters (cm)			X	0.3937	=	inches
AREA										
inches^2	X	645.16	=	millimeters ^{2}(mm^2)			X	0.00155	=	inches^2
inches^2	X	6.452	=	centimeters^2(cm^2)			X	0.155	=	inches^2
VOLUME										
quarts	X	0.94635	=	liters (l)			X	1.0567	=	quarts
fluid oz	X	29.57	=	milliliters (ml)			X	0.03381	=	fluid oz
MASS										
pounds (av)	X	0.4536	=	kilograms (kg)			X	2.2046	=	pounds (av)
tons (2000 lb)	X	907.18	=	kilograms (kg)			X	0.001102	=	tons (2000 lb)
tons(2000 lb)	X	0.90718	=	metric tons(t)			X	1.1023	=	tons(2000 lb)
FORCE										
pounds—f(av)	X	4.448	=	newtons (N)			X	0.2248	=	pounds—f(av)
kilograms—f	X	9.807	=	newtons (N)			X	0.10197	=	kilograms—f

TEMPERATURE

Degrees Celsius (C) = 0.556 (F - 32)   Degree Fahrenheit (F) = 1.8C + 32

```
°F   -40        32  98.6              212
          0    40   80   120   160  200  240  280   320      °F
     |||||||||||||||||||||||||||||||||||||||||||||||||

°C   -40   -20   0   20   40   60   80   100   120   140   160   °C
```

ENERGY OR WORK										
foot-pounds	X	1.3558	=	joules (J)			X	0.7376	=	foot-pounds

FUEL ECONOMY 8 FUEL CONSUMPTION

miles/gal	X	0.42514	=	kilometers/liter(km/l)			X	2.3522	=	miles/gal

Note:
235.2/(mi/gal) = liters/100km
235.2/(liters/100km) = mi/gal

PRESSURE OR STRESS										
inches Hg (60F)	X	3.377	=	kilopascals (kPa)			X	0.2961	=	inches Hg
pounds/sq in.	X	6.895	=	kilopascals (kPa)			X	0.145	=	pounds/sq in
pounds/sq ft	X	47.88	=	pascals (Pa)			X	0.02088	=	pounds/sq ft
POWER										
horsepower	X	0.746	=	kilowatts (kW)			X	1.34	=	horsepower
TORQUE										
pound-inches	X	0.11298	=	newton-meters (N-m)			X	8.851	=	pound-inches
pound-feet	X	1.3558	=	newton-meters (N-m)			X	0.7376	=	pound-feet
pound-inches	X	0.0115	=	kilogram-meters (Kg-M)			X	87	=	pound-inches
pound-feet	X	0.138	=	kilogram-meters(Kg-M)			X	7.25	=	pound-feet
VELOCITY										
miles/hour	X	1.6093	=	kilometers/hour(km/h)			X	0.6214	=	miles/hour

Conversion Chart courtesy Ford Motor Company

Appendix

STANDARD BOLT TORQUE SPECIFICATIONS

Bolt Diameter (mm)	Grade*	Thread Pitch (mm)	ft-lb	Tightening Torque kg-m	N-m
6	4	1.0	2.2–2.9	0.3–0.4	3–4
8	4	1.0–1.25	5.8–8.0	0.8–1.1	8–11
10	4	1.25–1.5	12–16	1.6–2.2	16–22
12	4	1.25	22–30	3.1–4.1	30–40
12	4	1.75	20–27	2.7–3.7	26–36
14	4	1.5	34–46	4.7–6.3	46–62
6	7	1.0	4.3–5.1	0.6–0.7	6–7
8	7	1.0–1.25	10–13	1.4–1.8	14–18
10	7	1.25–1.5	19–27	2.6–3.7	25–36
12	7	1.25	37–50	5.1–6.9	50–68
12	7	1.75	33–45	4.6–6.2	45–61
14	7	1.50	56–76	7.7–10.5	76–103
6	9	1.0	5.8–8.0	0.8–1.1	8–11
8	9	1.0–1.25	14–19	1.9–2.6	19–26
10	9	1.25–1.5	27–38	3.7–5.2	36–51
12	9	1.25	53–72	7.3–9.9	72–97
12	9	1.75	48–65	6.6–9.0	65–88
14	9	1.5	80–108	11.1–15.0	109–147

*Bolt grade embossed on bolt head

ENGINE BOLT & NUT TORQUE
ft-lb (kg-m)

Camshaft-cover bolts	5–6 (0.7–0.9)
Camshaft-sprocket bolts	100–108 (13.8–14.9)
Camshaft thrust-plate bolts	4–7 (0.5–1.0)
Camshaft-tower bolts	10–12 (1.3–1.6)
Chain-guide bolts	7 (1.0)
Chain-tensioner bolts	7 (1.0)
Connecting-rod bolts	
8mm	20–24 (2.8–3.3)
9mm	33–40 (4.4–5 4)
Crank-damper/pulley bolts	100–108 (13.8–14.9)
Cylinder-head bolts	
L13, 16, 20A	40 (5.5)
L18, 20B, 24, 26, 28	61 (8.5)
L28 Turbo	65 (1.0
Flywheel bolts	100–108 (13.8–14.9)
Front-cover bolts	
6mm	4–6 (0.6–0.8)
8mm	9–11 (1.2–1.5)
Intake/exhaust-manifold	
Bolts 8mm	8.7–11.6 (1.2–1.6)
10mm	25–35 (3.4–4.7)
Nuts	8.7–11.6 (1.2–1.6)
Main-bearing-cap bolts	30–40 (4.5–5.5)
Oil-pan bolts	5–7 (0.7–1.0)
Oil-pump bolts	9–11 (1.2–1.5)
Oil-pump-pickup bolts	8–10 (1.1–1.4)
Rocker-arm-pivot lock nut	40–44 (5.5–6.0)
Spark plugs	12–15 (1.2–2.0)
Spray-bar bolts	5–6 (0.7–0.9)

Index